SECTIONAL MA

OF
BRITAIN'S RAILWAYS

WITH GAZETTEER

LONDON

IAN ALLAN LTD

Scale = approx 4mm to 1 mile.

Updated by G. A. Jacobs (Consultant Editor and Liaison British Rail)

First published 1982
Second edition 1985
Revised edition 1989

ISBN 0 7110 1799 9

Published by Ian Allan Ltd, Shepperton, Surrey;
and printed by Ian Allan Printing Ltd at their works
at Coombelands in Runnymede, England

FOREWORD

This edition features a number of new or re-opened passenger stations, particularly in South Wales and West Yorkshire.

There have been some further reductions in the extent of the freight network. Notably with closures around Wath/Stairfoot a considerable area completely devoid of any line is apparent. Several lines in South Wales have also been closed.

An Anglia Region has been formed out of the Eastern Region, comprising mainly the former lines of the Great Eastern and LT&S railways. London (Marylebone) and services to the Chilterns and Banbury have been transferred from the London Midland Region to the Western Region.

The designated principal passenger lines have been aligned with the British Rail description.

New cross-city links have been established in London and Manchester.

There have been some developments with Independent railways, eg London Docklands. Further aspirations by 'Preserved' lines have been included.

GAJ 161288

Herein we show the British railway system as at January 1989. The various British Rail regions are shown in their own distinctive colourings and are differentiated from independent operating companies. Lines closed to all traffic are shown in yellow and an appropriate selection of closed stations is provided for geographical identification purposes.

Stations open to passenger traffic are shown with an open circle; closed stations with a solid circle; points open for freight or limited use by an 'x'.

BR lines which are open for freight services only are shown in hatched form and the principal main lines are shown in heavier style.

The distinctive colours used are:

LIGHT BLUE	—	Anglia Region
DARK BLUE	—	Eastern Region
RED	—	London Midland Region
LIGHT BLUE	—	Scottish Region
GREEN	—	Southern Region
BROWN	—	Western Region
PURPLE	—	Independent railways including London Underground Ltd, Tyne & Wear Metro and Docklands Light Railway
YELLOW	—	Lines closed to all traffic or sites thereof

Tube railways where running below the surface are not shown.

The initials of the original pre-Grouping owner/operating company are shown on the various lines depicted on each of the maps.

INDEX

Station	Region	Pre Group	Map Ref.
Barons Court	LUL	Dist	39, D4
Barnt Green	LM	Mid	9, A4
Barnton	Sc	NB	30, B3
Barrhead	Sc	GBK	29, C4; 44, F2
Barrhill	Sc	G & SW	25, A3
Barrow Haven	E	GC	22, E3
Barrow-in-Furness	LM	Fur	24, B5
Barrow Hill		Mid	16, A4; 41, B3
Barrow-in-Furness	LM	Fur	24, B5
Barrow-on-Soar & Quorn	LM	Mid	16, E3
Barry	W	BRY	8, D4; 43, C5
Barry Docks	W	BRY	8, D4; 43, C5
Barry Island	W	BRY	8, D4; 43, C5
Barry Links	Sc	D & A	34, E3
Bartlow		GE	11, D4
Barton-on-Humber	E	GC	22, E4
Barton	E	NE	27, F5
Basford Vernon	LM	GN	16, C4; 41, F4
Basildon	A	LT & S	6, A5
Basingstoke	S	LSW & GW	4, B2
Bat & Ball (Sevenoaks)	S	SEC	5, C4
Bath Green Park	W	SD	3, A3
Bath Spa	W	GW	3, A3; 8, D1
Bathgate	Sc	NB	30, C4
Batley	E	GN & LNW	21, E3; 42, B3
Battersby	E	NE	28, F4
Battersea	S	WLE	39, D5 and inset E4
Battersea Park	S	LBSC	39, D5 and inset F4
Battle	S	SEC	6, F5
Battlesbridge	A	GE	6, A5
Baverstock	S	LSW	3, C5
Bawtry	E	GN	21, G5
Bayford	E	GN	11, F2
Bayston Hill	LM	GW & LNW Jt	15, F1
Bayswater	LUL	Dist	39, C5
Beaconsfield	W	GW & GC Jt	5, A1; 10, F1
Bearley	LM	GW	9, B5
Bearsden	Sc	NB	29, B4; 44, E5
Bearstead & Thurnham	S	SEC	6, C5
Beasdale	Sc	NB	32, B5
Beaulieu Rd	S	LSW	4, E4
Bebington	LM	BJ	20, C4; 45, F4
Beccles	A	GE	12, A2; 18, G2
Beckenham Hill	S	SEC	40, F3
Beckenham Jcn	S	SEC	40, F3
Beckfoot	RE		26, F2
Beckhole		NE	28, F2
Becontree	LUL		5, A4
Beddgelert		NWNG	19, E2
Beddington Lane Halt	S	LBSC	40, G5
Bede	TWM		28, B5
Bedenham		LSW	4, E3
Bedford (Midland)	LM	Mid	10, C1; 11, D1
Bedford (St John's)	LM	LNW	10, C1; 11, D1
Bedhampton	S	LBSC	4, E2
Bedlington	E	NE	27, A5
Bedminster	W	GW	3 Inset
Bedwas	W	BM	8, B4; 43, B3
Bedworth	LM	LNW	16, G5
Bedwyn	W	GW	4, A5
Beechburn	E	NE	27, D5
Beechgrove	W	GW	3, C4
Beeston (Notts)	LM	Mid	16, D4; 41, G4
Beeston Castle & Tarporley	LM	LNW	15, B1; 20, E3
Beighton	LM	GC	41, A3
Beith Town	Sc	G & SW	29, D3
Bekesbourne	S	SEC	6, C2
Belasis North	E	NE	28, E4
Belford	E	NE	31, E4
Belgrave & Birstall	MLST	GC	16, E3
Belle Vue	LM	GC & Mid Jt	45, A3
Bellgrove	Sc	NB	44, D4
Bellingham (Kent)	S	SEC	40, F3
Bellshill	Sc	Cal	30, C5; 44, B3
Belmont	S	LBSC	5, C3
Belper	LM	Mid	16, C5; 41, F2
Beltring	S	SEC	5, D5
Belvedere	S	SEC	5, B4
Bembridge	S	IW	4, F2
Bempton	E	NE	22, B3
Benfleet (for Canvey Island)	A	LTS	6, A5
Bennerley Open Cast	LM	Mid	41, F4
Ben Rhydding	E	O & I	21, C2
Bentham	LM	Mid	24, B2
Bentley (Hants)	S	LSW	4, C1
Bentley (Suffolk)		GE	12, D4
Bentinck Colliery	LM	Mid	41, E3
Benton	TWM	NE	27, B5
Benwick		GE	11, A3; 17, G3
Bere Alston	W	LSW	1, D5
Bere Ferrers	W	LSW	1, D5
Berkeley Rd	W	Mid	8, B1; 9, F2
Berkhamsted	LM	LNW	10, E1
Berkswell	LM	LNW	9, A5
Berney Arms	A	GE	18, F1
Berrylands	S		39, G3
Berwick (Sussex)	S	LBSC	5, F4
Berwick-upon-Tweed	E	NE & NB Jt	31, C3
Berwyn	Ind	GW	20, F5
Bescar Lane	LM	LY	20, A4; 24, E3; 45, F1;
Bescot	LM	LNW	13, A3; 15, F4
Besses O' the Barn	LM	L & Y	45, B2
Betchworth	S	SEC	5, C2
Bethesda		LNW	19, D2
Bethnal Green	A	GE	40, C4
Betteshanger Colliery	S	SEC	6, C1
Bettws-y-Coed	LM	LNW	19, E4
Bevercotes Colliery	E	GC	16, B3
Beverley	E	NE	22, D3
Bewdley	SVR	GW	9, A3
Bexhill	S	LBSC	6, F5
Bexley	S	SEC	5, B4
Bexleyheath	S	SEC	5, B4
Bicester North	W	GW	10, D3
Bicester Town	W	LNW	10, D4
Bickershaw & Abram	LM	GC	45, C2
Bickley	S	SEC	40, G2
Bideford	W	LSW & BWHA	7, F2
Bidston	LM	Wir	20, C4; 24, G4; 45, F4
Bidston Dock	LM	GC	45, F4
Biggleswade	E	GN	11, D2
Bilbrook	WR	GW	15, F3
Billericay	A	GE	5, A5; 11, G5
Billingham-on-Tees	E	NE	28, E4
Billingshurst	S	LBSC	5, E2
Bilson	W	GW & SVW	8, A1; 9, E2
Bilsthorpe Colliery	E	GC	16, B2 and 41, D5
Bilston Central	LM	GW	15, F4; 13, A2
Bilton	LM	LNW	10, A4
Bingham	LM	GN	16, C3
Bingham Road		SEC/ LBSC Jt	40, G4
Bingley	E	Mid	21, D2; 42, A5
Birch Coppice Colliery	LM	Mid	16, F5
Birchington-on-Sea	S	SEC	6, B2
Birchgrove	W	RR	8, C4; 43, B4
Birchwood	LM	CLC	20, C2; 24, G2; 45, C3
Birdwell	E	GC	42, E2
Birkbeck	S		40, F4
Birkdale	LM	LY	20, A4; 24, E4; 45, F1
Birkenhead Central	LM	Mer	20, C4; 24, G4; 45, F4
Birkenhead Hamilton Sq	LM	Mer	20, C4; 24, G4; 45, F4
Birkenhead North	LM	Mer	20, C4; 24, G4; 45, F4
Birkenhead Park	LM	Mer/Wir	20, C4; 24, G4; 45, F4
Birkenhead Woodside		GW/ LNW	20, C4; 24, G4; 45, F4
Birmingham Curzon Street (Goods)	LM	LNW	13, C4
Birmingham International	LM		15, G5
Birmingham Moor Street	LM	GW	13, C4; 15, G4
Birmingham New Street	LM	LNW/ Mid	13, C3; 15, G4
Birmingham Snow Hill	LM	GW	13, C3; 15, G4
Birstall	E		21, E2
Bishop Auckland	E	NE	27, E5
Bishopbriggs	Sc	NB	29, C5; 44, D4
Bishops Castle		Ind	14, C1
Bishop's Lydeard	WSR	GW	8, F4
Bishop's Stortford	A	GE	11, E3
Bishop's Waltham		LSW	4, D3
Bishopstone	S	LBSC	5, G4
Bishopton	Sc	Cal	29, C4
Bisley Camp		LSW	5, C2
Bitterne	S	LSW	4, E4
Bitton	W	Mid	3, A3; 8, D1
Blackburn	LM	LY	24, D2
Blackfriars	S	SEC	40, C5
Blackheath (London)	S	SEC	40, E2
Blackhill	E	NE	27, C4
Blackhorse Rd	A	TFG	40, A3
Blackpool North	LM	PWY	24, D4
Blackpool Pleasure Beach	LM	L & Y/ LNW Jt	24, D4
Blackpool South	LM	PWY	24, D4
Blackwater	S	SEC	4, B1
Blackwell	LM	Mid	41, D3
Blackwood (Lanark)	Sc	Cal	30, D5
Blaenant	W	N&B	7, A5 and 43, E2
Blaenau Ffestiniog Central	LM	LNW	19, F3
Blaenavon	Ind	LNW	8, A4; 43, A1
Blaengarw	W	GW	7, B5; 43, D3
Blaengwynfi	W	RSB	7, B5
Blaenrhondda	W	RSB	7, B5; 43, D2
Blagdon		GW	3, B2; 8, 2D
Blair Atholl	Sc	HR	33, C3
Blairgowrie	Sc	Cal	33, D5
Blairhill	Sc	NB	44, B4
Blakedown	LM	GW	9, A3
Blake Street	LM	LNW	15, F5
Blanchland	E	NE	27, D4
Blantyre	Sc	Cal	29, C5; 44, C2
Blaydon		NER	28, Inset
Bleasby	E	Mid	16, C3
Blenheim & Woodstock	W	GW	10, E4
Bletchington	W	GW	10, E4
Bletchley	LM	LNW	10, D2
Blidworth Colliery	E	GC	16, B3 and 41, D5
Blindwells	Sc	NB	30, B1
Blodwell	W	Cam	14, A2; 20, G5
Blue Anchor	WSR	GW	8, E5
Blundellsands & Crosby	LM	LY	20, B4; 24, F4; 45, F3
Blunsdon	Ind	MSWJ	9, F5
Blyth	E	NE	28, A5
Blythe Bridge	LM	NS	15, C4
Boat of Garten	Stra	HR & GNS	36, F3
Boddam	Sc	GNS	37, D5
Bodmin Parkway	W	GW	1, D3
Bodorgan	LM	LNW	19, D1
Bognor Regis	S	LBSC	5, G1
Bogside	Sc	GSW	29, D3
Bogside (Fife)	Sc	NB	30, A4
Bogston	Sc	Cal	29, B3
Bolden Colliery	E	NE	28, C5
Bollington	LM	GC & NS Jt	15, A4
Bolsover	E	GC & Mid	16, B4; 41, C3
Bolton (Trinity Street)	LM	LY	20, B2; 24, F1; 45, B2
Bolton-le-Sands	LM	LNW	24, B3
Bolton-on-Dearne	E	SK	21, F4; 42, E1
Bo'ness	B & K	NB	30, B4
Bookham	S	LSW	5, C2
Boothferry Park	E	H&B	22, Inset
Bootle (Cumb)	LM	Fur	24, A5; 26, G3
Bootle New Strand (Merseyside)	LM	LY	45, F3
Bootle (Merseyside) (Oriel Road)	LM	LY	45, F3
Bordesley	LM	GW	13, C4; 15, G5
Bordon		LMR	4, C1
Borough Green & Wrotham	S	SEC	5, C5
Borth, Cam	LM	Cam	13, C5
Boscarne Jcn		LSW	1, D3
Bosham	S	LBSC	4, E1
Boston	E	GN	17, C3
Boston Lodge	Fest		19, F2
Boston Manor	LUL		39, D2
Botanic		NB/Cal	44, C2
Botley	S	LSW	4, E3
Bottesford	E	GN	16, D2
Bourne	M	GN	17, E1
Bourne End	W	GW	5, A1; 10, G2
Bournemouth	S	LSW	3, F5
Bournemouth West	S	LSW	3, F5
Bournville	LM	Mid	9, A4
Bow Brickhill	LM	LNW	10, D2
Bow Church	DLR	(NL)	40, C3
Bow Creek	A	GE	40, C3
Bowers Row Open Cast	E	NE	42, B1
Bowes Park	E	GN	5, A3
Bow Goods	A	Mid	40, B3
Bowhill	Sc	NB	30, A2
Bowker Vale	LM		45, B2
Bow Road	LUL		40, C3
Bowling	Sc	Cal & NB	29, B4
Boxhill & Westhumble	S	LBSC	5, C2
Brackley	LM	GC	10, C3
Brackmills	LM	Mid	10, B2
Bracknell	S	LSW	4, A1
Bradford Interchange	E	GN/LY	42, A4
Bradford Forster Square	E	Mid	21, D2; 42, A4
Bradford-on-Avon	W	GW	3, B4
Brading	S	IW	4, F3
Bradley Fold	LM	LY	20, B2
Braidhurst	Sc	Cal	44, B2
Braintree & Bocking	A	GE	11, E5
Bramhall	LM	LNW	15, A3; 20, C1; 45, A4
Bramley (Hants)	S	GW	4, B2
Bramley (W. Yorks)	E	GN	21, D3 and 42, A3
Brampton (Suffolk)	A	GE	12, B2
Brampton Jcn (Cumb)	E	NE	27, C1
Branchton	Sc	Cal	29, B3
Brandon (Norfolk)	A	GE	11, A5; 17, G5
Branksome	S	LSW	3, F5
Bransty	LM	LNW	26, E4
Braunstone Gate (Leics)	LM	GC	16, F4
Braystones	LM	Fur	26, F3
Brechin	Ind	Cal	34, C3
Brecon	W	N & B	14, F3
Bredbury	LM	GC & Mid Jt	21, G1; 45, A3
Breich	Sc	Cal	30, C4
Brent/Cricklewood Sdgs	LM	Mid	39, B4
Brent (Devon)	W	GW	2, D4
Brent Cross	LUL		39, A4
Brentford	S	LSW	39, D2
Brentford Town	WR	GW	39, D2
Brentwood	A	GE	5, A5
Bretby		Mid	16, E5
Bricket Wood	LM	LNW	11, G1
Bridgend	W	GW	7, C5; 43, D4
Bridge of Allan	Sc	Cal	30, A5
Bridge of Dun	Sc	Cal	34, C3
Bridge of Earn	Sc	NB	33, F5
Bridge of Orchy	Sc	NB	32, E1
Bridge of Weir	Sc	G & SW	29, C3
Bridgnorth	SVR	GW	15, F2
Bridgeton	Sc	Cal	44, D3
Bridport		GW	3, F2
Bridgwater	W	GW & SD	3, C1; 8, F3
Bridlington	E	NE	22, B3
Brierfield	LM	LY	24, D1
Brierley Hill	LM	GW	15, G3
Brigg	E	GC	22, F4

Station	Region	Pre Group	Map Ref.
Brigham	LM	LNW	26, E3
Brightlingsea		GE	12, F4
Brighton	S	LBSC	5, F3
Brightside	E	Mid	21, G3 and 42, G2
Brill & Ludgershall	W	GW	10, E3
Brimsdown	A	GE	5, A3; 11, G3
Brinnington	LM	GC & NS	21, G1 and 45, A3
Bristol Parkway	W		8, C1; 9, G2
Bristol (Temple Meads)	W	GW/Mid	3, A2 and Inset; 8, C1/2
Brithdir	W	Rhy	8, B4; 43, B2
British Steel Redcar	E	NE	28, E4
Brixham		GW	2, D3
Brixton	S	SEC	40, E5
Broadbottom	LM	GC	21, G1
Broadfield	LM	LY	20, B1; 45, A2
Broad Green	LM	LNW	20, C4; 24, G3; 45, E4
Broadstairs	S	SEC	6, B1
Broadstone	S	LSW	3, F5
Broad St (London)	LM	NL	5, A3; 40, C4
Broadway	G & WR	GW	9, C4
Brodsworth Colliery	E	GN	21, F4
Brockenhurst	S	LSW	4, E4
Brockholes	LM	LY	21, F2; 42, D5
Brocklesby	E	GC	22, E3
Brockley	S	LBSC	40, E3
Bromborough	LM	BJ	20, C4; 45, F5
Bromborough Rake	LM	GW/LNW Jt	45, F4; 20, C4
Bromley	LUL	Dist	40, C3
Bromley Cross	LM	LY	20, A2; 24, F1; 45, B1
Bromley North	S	SEC	5, B4; 40, F2
Bromley South	S	SEC	40, G2
Bromsgrove	W	Mid	9, A4
Brondesbury	LM	LNW	39, B4
Brondesbury Park	LM	LNW	39, B4
Bronwydd Arms	Ind	GW	13, G4
Brooklands	LM	MSJA	20, C1; 24, G1; 45, B3
Brookmans Park	E	GN	11, F2
Brookwood	S	LSW	5, C1
Broom	LM	SMJ	9, B5
Broome	W	LNW	14, C1
Broomfleet	E	NE	22, E4
Brora	Sc	HR	36, A4; 38, E5
Brough	E	NE	22, E4
Broughty Ferry	Sc	D & A	34, Inset E1
Broxbourne & Hoddesdon	A	GE	11, F3
Bruce Grove	A	GE	40, A4
Brundall	A	GE	18, F2
Brundall Gardens	A		18, F2
Bruton	W	GW	3, C3; 8, F1
Bryn (Lancs)	LM	LNW	20, B3; 24, F2; 45, D3
Brynamman	W	Mid	7, A4
Brynglas	Tal		13, B5
Bryngwyn		NWNG	19, E2
Brynmawr	W	LNW	8, A4; 43, B1
Buchlyvie	Sc	NB	29, A5
Buckenham	A	GE	18, F2
Buckfastleigh	DVR	GW	2, D4
Buckhill	LM	C&W Jcn	26, D3
Buckhurst Hill	LUL	GE	5, A4
Buckley	LM	GC	20, E4
Bucknell	W	LNW	14, D1
Bugle	W	GW	1, D2
Buildwas	LM	GW	15, F2
Builth Road (High Level)	W	LNW	14, E3
Builth Road (Low Level)	W	Cam	14, E3
Builth Wells	W	Cam	14, E3
Bulford Camp		LSW	4, C5
Bull Point (St Budeaux)	W	GW	1, Insert
Bulwell Forest	LM	Mid	16, C4; 41, F4
Buntingford	A	GE	11, E3
Bures	A	GE	12, E5
Burgess Hill	S	LBSC	5, E3
Burghead	Sc	HR	36, C2
Burley-in-Wharfedale	E	O & I	21, C2
Burley Park	E	NE	21, D3; 42, A3
Burnage	LM	LNW	45, A3
Burneside	LM	LNW	27, G1
Burngullow	W	GW	1, D2
Burnham (Bucks)	W	GW	5, B1; 10, G1
Burnham-on-Crouch	A	GE	6, A4; 12, G5
Burnham-on-Sea		SDJ	3, B1; 8, E3
Burnley Barracks	LM	LY	24, D1
Burnley Central	LM	LY	24, D1
Burn Naze	LM	L&Y/LNW Jt	24, B4
Burnside	LM	Cal	44, D3
Burntisland	Sc	NB	30, A2
Burnt Oak	LUL		5, A2
Burscough Bridge	LM	LY	20, A4; 24, F3; 45, E1
Burscough Jcn	LM	LY	20, B4; 24, F3; 45, E1
Bursledon	S	LSW	4, E3
Burton Dassett	W	SMJ	10, B5
Burton Joyce	E	Mid	16, C3; 41, F5
Burton-on-Trent	LM	Mid	15, D5 and Inset
Bury (Lancs)	LM	LY	20, B1; 24, F1; 45, B2
Bury (Bolton St) (Lancs)	Ind	LY	20, B1; 24, F1; 45, B1/2
Bury St Edmunds	A	GE	12, C5
Busby	Sc	Cal	29, C5; 44, E2
Bushey	LM	LNW	5, A2; 11, G1
Bush Hill Park	A	GE	5, A3; 11, G3
Bute Road Cardiff	W	GW	8, C4; 43, B5
Butler's Lane	LM	LNW	15, F5
Butterley	LM	Mid	41, E2
Butterwell		BR	27, A5
Buxted	S	LBSC	5, E4
Buxton	LM	LNW	15, A4
Buxton (Midland)	LM	Mid	15, A4
Byfleet & New Haw	S	LSW	5, C1
Byker	TWM		28, Inset
Bynea (Carmar)	W	GW	7, B3
Cadder	Sc	NB	44, D5
Cadoxton	W	BRY	8, D4; 43, B5
Cae Harris	W	RR	8, A5; 43, C2
Caergwrle	LM	GC	20, E4
Caerphilly	W	Rhy	8, C4; 43, B3
Caersws	LM	Cam	14, C3
Cairnie Jcn	Sc	GNS	37, D1
Caldicot	W	GW	8, B2; 9, F1
Caledonian Rd & Barnsbury	LM	NL	40, B5
Calder	Sc	Cal	44, B4
Caldon Low	LM	NS	15, C4
Callander	Sc	Cal	33, G2
Callington		BAC	1, C5
Calstock	W	BAC	1, C5
Calne		GW	3, A5
Calvert Lane	E	H&B	22, Inset
Calverton Colliery	LM		41, E4
Camberley	S	LSW	4, B1; 5, C1
Camborne	W	GW	1, Inset E5
Cambridge	A	GE	11, C3
Cambridge Heath	A	GE	40, B4
Cambus	Sc	NB	30, A5
Cambuslang	Sc	Cal	44, D3
Camden Road	LM	NL	40, B5
Cameron Bridge	Sc	NB	30, A2; 34, G5
Campbeltown	CM		29 Inset
Camp Hill	LM	Mid	13, C4; 15, G4
Canley	LM	LNW	10, A5
Canning Town	A	GE	40, C2
Cannock	LM	LNW	15, E4
Cannon St (London)	S	SEC	5, B3; 40, C4
Canonbury		NL	40, B4
Canterbury East	S	SEC	6, C3
Canterbury West	S	SEC	6, C3
Cantley	A	GE	18, F2
Capel Bangor	LM	VR	13, B5
Capenhurst	LM	BJ	20, D4; 45, F5
Carbean		GW	1, D2
Carbis	W	GW	1, D2
Carbis Bay	W	GW	1, Inset E4
Cardenden	Sc	NB	30, A2
Cardiff Bute Road	W	TV	8, C4; 43, B5
Cardiff Clarence Road	W	GW	43, B5
Cardiff Central	W	GW	8, C4; 43, B5
Cardiff Queen Street	W	GW	8, C4; 43, B5
Cardigan	W	GW	13, E2
Cardonald	Sc	G & P	44, F3
Cardross	Sc	Cal	29, B3
Carfin	Sc	Cal	44, A2
Cargo Fleet	E	NE	28, E4
Cark & Cartmel	LM	Fur	24, B4
Carlisle Citadel	LM	CJC	26, C1
Carlisle Yard	LM	LNW	26, C1
Carlton	LM	Mid	16, C3; 41, F5
Carluke	Sc	Cal	30, D5
Carmarthen	W	GW	7, A2; 13, G4
Carmyle	Sc	Cal	29, C5; 44, D3
Carmyllie	Sc	D & A	34, D3
Carne Point	W	GW	1, D3
Carnforth	LM	Fur & LNW Jt	24, B3
Carnoustie	Sc	D & A	34, E3
Carntyne	Sc	NB	44, D3
Carpenders Park	LM	LMS	5, A2
Carrbridge	Sc	HR	36, F3
Carron	Sc	GNS	36, E1
Carshalton	S	LBSC	5, C3
Carshalton Beeches	S		5, C3
Carstairs	Sc	Cal	30, D4
Cartsdyke	Sc	Cal	29, B3
Castle Bar Park	W	GW	39, C2
Castle Bromwich	LM	Mid	25, G5
Castle Caereinion	W & L		14, B3
Castle (Som)	W	GW	3, C2; 8, F1
Castle Donnington	LM	Mid	16, D4
Castle Douglas	Sc	G & SW	26, C5
Castle Headingham	Ind	CVH	22, D1/E1
Castleford Cutsyke	E	LY	22, E4; 42, B1
Castleton (Lancs)	LM	LY	20, B1; 45, A1
Castleton Moor (Yorks)	E	NE	28, F3
Caterham	S	SEC	5, C3
Catford	S	SEC	40, E3
Catford Bridge	S	SEC	40, E3
Cathays	W	TV	8, C4 and 43, B4
Cathcart	Sc	Cal	44, E3
Catrine	Sc	GSW	29, E5
Cattal	E	NE	21, C4
Cattewater	W	GW	2, D5 and Inset
Causeland	W	GW	1, D4
Cawood	E	NE	21, D5
Cemmes Road	LM	Cam	14, B5
Cefn-y-Bedd	LM	GC	20, E4
Cei Llydan	Ind		29, F2
Chadwell Heath	A	GE	5, A4
Chalfont & Latimer	LUL	Met & GC	10, F1
Chalkwell	A	LTS	6, A5
Chalmerston	Sc		29, G4
Chapel-en-le-Frith	LM	Mid & LNW	25, A4
Chapel Hall	Sc	Cal	44, A3
Chapelton	W	LSW	7, F3
Chapeltown	E	Mid & GC	21, F3; 42, F2
Chappel & Wakes Colne	A & Ind	GE	22, E5
Chard		GW	3, E1
Chard Jcn	W	LSW	3, E1
Charing	S	SEC	6, C4
Charing Cross (Glasgow)	Sc	NB	44, E4
Charing Cross (London)	S	SEC	5, B3; 40, C5
Charlbury	W	GW	10, D5
Charlestown	Sc	NB	30, B3
Charlton (Kent)	S	SEC	40, D2
Chartham	S	SEC	6, C3
Chasewater	W	GW	Inset, E5
Chassen Road	LM		20, C1; 24, G1; 45, B3
Chatham	S	SEC	6, B5
Chathill	E	NE	32, E5
Chatterley Valley	LM	SC	15, C3; 20, E1
Cheadle (Staffs)	LM	NS	25, C4
Cheadle Hulme	LM	LNW	25, A3; 20, C1; 45, A4
Cheam	S	LBSC	5, C3
Cheddar		GW	3, B1; 8, E2
Cheddington	LM	LNW	20, E1
Cheddleton	LM & Ind	NS	15, C4
Cheesewring Quarry		LC	1, C4
Chelford	LM	LNW	25, A3; 20, D1; 45, B5
Chelmsford	A	GE	11, F5
Chelsea Basin	S	WLE Jt	39, D5
Chelsfield	S	SEC	5, C4
Cheltenham Spa Lansdown	W	Mid	9, D4
Cheltenham Spa Malvern Rd	W	GW	9, D4
Cheltenham Spa St James	W	GW	9, D4
Chepstow	W	GW	8, B2; 9, F1
Cherry Tree	LM	LY	20, A2; 24, E2
Chertsey	S	LSW	5, B1
Chesham	LUL	Met & GC Jt	20, F1
Cheshunt	A	GE	11, G3
Chesil		GW	4, D3
Chessington North	S		5, C2; 39, G3
Chessington South	S		5, C2; 39, G3
Chester (General)	LM	BJ CLC GC LNW & GW	20, D4
Chesterfield (Midland)	LM	Mid	26, B5; 42, C2
Chester-le-Street	E	NE	27, C5
Chester Road	LM	LNW	15, F5
Chestfield & Swalecliffe Halt	S		6, B3
Chetnole	W		3, E2
Chichester	S	LBSC	4, E1
Chichester	TWM		28, B5
Chigwell	LUL	GE	5, A4
Chilcompton	W	SD	3, B3; 8, E1
Chilham	S	SEC	6, C3
Chillingham Road	TWM		28, Inset
Chilworth & Albury	S	SEC	5, D1
Chinnor	W	GW	10, F3
Chingford	A	GE	5, A4
Chinley	LM	Mid	15, A4
Chippenham	W	GW	3, A4
Chipping Sodbury	W	GW	8, C1; 9, G2
Chipstead	S	SEC	5, C3
Chirk	LM	GW	20, F4
Chislehurst	S	SEC	40, F2
Chiswick	S	LSW	39, D3
Chiswick Park	LM	NSW	39, D3
Cholsey & Moulsford	W	GW	10, G4
Chorley	LM	LY	20, A3; 24, E2; 45, D1
Chorleywood	LUL	Met & GC Jt	5, A1; 20, F1; 11, G1
Chorlton-cum-Hardy	LM	CLC	20, C1; 45, B3
Christchurch	S	LSW	4, F5
Christ's Hospital (West Horsham)	S	LBSC	5, E2
Church & Oswaldtwistle	LM	LY	24, E1
Church Fenton	E	NE	11, D4
Church Stretton	LM	S & H	14, B1; 15, F1
Churston	DVR	GW	2, D3
Cilmeri	W	LNW	14, E3
Cinderford Town	W	GW	8, A1; 9, E2
Cirencester Town	W	GW	9, F4
City Basin (Exeter)	W	GW	2, B3
Clacton	A	GE	12, F3
Clandon	S	LSW	5, C1
Clapham (London)	S	LBSC	40, F5
Clapham (N. Yorks)	LM	Mid	24, B1
Clapham Jcn (London)	S	LSW LBSC	5, B3; 39, E5, Inset F3 and Inset 39
Clapton	A	GE	40, B4
Clarbeston Road	W	GW	23, G1
Clarkston	Sc	NB	44, A4
Clarkston (Renfrew)	Sc	Cal	29, C5; 44, E2
Claverdon	LM	GW	9, B5
Clay Cross	LM	Mid	16, B5; 41, D2
Clarkston	Sc	NB	44, A4
Claydon	A	GE	12, D4
Claygate	S	LSW	5, C2

Station	Region	Pre Group	Map Ref.
Dovey Jcn	LM	Cam	14, B5
Dowlais (Cae Harris)	W	TBJ	8, A5; 43, C2
Downham Market	A	GE	17, F4
Drakelow Power Station	LM	Mid	15, Inset
Draycott	LM	Mid	16, D4
Drayton		MGN	18, E3
Drayton	S	LBSC	4, E1 and 5, F1
Drayton Green (Ealing)	W	GW	39, C1
Drayton Park	E	GN	40, B5
Drax	E	HB	21, E5
Drem	Sc	NB (NE)	30, B1
Driffield	E	NE	22, C4
Drigg	LM	Fur	26, F3
Drighlington	E	GN	42, B4
Drinnick Mill	W	GW	1, D2
Droitwich Spa	W	GW	9, B3
Dronfield	E	Mid	16, A5; 41, B2
Droylsden	LM	LY & LNW	21, F1 and Inset A2; 45, A3
Drumchapel	Sc	NB	44, F4
Drummuir	Sc	GNS	36, D1
Drumry	Sc	NB	44, F5
Dudbridge	W	Mid	9, E3
Duddeston	LM	LNW	15, G4; 13, C4
Dudley Port	LM	GW	13, B2; 15, G4
Dudley Hill	E	GN	21, D2
Dudley Port	LM	LNW	13, B2; 15, G4
Duffield	LM	Mid	16, C5; 41, F2
Dufftown	Sc	GNS	36, E1
Duirinish	Sc	HR	35, F1
Duke St (Glasgow)	Sc	NB	44, D4
Dullingham	A	GE	11, C4
Dumbarton Central	Sc	D & B	29, B3
Dumbarton East	Sc	Cal	29, B4
Dumfries	Sc	G & SW & Cal	26, B3
Dumpton Park	S		6, B1
Dunbar	Sc	NB	31, B1
Dunblane	Sc	Cal	30, A5; 33, G3
Dunbridge	S	LSW	4, D4
Duncraig	Sc	HR	35, E1
Dundee	Sc	NB	34, E4
Dundee East	Sc	D&A Jt	34 Inset
Dundee (West)	Sc	Cal	34, E4
Dunfermline	Sc	NB	30, A3
Dunford Bridge	E	GC	21, F2; 42, E4
Dungeness	S & RHD	SEC	6, E3
Dunkeld	Sc	HR	33, D4
Dunlop	Sc	GBK	29, D4
Dunnington	DVL		21, C5
Dunragit	Sc	P&W	25, C2
Dunrobin Castle	Sc	HR	36, A4 and 38, G5
Dunstable North	LM	LNW	10, D1; 11, E1
Dunster	WSR	GW	8, E5
Dunston	E	NE	28, Inset
Dunton Green	S	SEC	5, C4
Durham	E	NE	27, D5
Durrington-on-Sea	S	LBSC	5, F1
Dursley	W	Mid	8, B1; 9, F2
Dyce	Sc	GNS	37, F4
Dyffryn Ardudwy	LM	Cam	13, A5; 19, G2
The Dyke		LBSC	5, F3
Dymchurch	RHD		6, E3
Dysart	Sc	NB	30, A2
Dyserth		LNW	19, C5
Eaglescliffe	E	NE	28, E5
Ealing Broadway	W	GW	5, B2; 39, C2
Ealing Common	LUL	Dist	39, C3
Earby	LM	Mid	21, Inset A1
Eardington	SVR	GW	15, G2
Eardisley	W	Mid	14, E2
Earlestown	LM	LNW	20, C3; 24, G2; 45, D3
Earley	S	SEC	4, A2
Earls Court	LUL	Dist	39, D5
Earlsfield	S	LSW	39, E5
Earleswood (W. Mids)	LM	GW	9, A5
Earlswood (Surrey)	S	LBSC	5, D3
Easington Colliery	E	NE	28, D5
Easingwold		Eas	21, B4
East Boldon	E	NE	28, C5
Eastbourne	S	LBSC	5, G5
Eastbrook	W	BR	43, B5
Eastcote	LUL	Dist	39, A1
East Croydon	S	LBSC	5, C3
East Didsbury	LM	LNW	20, C1; 24, G1; 45, A4
East Dulwich	S	LBSC	40, E4
Easterbrook	W	BR	43, B5
Easterhouse	Sc	NB	44, C3
East Farleigh	S	SEC	6, C5
East Finchley	LUL	GN	39, A5
East Garfield	E	NE	21, D4; 42, A1
Eastgate	E	NE	27, D3
East Grimstead	S	LSW	4, D5
East Grinstead	S	LBSC	5, D4
East Ham	LUL	LTS	40, B2
East Kilbride	Sc	Cal	29, D5; 44, D2
East Leake		GC	16, D4
Eastleigh	S	LSW	4, D3
East Malling	S	SEC	5, C5
Easton		GW	3, G3
East Putney	S	LSW	39, E4
Eastriggs	Sc	GSW	26, B2
Eastrington	E	NE	22, D5
East Tilbury	A	LTS	5, B5
East Usk Yard	W	GW	43, A3
East Worthing	S	LBSC	5, F2
Ebbw Vale	W	GW & LNW	8, A4; 43, B1; 45, B3
Eccles	LM	LNW	45, B3
Ecclesfield West	E	Mid & GC	21, G3
Eccles Rd	A	GE	12, A4; 18, G4
Eccleston Park	LM	LNW	20, C3; 24, G3; 45, E3
Edale	LM	Mid	15, A5
Edenbridge	S	SEC	5, D4
Edenbridge Town	S	LBSC	5, D4
Eden Park	S	SEC	40, G3
Edge Hill	LM	LNW	20, C4; 24, G4; 45, F4
Edgware	LUL	GN	5, A2
Edgware Road	LUL	Met	39, C5
Edinburgh Princes Street	Sc	Cal	30, B2 and Inset
Edinburgh Scotland Street	Sc	NB	30 Inset
Edinburgh Waverley	Sc	NB	30, B2 and Inset
Edington Burtle	W	GW	3, B4
Edmonton	A	GE	5, A4
Edwinstowe	LM	GC	41, C5
Edzell	Sc	Cal	34, C3
Effingham Jcn	S	LSW	5, C2
Eggesford	W	LSW	2, A5; 7, G4
Egham	S	LSW	5, B1
Egton	E	NE	28, F2
Elderslie	Sc	G & SW	44, G3 and 29, C4
Elephant & Castle	S	SEC	40, D5
Elgin	Sc	GNS & HR	36, C2
Elland	E	L&Y	42, C5
Ellesmere	LM	Cam	20, F4
Ellesmere Port	LM	BJ	20, D4; 45, E5
Ellon	Sc	GNS	37, E4
Elmers End	S	SEC	40, G4
Elm Park	A	LTS	5, A4
Elmstead Woods	S	SEC	40, F2
Elmswell	A	GE	12, C4
Elton & Creswell	E	Mid	16, A4; 41, B4
Elsecar	E	Mid	21, F3; 42, F2
Elsecar East		GC	21, F4; 42, F1
Elsenham	A	GE	11, E4
Elsham	E	GC	22, F4
Elstree	LM	Mid	5, A2; 11, G2
Elswick	E	NE	28 Inset
Elton & Orston (Notts)	E	GN	16, C2
Ely (Cambs)	A	GE	11, B4
Elvet	E	NE	28, D5
Embankment	LUL		40, C5
Embsay	YDR	Mid	21, C1
Embsay Jcn	LM	Mid	21, C1
Emerson Park	A	LTS	5, A5
Emsworth	S	LBSC	4, E1
Enderby		LNW	16, F4
Enfield Chase	E	GN	5, A3; 11, G2
Enfield Lock	A	GE	11, G3
Enfield Town	A	GE	5, A3; 11, G3
Entwistle	LM	LY	20, A2; 24, E1; 45, B1
Epping	LUL	GE	11, G3
Epsom	S	LSW/ LBSC	5, C2;
Epsom Downs	S	LBSC	5, C3
Erdington	LM	LNW	15, F5
Eridge	S	LBSC	5, D5
Erith	S	SEC	5, B4
Ernesettle	W	LSW	1, D5
Errol	Sc	Cal	34, E5
Eryholme	E	NE	28, F5
Esher	S	LSW	5, B2; 39, G1
Eskbank & Dalkeith	Sc	NB	30, C2
Eskdale (Dalegarth)	RE		26, F2
Eskdale Green (The Green)	RE		26, F3
Essendine	E	GN	16, E1; 17, E1
Essex Road	E	GN	40, B5
Etchingham	S	SEC	6, E5
Etherley	E	NE	27, D5
Etruria	LM	NS	15, C3; 20, F1
Euston	LM	LNW	5, A3; 40, C5
Euston Square	LUL	Met	40, C5
Evercreech Jcn	SD		3, C3; 8, F1
Evesham	W	GW & Mid	9, C4
Ewell East	S	LBSC	5, C3
Ewell West	S	LSW	5, C3
Exeter Central	W	LSW	2, B3
Exeter St Davids	W	GW & LSW	2, B3
Exeter St James's Park	W	LSW	2, B3
Exeter St Thomas	W	GW	2, B3
Exhibition Centre	Sc	NB	44, E4
Exminster	W	GW	2, B3
Exmouth	W	LSW	2, C2
Exton	W	LSW	2, B3
Eye		GE	12, B3
Eyemouth	Sc	NB	31, C3
Eynsford	S	SEC	5, C5
Failsworth	LM	LY	45, A2
Fairbourne	LM	Cam	13, A5
Fairfield	LM	GC	45, A3
Fairford	W	GW	9, F5
Fairlie High	Sc	G & SW	29, D2
Fairlie Pier	Sc	G & SW	29, D2
Fairwater	W		43, B4
Fakenham East	A	GE	18, D5
Falconwood	S	SEC	40, E1
Falkirk Camelon	Sc	NB	30, B4
Falkirk Grahamston	Sc	NB & Cal	30, B4
Falkirk (High)	Sc	NB	30, B4; 29, F3
Falkland Yard	Sc		29, F3
Falmer	S	LBSC	5, F3
Falmouth Docks	W	GW	1, F1
Falmouth Town	W	GW	1, F1
Fambridge	A	GE	12, G5
Fareham	S	LSW	4, E3
Faringdon	W	GW	10, F5
Farnborough Main	S	LSW	4, B1
Farnborough North	S	SEC	4, B1; 5, C1
Farncombe	S	LSW	5, D1
Farnham	S	LSW	4, C1
Farningham Rd	S	SEC	5, B5
Farnworth	LM	LY	20, B2; 24, F1; 45, B2
Farringdon	LUL	Met	40, C5
Fauldhouse	Sc	Cal & NB	30, C4
Faversham	S	SEC	6, C3
Fawdon		TWM	27, B5
Fawley (Hants)	S		4, E3
Faygate	S	LBSC	5, D3
Fazakerley	LM	LY	20, B4; 24, G4; 45, F3
Fearn	Sc	HR	36, B4
Felixtowe FLT	A		12, E3
Felixstowe	A	GE	12, E2
Felling		TWM	28, Inset
Feltham	S	LSW	5, B2
Fenchurch Street	A	GE	5, B3; 40, C4
Fen Drayton	A	GE	11, B3
Feniscowles	LM	LY	24, E2
Feniton	W	LSW	2, B2
Fenny Compton Jcn	LM	GW	10, B4
Fenny Stratford	LM	LNW	10, D2
Fernhill		TV	43, C2
Ferriby	E	NE	22, E4
Ferrybridge for Knottingley	E	SK	21, E4; 42, C1
Ferryhill (Aberdeen)	Sc	Cal	37, G4
Ferry Meadows	NVR	LNW	11, A1
Ferry Road (St Budeaux)	W	GW	1, D5 and Inset
Ferryside	W	GW	7, A2
Ffairfach Halt	W	GW	13, G5
Fiddlers Ferry Power Station	LM	LNW	15, A1 and 45, D4
Filey	E	NE	22, A3
Filey Holiday Camp			22, A3
Filton	W	GW	3, A2; 8, C1; 9, G1
Finchley Central	LUL	GN	39, A5
Finchley Road	LM	GC & Met	39, B5
Finchley Rd & Frognal	LM	LNW	39, B5
Finsbury Park	E	GN	40, B5
Finstock	W	GW	10, E5
Fishbourne	S	LBSC	4, E14
Fishersgate	S	LBSC	5, F3
Fisherrow	Sc	NB	30 Inset
Fiskerton	E	Mid	16, C3
Fitzwilliam	E	GN	42, D1
Fiveways	LM	Mid	13, C3
Fleet (Hants)	S	LSW	4, B1
Fleetwood	LM	PWY & LY	24, C4
Fletton		GN	11, A2; 17, G2
Flimby	LM	LNW	26, D3
Flint	LM	LNW	20, D5; 45, G5
Flintstock	W	GW	10, E5
Flitwick	LM	Mid	10, D1; 11, E1
Flixton	LM	CLC	20, C2; 24, G1; 45, B3
Flowery Field	LM	GC	21, G1
Fochabers Town	Sc	HR	36, C1
Fockerby		LY & NE	22, E5
Folkestone Central	S	SEC	6, D2
Folkestone Harbour	S	SEC	6, D2
Folkestone West	S	SEC	6, D2
Forcett	E	NE	27, F5
Ford (Sussex)	S	LBSC	5, F1
Fordham	A	GE	11, B4
Forest Gate	A	GE	40, B2
Forest Hill	S	LBSC	40, E4
Forfar	Sc	Cal	34, D4
Formby	LM	LY	20, B4; 24, F4; 45, G2
Forncett	A	GE	12, A3; 18, G3
Forres	Sc	HR	36, D3
Forsinard	Sc	HR	38, E5
Fort Augustus	Sc	NB	32, A1; 35, G4
Fort George	Sc	HR	36, D4
Forthside (Stirling)	Sc	NB	30, A5
Fort Matilda	Sc	Cal	29, B3
Fortrose	Sc	HR	36, D5
Fort William	Sc	NB	32, C3
Foss Islands	E	NE	21, C5 and Inset
Fountainhall	Sc	NB	30, D1
Four Ashes	LM	LNW	15, E3
Four Lane Ends		TWM	27, B5
Four Oaks	LM	LNW	15, F5
Fowey	W	GW	1, D3
Foxdale (IoM)		IoMR	23, B2

Station	Region	Pre Group	Map Ref.
Foxfield	LM	Fur	24, A5
Foxton	A	GE	11, D3
Framlingham		GE	12, C3
Frant	S	SEC	5, D5
Fraserburgh	Sc	GNS	37, C4
Fratton	S	LSW & LBSC Jt	4, E2
Freshfield	BBL	LBSC	5, E4
Freshfield	LM	LY	20, B4; 24, F4; 45, G2
Freshford	W	GW	3, B4
Freshwater		FYN	4, F4
Friary (Plymouth)	W	LSW	1, D5 and Inset
Frickley Colliery	E	Mid & NE Jt	42, D1
Friday Street	LM	L & Y	20, A3; 24, E2; 45, D1
Frimley	S	LSW	4, B1; 5, C1
Frinton	A	GE	12, E3
Frizinghall	E	Mid	21, D2; 42, A5
Frodsham	LM	BJ	15, A1; 20, D3; 45, D5
Frome	W	GW	3, C3
Fulbourne	A	GE	11, C4
Fulham Broadway	LUL	Dist	39, D4
Fullerton		LSW	4, C4
Fulwell (Middx)	S	LSW	39, F1
Furness Vale	LM	LNW	15, A4
Furzebrook	S	LSW	3, F4
Furze Platt	W	GW	5, A1
Gaerwen	LM	LNW	19, D2
Gainsborough (Central)	E	GC	16, A2; 22, G5
Gainsborough (Lea Road)	E	GN & GC Jt	16, A2; 22, G5
Galashiels	Sc	NB	30, E1
Galley Hill	S	LBSC	6, F5
Gants Hill	LUL		40, A1
Garelochhead	Sc	NB	29, A3
Gartcosh	Sc	Cal	44, C4
Gartsherrie (Coatbridge CB)	Sc	Cal	44, B4
Garforth	E	NE	21, D4; 42, A1
Gargrave	LM	Mid	21, C1
Garlieston	Sc	P & W	25, D4
Garmouth	Sc	GNS	36, C1
Garrowhill	Sc	NB	44, C3
Garscadden	Sc	NB	44, F4
Garsdale	LM	Mid	27, E2
Garstang & Catherall	LM	LNW & G & KE	24, D3
Garston (Herts)	LM	LNW	11, G1
Garston (Merseyside)	LM	CLC & LNW	45, E4
Garston Dock	LM	LNW	45, E4
Garswood	LM	LNW	20, B3; 24, F2; 45, D3
Gartcosh	Sc	Cal	44, C4
Garth	W	LNW	14, E4
Garth Road		Van (Cam)	14, C4
Gartshore	Sc	NB	44, B5
Garve	Sc	HR	35, C4
Gateacre	LM	CLC	20, C4; 45, E4
Gateshead	TWM	NE	28, Inset
Gateshead Metro Centre	E	NE	28 Inset
Gateshead Stadium	TWM	NE	28, Inset
Gatewen Open Cast	LM	GW	20, E4
Gathurst	LM	LY	20, B2; 24, F3; 45, D2
Gatley	LM	LNW	20, C1; 24, G1; 45, A4
Gatwick Airport	S	LBSC	5, D3
Gedling Colliery	LM	GN	41, F5
Georgemas Jcn	Sc	HR	38, C3
Gerrards Cross	W	GW & GC Jt	5, A1; 10, F1
Gidea Park	A	GE	5, A4
Giffnock	Sc	Cal	44, E2
Gifford	Sc	NB	31, C1
Giggleswick	LM	Mid	24, B1
Gilberdyke	E	NE	22, E5; 27, C2
Gilderdale	Ind		
Gilfach Fargoed	W	RR	8, B4; 43, B2
Gilling	E	NE	21, A5
Gillingham (Dorset)	S	LSW	3, D4
Gillingham (Kent)	S	SEC	6, B5
Gipsy Hill	S	LBSC	40, F4
Girvan	Sc	G & SW	29, G2
Gladstone Dock	LM		45, F3
Glaisdale	E	NE	28, F2
Glan Conwy	LM	LNW	19, D4
Glanrafon	LM	VR	13, C5
Glascoed	W	GW	8, B3
Glasgow Argyle Street	Sc		44, E4 and Inset
Glasgow (Central)	Sc	Cal	29, C5; 44, E4 and Inset E2
Glasgow Cross	Sc	Cal	44, D4 and Inset E2
Glasgow (St Enoch)		G & SW	29, C5; 44, E4 and Inset E2
Glasgow (Queen St)	Sc	NB	29, C5; 44, E4 and Inset E2
Glassel	Sc	GNS	34, A3; 37, G2
Glasson Dock	LM	Mid	24, C3
Glazebrook	LM	CLC	20, C2; 24, G2; 45, C3
Glemsford		GE	12, D5
Glen Douglas	Sc	NB	29, A3
Gleneagles	Sc	Cal	33, F4
Glenfinnan	Sc	NB	32, B4
Glengarnock	Sc	G & SW	29, D3
Glen Parva	LM	LNW	16, F4
Glossop	LM	GC	21, G1
Gloucester	W	Mid	9, E3
Gloucester (Eastgate)	W	GW	9, E3
Gloucester Road	LUL	Dist	39, D5
Glynceiriog		GVT	20, F5
Glynde	S	LBSC	5, F4
Goathland	NYMR	NE	28, F2
Gobowen	LM	GW	20, F4
Godalming	S	LSW	5, D1
Godley	LM	GC	21, G1
Godley East	LM	GC	21, G1
Godstone	S	SEC	5, D3
Gogarth	LM	Cam	13, B5
Goldhawk Road	LUL	H & C	39, D4
Golders Green	LUL		39, A5
Goldthorpe	E	NE & Mid Jt	21, F4; 42, E1
Goldthorpe Colliery	E		21, F4 and 42, E1
Golfa		W & L	14, B2
Golf Street	Sc	NB	34, E3
Gollanfield Jcn	Sc	HR	36, D4
Golspie	Sc	HR	36, A4
Gomshall	S	SEC	5, D2
Goodmayes	A	GE	5, A4
Goodrington Sands	DVR	NE	2, D3
Goole	E	NE	22, E5
Goostrey	LM	LNW	15, B3; 20, D1
Gordon Hill	E	GN	11, G2
Gorgie East	Sc	NB	30 Inset
Goring & Streatley	W	GW	10, G3
Goring-by-Sea	S	LBSC	5, F2
Gorseinon	W	LNW	7, B3
Gorton	LM	GC	45, A3
Gosford Green		LNW	10, A5
Gospel Oak	LM	LNW & THJ	39, B5; 40, Inset
Gosport	S	LSW	4, E3
Gotham		GC	16, D4
Gourock	Sc	Cal	29, B3
Govan	Sc	GSW	44, E4
Gowerton	W	GW	7, B3
Goxhill	E	GC	22, E3
Grange Hill	LUL	GE	5, A4
Grange Court	W	GW	9, E2
Grange-over-Sands	LM	Fur	24, B3
Grange Park	E	GN	5, A3
Grangetown (Glam)	W	TV	8, C4; 43, C4
Grangetown (Cleveland)	E	NE	28, E4
Grantham	E	GN	16, D1
Granton	Sc	Cal	30 Inset
Grantown-on-Spey East	Sc	GNS	36, F3
Grassington & Threshfield	LM	Mid	21, B1
Grateley	S	LSW	4, C5
Gravely Hill	LM	LNW	15, C5
Gravesend	S	SEC	5, B5
Grays	A	LTS	5, B5
Great Ayton	E	NE	28, F4
Great Bentley	A	GE	12, E4
Great Chesterford	A	GE	11, D4
Great Coates	E	GC	22, F2
Greatham	E	NE	28, E4
Great Malvern	W	GW	9, C3
Great Missenden	W	Met & GC Jt	10, F2
Great Moor St	LM	LNW	45, C2
Greatstone-on-Sea Halt	RHD		6, E3
Great Orme	Ind		19, C3
Great Portland St	LUL	Met	39, C5
Great Yarmouth	A	GE	18, F1
Greenbank	LM	CLC	15, A2; 20, D2; 45, C5
Greenfield (Yorks)	LM	LNW	21, F1
Greenford	LUL	GW	39, B1
Greenhithe	S	SEC	5, B5
Green Lane	LM	GW/ LNW	45, F4
Greenock Central	Sc	G & SW	29, B3
Greenock West	Sc	Cal	29, B3
Green Park (Bath)		Mid (SD)	3, A3
Green Road	LM	Fur	24, A5
Greenwich	S	SEC	40, D3
Greenwich Park	S	SEC	40, D3
Gresley	LM	Mid	16, E5
Griffin Wharf (Ipswich)	A	GE	12, D3
Grimethorpe Colliery	E		21, F4 and 42, E1
Grimsby Docks	E	GC	22, F2
Grimsby Town	E	GC	22, F2
Grindleford	LM	Mid	16, A5; 41, B1
Groombridge	S	LBSC	5, D5
Grosmont	E & NYMR	NE	28, F2
Grove Park		SEC	40, E2
Guard Bridge	Sc	NB	34, F4
Guide Bridge	LM	GC	21, Inset A2; 45, A3
Guildford	S	LSW	5, C1
Guild Street (Aberdeen)	Sc	Cal	37, G4
Guisborough	E	NE	28, E3
Guiseley	E	Mid	21, D2
Gullane	Sc	NB	30, B1
Gunheath		GW	1, D2
Gunnersbury	S	LSW	39, D3
Gunnie	Sc	NB	44, B4
Gunnislake	W	BAC	1, C5
Gunton	A	GE	18, D3
Guyhirne		GN & GE Jt	17, F3
Gwaun-cae-Gurwen	W	GW	7, A4
Gwersyllt	LM	GC	20, E4
Gwinear Rd	W	GW	1 Inset, E4
Gypsy Hill	E	NE	28, E4
Habrough	E	GC	22, E3
Hackbridge	S	LBSC	39, G5
Hackney Central	A	NL	40, B3
Hackney Downs	A	GE	40, B4
Hackney Wick	A	NL	40, B3
Haddenham & Thame Parkway	W	GW	10, E3
Haddington	Sc	NB	30, B1
Haddiscoe	A	GE	12, A2; 18, F1
Hadfield	LM	GC	21, G1
Hadley Wood	E	GN	11, G2
Hadleigh		GE	12, D4
Hadrian Road	TWM		28, B5
Hag Fold	LM	L&Y	20, B2; 24, F2 and 45, C2
Hagley	LM	GW	9, A3
Hailsham	S	LBSC	5, F5
Hainault	LUL		5, A4
Hairmyres	Sc	Cal	29, D5; 44, D1
Hale	LM	CLC	15, A2; 20, C1; 45, B4
Halesowen	W	GW	13, C1; 15, G4
Halesworth	A	GE & SWD	12, B2
Halewood	LM	CLC	20, C3; 45, E4
Halfway	SMR		19, E2
Halifax	E	LY	21, E2; 42, B5/C5
Hall Green	LM	GW	9, A5
Halling	S	SEC	6, C5
Hall I 'Th' Wood	LM	L&Y	20, B2; 24, F1 and 45, B1
Halliwell	LM	L & Y	20, B2; 24, F1; 45, B1
Hall Road	LM	LY	20, B4; 24, F4; 45, F2
Haltwhistle	E	NE	27, B2
Halwill Jcn		LSW	1, B5
Hamble	S	LSW	4, E3
Hamilton Central	Sc	Cal & NB	30, D5; 44, B2
Hamilton Sq (Birkenhead)	LM	Mer	45, F4
Hamilton West	Sc	Cal	30, D5; 44, B2
Hammersmith	LUL	Dist & H & C	39, D4
Hammersmith & Chiswick	LUL	Dist	39, D4
Hammerton	E	NE	21, C4
Hampden Park	S	LBSC	5, F5
Hampstead Heath	LM	LNW	39, B5; 40, Inset
Hampton	S	LSW	39, F1
Hampton Court	S	LSW	5, B2; 39, G2
Hampton-in-Arden	LM	LNW	9, A5; 15, G5
Hampton Loade	SVR	GW	15, G2
Hampton Wick	S	LSW	39, F2
Hamstead	LM	LNW	13, B3
Ham Street	S	SEC	6, D4
Hamworthy	S	LSW	3, F5
Handborough	W	GW	10, E4
Handforth	LM	LNW	15, A3; 20, C1; 45, A4
Handsworth & Smethwick	LM	GW	13, B3
Hanger Lane	LUL	GW & GC Jt	39, C2
Hanley	LM	NS	15, C3; 20, E1
Hanwell & Elthorne	W	GW	39, C2
Hapsford	W	GW	3, B3
Hapton	LM	LY	24, D1
Harborne	WR	LNW	15, G4; 13, C3
Harby	LM	GC & LNWR	41, D1
Hare Park	E	GC/GN Jt	42, C2
Harker	LM	NB	26, C1
Harlech	LM	Cam	19, F2
Harlesden	LM	LNW	39, B3
Harleston		GE	12, B3
Harling Road	A	GE	12, A4; 18, G4
Harlington (Beds)	LM	Mid	10, D1; 11, E1
Harlow Mill	A		11, F3
Harlow Town	A	GE	11, F3
Harold Wood	A	GE	5, A5
Harpenden	LM	Mid	11, F1
Harrietsham	S	SEC	6, C4
Harringay Stadium	A	THJ	40, A5
Harringay West	A	GN	40, A5
Harrington	LM	LNW	26, E3
Harrogate	E	NE	21, C3
Harrow & Wealdstone	LM & LUL	LNW	5, A2; 39, A2
Harrow-on-the-Hill	W	Met & GC Jt	39, A2
Hartford	LM	LNW	15, B2; 20, D2; 45, C5
Hartington	LM	LNW	15, B5
Hartlebury	LM	GW	9, A3
Hartlepool	E	NE	28, D5
Hartwood	Sc	Cal	30, C5

Station	Region	Pre Group	Map Ref.
Harwich Parkeston Quay	A	GE	12, E3
Harwich (Town)	A	GE	12, E3
Harworth Colliery	E	SY Jt	21, G5
Haslemere	S	LSW	4, C1; 5, D1
Hassocks	S	LBSC	5, F3
Hastings	S	SEC	6, F5
Haswell	E	NE	28, D5
Hatch End	LM	LNW	5, A2
Hatfield (Herts)	E	GN	11, F2
Hatfield Moor		LY & NE Jt	22, F5
Hatfield Peverel	A	GE	11, F5
Hathersage	LM	Mid	15, A5
Hattersley	LM	GC	21, G1
Hatton Cross	LUL		5, B2; 39, D1
Hatton (Warwickshire)	LM	GW	9, B5
Haughley		GE & MSL	12, C4
Havant	S	LBSC	4, E2
Havenhouse	E	GN	17, B4
Haven Street	IWSR	IWC	4, F3
Haverfordwest	W	GW	7, C2
Haverhill	A	GE & CVH	11, D5
Haverthwaite	L & HR	Fur	24, A4
Haverton Hill	E	NE	28, E4
Hawarden	LM	GC	20, D4
Hawarden Bridge	LM	GC	20, D4
Hawick	Sc	NB	31, F1
Hawkhurst	S	SE	6, D5
Haworth	KWV	Mid	21, D1
Haxey Jcn	E	GN/GE	22, F5
Hay	W	Mid GW	14, F2
Haydon Bridge	E	NE	27, B3
Haydons Rd	S	LBSC & LSW Jt	39, F5
Hayes (Kent)	S	SEC	5, B4; 40, G2
Hayes & Harlington (London)	W	GW	5, B2
Hayfield	LM	GC & Mid Jt	15, A4
Hayle	W	GW	1, Inset E4
Hayling Island		LBSC	4, E2
Haymarket (Edinburgh)	Sc	NB	30, Inset
Haymarket (Newcastle)	TWM		28, Inset
Haywards Heath	S	LBSC	5, E3
Hazel Grove	LM	LNW	15, A4; 20, C1; 21, G1; 45, A4
Headcorn	S	SEC & KES	6, D5
Headingley	E	NE	21, D3; 42, A3
Heads of Ayr	Sc	G & SW	29, F3
Headstone Lane	LM		5, A2; 39, A1
Heald Green	LM	LNW	15, A3; 20, C1; 45, A4
Healey Mills Yard	E	L&Y	21, E3 and 42, C3
Healing	E	GC	22, F2
Heanor		GN	16, C4; 41, F3
Heap Bridge	LM	L & Y	20, B1; 24, F1; 45, A1
Heath (High Level)	W	Rhy	8, C4; 43, B4
Heath (Low Level)	W	Car	8, C4; 43, B4
Heathfield (Devon)	W	GW	2, C4
Heathrow 1, 2, 3	LUL		5, B2; 39, D1
Heathrow 4	LUL		5, B2; 39, D1
Heathway	LUL		5, A4
Heaton Chapel	LM	LNW	45, A3
Heaton Park	LM	LY	20, B1; 24, F1; 45, A2
Hebburn	TWM	NE	28, B5
Hebden Bridge	E	LY	21, E1
Hebron	SMR		19, E2
Heck	E	NE	21, E5
Heckington	E	GN	17, D1
Heighington (Durham)	E	NE	27, E5
Helensburgh Central	Sc	NB	29, B3
Helensburgh Upper	Sc	NB	29, B3
Hellifield	LM	Mid	24, C1
Helmsdale	Sc	HR	38, F4
Helsby	LM	BJ & CLC	15, A1; 20, D3; 45, E5
Helston		GW	1, Inset F5
Hemel Hempstead	LM	Mid	10, E1; 11, F1
Hemingborough	E	NE	21, D5
Hemsworth	E	WRG	42, D1
Hemyock		GW	2, A2; 8, G4
Hendford		GW	3, D2
Hendon	LM	Mid	39, A4
Hendon Central	LUL		39, A4
Hengoed High Level	W	GW	8, B4; 43, B3
Hengoed Low Level	W	Rhy	8, B4; 43, B3
Heniarth	W & L		14, B3
Henley-in-Arden	LM	GW	9, B5
Henley-on-Thames	W	GW	10, G2
Henshall		LY	21, E5
Hereford (Barrs Court)	W	S & H	9, C1
Herne Bay	S	SEC	6, B2
Herne Hill		SEC	40, F5
Heron Quays	DLR		40, C3
Hersham	S		5, C2 and 39, G1
Hertford North	E	GN	11, F2
Hertford East	A	GE	11, F2
Hessle	E	NE	22, E4
Hest Bank	LM	LNW	24, B3
Heswall	LM	GC	20, C4; 45, F4
Hethersett	A	GE	18, F3
Hever	S	LBSC	5, D4
Heworth	TWM		28, Inset
Hexham	E	NE	27, B3
Heyford	W	GW	10, D4
Heysham	LM	Mid	24, C3
Heywood	LM	LY	20, B1; 24, F1; 45, A2
Higham (Kent)	S	SEC	6, B5
Higham Ferrers	LM	LNW	10, B1
Highams Park	A	GE	5, A4
High Barnet	LUL	GN	5, A3; 11, G2
High Blantyre	Sc	Cal	44, C2
Highbridge for Burnham-on-Sea	W	GW & SD	3, B1; 8, E3
High Brooms	S	SEC	5, D5
Highbury & Islington	NL		40, B5
Highley	SVR	GW	15, G2
High Marnham Power Station	E	GC	16, B2
Hightown	LM	LY	20, B4; 24, F4; 45, F2
Highworth	W	GW	9, F5
High Wycombe	W	GW & GC Jt	10, F2
Hildenborough	S	SEC	5, C5
Hillfoot	Sc	NB	29, B4; 44, E5
Hillhouse	E	LNW	21, E2; 42, C5
Hillingdon	LUL	Dist	5, A2
Hillington East	Sc	G & SW	44, F3
Hillington West	Sc	G & SW	44, F3
Hilsea	S	LBSC	4, E2
Hillside	LM	LY	20, A4; 24, E4; 45, F1
Hillside	Sc	NB	34, C2
Hinchley Wood	S	LSW	5, C2
Hinckley	LM	LNW	16, F4
Hindley North	LM	LY	20, B2; 24, F2; 45, C2
Hindley South	LM	LY	20, B2; 24, F2; 45, C2
Hinton Admiral	S	LSW	4, F5
Hirwaun	W	GW	8, A5 and 43, D1
Histon	A	GE	11, C3
Hitchin	E	GN	11, E2
Hither Green	S	SEC	40, E3
Hockley (Birmingham)	LM	GW	13, C3; 15, G4
Hockley (Essex)	A	GE	6, A5
Hoddlesden	LM	L & Y	20, A2; 24, E1
Holborn Viaduct	S	SEC	5, B3; 40, C5
Holcombe Brook	LM	LY	20, A1; 24, F1; 45, B1
Holditch Colliery	LM	NS	15, C3
Hollingbourne	S	SEC	6, C5
Hollins	LM	L & Y	24, E2
Hollinwood	LM	L & Y	45, A2
Holme	E	GN	11, A2; 17, G2
Holmes Chapel	LM	LNW	15, B3; 20, D1
Holmfirth	E	L & Y	21, F2; 42, D5
Holmwood	S	LBSC	5, D2
Holt	NNR	MGN	18, D4
Holton Heath	S	LSW	3, F4
Holybourne	S	LSW	4, C2
Holyhead	LM	LNW	19, B2
Holytown	Sc	Cal	30, C5; 44, A3
Holywell Jcn & Town	LM	LNW	20, D5; 45, G5
Homerton	A	NL	40, B3
Honeybourne	W	GW	9, C5
Honiton	W	LSW	2, A2
Honley	E	LY	21, F2; 42, D5
Honor Oak Park	S	LBSC	40, E4
Hook	S	LSW	4, B2
Hooton	LM	BJ	20, D4; 45, F5
Hope (Derbys)	LM	Mid	15, A5
Hopeman	Sc	HR	36, C2
Hope Village	LM	GC	20, E4
Hopton Heath	W	LNW	14, C1
Horbury & Osset	E	LY	42, C3
Horley	S	LBSC	5, D3
Hornby Dock	LM		45, F3
Horncastle		GN	17, B2
Hornchurch	A	LTS	5, A5
Hornsea	E	NE	22, C2
Hornsey	E	GN	40, A5
Horrocksford		L&Y	24, D1
Horsforth	E	NE	21, D3; 42, A3
Horsham	S	LBSC	5, E2
Horsley	S	LSW	5, C2
Horsted Keynes	BBL	LBSC	5, E4
Horton-in-Ribblesdale	LM	Mid	24, B1
Horwich	LM	LY	20, B2; 24, F2; 45, C1
Hoscar	LM	LY	20, B3; 24, F3; 45, E1
Hotchley Hill	LM	Mid	16, D4
Hothfield	S	SEC	6, D4
Hough Green	LM	CLC	15, A1; 20, C3; 45, E4
Hounslow	S	LSW	39, E1
Hounslow Central	LUL	Dist	5, B2; 39, D1
Hounslow East	LUL	Dist	39, D1
Hounslow West	LUL	Dist	5, B2; 39, D1
Houston & Crosslee	Sc	Cal	29, C4; 44, G4
Hove	S	LBSC	5, F3
Hoveton & Wroxham	A	GE	18, E2
Howden	E	NE	22, D5
Howdon-on-Tyne	TWM	NE	28, B5
How Wood	LM	LNW	11, G1
Hoylake	LM	Wir	20, C5; 45, G4
Hubbert's Bridge	E	GN	17, C2
Hucknall	LM	Mid	41, E4
Huddersfield	E	LNW & LY Jt	21, E2; 42, C5
Hull Paragon	E	NE & HB	22, D3/E3; and Inset
Hulme End	L & M		15, B5
Humber Oil Refinery	E	GC	22, E3
Humphrey Park	LM	CLC	45, B3
Huncoat	LM	LY	24, D1
Hungerford	W	GW	4, A4
Hunmanby		NE	22, B3
Hunslet East	E	NE	42, A2
Hunstanton		GE	17, D5
Hunterston	Sc	GSW	29, D2
Huntingdon	E	GN	11, B2
Huntly	Sc	GNS	37, E1
Hunt's Cross	LM	CLC	20, C4; 45, E4
Huntspill	W	GW	3, C1 and 8, E3
Hurst Green	S	CO	5, C4
Huskisson	LM	CLC	45, F3
Hutton Cranswick	E	NE	22, C4
Huyton	LM	LNW	20, C3; 24, G3; 45, E4
Hyde Central	LM	GC & Mid Jt	21, G1
Hyde North	LM	GC & Mid Jt	21, G1
Hykeham	E	Mid	16, B1
Hyndland	Sc	NB	44, E4
Hythe (Essex)	A	GE	12, E4
Hythe (Hants)	S		4, E4
Hythe (Kent)	RHD		6, D3
IBM (private)	Sc	Cal	29, B3
Ickenham	LUL	Dist	5, A2
Ickles	E	GC	42, G1
Idle	E	GN	42, A4
Ifield	S	LBSC	5, D3
Ilford	A	GE	5, A4; 40, B1
Ilfracombe	W	LSW	7, E3
Ilkeston North	LM	GN	16, C4; 41, F3
Ilkeston Jcn & Cossall	LM	Mid	16, C4; 41, F3
Ilkley	E	Mid & O & I	21, C2
Immingham Dock	E	GC	22, E2
Ince (Lancs)	LM	LY	20, B2; 24, F2; 45, D2
Ince & Elton	LM	BJ	15, A1; 20, D3; 45, E5
Inchture Village	Sc	Cal	34, E5
Ingatestone	A	GE	11, G4
Ingrow	KWV	Mid	21, D1
Insch	SC	GNS	37, E2
Inveramsay	Sc	GNS	37, E3
Inverbervie	Sc	NB	34, B2
Invergordon	Sc	HR	36, C5
Invergowrie	Sc	Cal	34, E5
Inverkeilor	Sc	NB	34, D3
Inverkeithing	Sc	NB	30, B3
Inverkip	Sc	Cal	29, C2
Inverness	Sc	HR	36, E5
Invershin	Sc	HR	35, A5
Inverurie	Sc	GNS	37, F3
Ipswich	A	GE	12, D3
Irlam	LM	CLC	20, C2; 24, G1; 45, C3
Irton Road	RE		26, F3
Irvine	Sc	G & SW & Cal	29, E3
Isfield	Ind	LBSC	5, E4
Island Gardens	DLR		40, D3
Isleworth	S	LSW	39, D2
Iver	W	GW	4, C3; 5, B1
Jamestown	Sc	NB	29, B4
Jarrow	TWM	E	28, B5
Jedburgh	Sc	NB	31, E1
Jefferstone Lane	RHD		6, E3
Jesmond	TWM	NE	27, B5; 28 Inset
Johnston (Dyfed)	W	GW	7, C1
Johnstone	Sc	G & SW	29, C4
Jordanhill	Sc	NB	44, E4
Justinhaugh	Sc	Cal	34, C4
Keadby	E	GC	22, F5
Kearsley	LM	LY	20, B2; 24, F1; 45, B2
Kearsney	S	SEC	6, D2
Kegworth	LM	Mid	16, D4
Keighley	KWV	Mid & E	21, D1
Keith	Sc	GNS & HR	37, D1
Kelling Camp Halt	NNR		18, D4
Kelton Fell	RKF		26, E3
Kelty	Sc	NB	30, A3
Kelvedon	A	GE	12, F5
Kemble	W	GW	9, F4
Kempston Hardwick	LM	LNW	10, C1; 11, D1
Kempton Park	S	LSW	39, F1
Kemp Town (Brighton)		LBSC	5, F3
Kemsing	S	SEC	5, C5
Kemsley	S	SR	6, B4
Kemsley Down	S & KL		6, B4
Kendal	LM	LNW	24, A3; 27, G1
Kenley	S	SEC	5, C5
Kennethmont	Sc	GNS	37, E2
Kennett	A	GE	11, C5
Kennishead	Sc	GBK	44, E3
Kensal Green	LM	LNW	39, B4

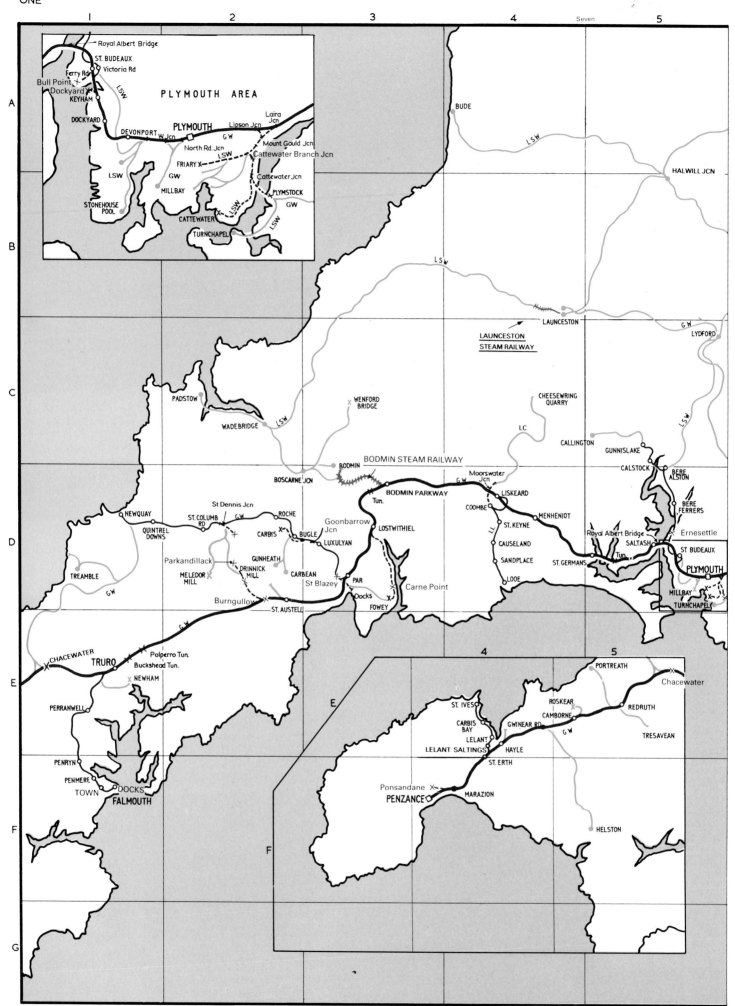

PLYMOUTH AREA

Royal Albert Bridge
ST. BUDEAUX
Ferry Rd
Victoria Rd
Bull Point
Dockyard
KEYHAM
DOCKYARD
LSW
DEVONPORT
W. Jcn
PLYMOUTH
North Rd. Jcn
FRIARY X
Lipson Jcn
Laira Jcn
GW
Mount Gould Jcn
Cattewater Branch Jcn
LSW
Cattewater Jcn
PLYMSTOCK
GW
LSW
GW
MILLBAY
LSW
STONEHOUSE POOL
CATTEWATER
LSW
TURNCHAPEL

BUDE
LSW
HALWILL JCN
Seven
LSW
GW
LYDFORD
LSW
LAUNCESTON
LAUNCESTON STEAM RAILWAY

PADSTOW
WENFORD BRIDGE
CHEESEWRING QUARRY
LC
CALLINGTON
GUNNISLAKE
WADEBRIDGE
LSW
BODMIN
BODMIN STEAM RAILWAY
CALSTOCK
BERE ALSTON
BOSCARNE JCN
GW
Moorswater Jcn
LISKEARD
BERE FERRERS
NEWQUAY
St Dennis Jcn
ST. COLUMB RD
GW
ROCHE
BODMIN PARKWAY
Tun.
COOMBE
Royal Albert Bridge
Ernesettle
QUINTREL DOWNS
CARBIS
X
BUGLE
Goonbarrow Jcn
ST. KEYNE
LL
SALTASH
Tun.
ST BUDEAUX
Parkandillack
GUNHEATH
LUXULYAN
LOSTWITHIEL
CAUSELAND
ST. GERMANS
PLYMOUTH
TREAMBLE
MELEDOR MILL
DRINNICK MILL
CARBEAN
PAR
SANDPLACE
MILLBAY
GW
CARNEAN
St Blazey
Docks
Carne Point
LOOE
TURNCHAPEL
Burngullow
X
ST. AUSTELL
FOWEY
X
CHACEWATER
TRURO
Polperro Tun.
Buckshead Tun.
GW
NEWHAM
PERRANWELL
PORTREATH
Chacewater
ST. IVES
ROSKEAR
CAMBORNE
REDRUTH
PENRYN
PENMERE
CARBIS BAY
GWINEAR RD
TRESAVEAN
TOWN
DOCKS
FALMOUTH
LELANT
LELANT SALTINGS
HAYLE
GW
ST. ERTH
Ponsandane X
PENZANCE
MARAZION
HELSTON
MENHENIOT

MEETH

EGGESFORD

LSW

LAPFORD

MORCHARD RD

COPPLESTONE

TIVERTON PARKWAY

TIVERTON

TIVERTON JCN

HEMYOCK

GW

Summit   Honiton Tun.

FENITON

HONITON

AXMINSTER

LSW

SEATON JCN

COLYTON

CREDITON

NEWTON ST. CYRES

Coleford Jcn

YEOFORD

LSW

OKEHAMPTON

Meldon Quarry

Summit

Cowley Bridge Jcn

ST DAVIDS

EXETER

ST. THOMAS

GW

Stoke Canon

PINHOE

St. James Park

CENT.

City Basin

Exmouth Jcn

POLSLOE BRIDGE

WHIMPLE

TIPTON ST. JOHNS

SIDMOUTH

LSW

SEATON TRAMWAY

COLYFORD

AXMOUTH

SEATON

MORETON HAMPSTEAD

GW

TOPSHAM

EXTON

LYMPSTONE COMMANDO

LYMPSTONE

STARCROSS

EXMOUTH

HEATHFIELD

DAWLISH WARREN

DAWLISH

TEIGNMOUTH

PRINCETOWN

YELVERTON

ASHBURTON

Aller Jcn

NEWTON ABBOT

GW

PLYM VALLEY RAILWAY
(UNDER CONSTRUCTION)

BUCKFASTLEIGH

Summit

Dainton Tun.

TORRE

STAVERTON BRIDGE

RIVERSIDE

Ashburton Jcn

TOTNES

TORQUAY

PAIGNTON

GOODRINGTON SANDS

BRENT

Marley Tun.

GW

Rattery Summit

DART VALLEY RAILWAY

BRIXHAM

CHURSTON

KINGSWEAR

MARSH MILLS

Tavistock Jcn.

GW

YEALMPTON

KINGSBRIDGE

A

Three

B

C

D

E

F

G

1   2   Eight   3   4   Nine   5

A

PORTISHEAD
CENTRAL
AVONMOUTH
SHIREHAMPTON
SEA MILLS
FILTON
GW (out of use)
GW
GW
MID
MANGOTSFIELD
CHIPPENHAM

BRISTOL (SEE INSET BELOW)
TEMPLE MEADS
AVON VALLEY RAILWAY
Thingley Jcn.
CALNE

CLEVEDON
Brislington Tun.
Middle Hill Tun.
Box Tun.

WC&P
NAILSEA & BACKWELL
KEYNSHAM
MIDLAND BRIDGE RD.
GREEN PARK
Bathampton Jcn.

YATTON
BITTON MID
MELKSHAM

B

WESTON MILTON
GW
Worle Jcn.
Twerton Tun
OLDFIELD PARK
BATH SPA

Uphill Jcn.
WESTON-SUPER-MARE
Combe Down Tun.
BRADFORD-ON-AVON
W N S
Bradford Jcn.

BLAGDON
FRESHFORD
AVONCLIFF
TROWBRIDGE

GW
GW
RADSTOCK
SDJ
Hawkeridge Jcn
Heywood Rd Jcn

CHEDDAR
Writhlington Colliery
Fairwood Jcn
WESTBURY
GW

BURNHAM-ON-SEA
HIGHBRIDGE
BASON BRIDGE
Masbury Summit
VOBSTER
Hapsford
Clink Rd Jcn
DILTON MARSH

SDJ
GW
WELLS
Whatley Quarry
FROME
WARMINSTER
Beechgrove

C

Huntspill
Winsor Hill Tun
SHEPTON MALLET
GW
Blatchbridge Jcn
RB

Docks
BRIDGWATER
SDJ
SDJ
GLASTONBURY & STREET
CRANMORE
Merehead Quarry
WITHAM
GW

EAST SOMERSET RAILWAY

EVERCREECH JCN
Baverstock

CASTLE CARY
BRUTON
CHILMARK DINTON
LSW

D

Curry Rivell Jcn.
GW
SDJ
TISBURY

GW
GILLINGHAM
Buckhorn Weston Tun.

GW
TEMPLECOMBE
LSW
SDJ

E

HENDFORD
PEN MILL
RB
SHERBORNE

GW
TOWN JCN
YEOVIL

CHARD
CREWKERNE
CLIFTON MAYBANK
THORNFORD
YETMINSTER

CHARD JCN
LSW
CHETNOLE
GW

F

MAIDEN NEWTON
WIMBORNE

Corfe Mullen Jcn
BROADSTONE

LYME REGIS
GW
BRANKSOME
BOURNEMOUTH

BRIDPORT
HAMWORTHY
POOLE
PARKSTONE WEST

WEST BAY
RB WEST
HOLTON HEATH
HAMWORTHY

GW
DORCHESTER
SOUTH
Dorchester Jcn
MORETON
Winfrith
WAREHAM
WOOL
Worgret Jcn

ABBOTSBURY
GW
Bincombe Tuns.
LSW
FURZEBROOK

UPWEY
CORFE CASTLE

G

Weymouth Jcn
HERSTON HALT
SWANAGE
HARMANS CROSS (1989)
SWANAGE RAILWAY

WEYMOUTH QUAY
LSW

EASTON

BRISTOL (inset)

REDLAND
Ashley Hill Jcn.
CLIFTON DOWN
MONTPELIER
STAPLETON RD.
HOTWELLS (out of use)
WAPPING WHARF
AVONSIDE WHARF
Lawrence Hill Jcn.
LAWRENCE HILL
Dr. Day's Bridge Jcn.
Ashton Jcn.
TEMPLE MEADS
KINGSLAND RD.
North Somerset Jcn.
Relief line Jcn.
BRISTOL EAST DEPOT
BEDMINSTER
Marsh Jcn.
PARSON ST.
West Depot FLT

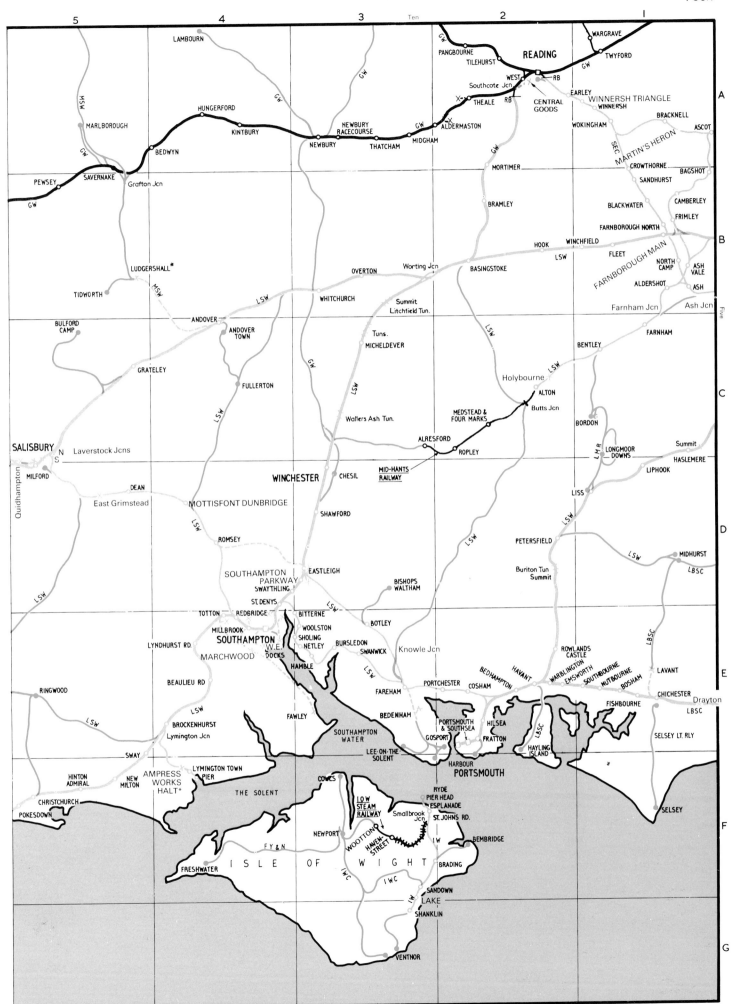

WARGRAVE
LAMBOURN
TWYFORD
PANGBOURNE
TILEHURST
READING
Southcote Jcn
WEST
RB
EARLEY   WINNERSH TRIANGLE
Theale   RB   WINNERSH
CENTRAL   WOKINGHAM   BRACKNELL
Aldermaston   GOODS   ASCOT
MARTIN'S HERON
MARLBOROUGH
HUNGERFORD   CROWTHORNE   BAGSHOT
KINTBURY   NEWBURY RACECOURSE   SANDHURST
NEWBURY   MORTIMER   BLACKWATER   CAMBERLEY
BEDWYN   THATCHAM   MIDGHAM   FRIMLEY
FARNBOROUGH NORTH
BRAMLEY   NORTH
PEWSEY   SAVERNAKE   HOOK   WINCHFIELD   CAMP   ASH
Grafton Jcn   VALE
FLEET
FARNBOROUGH MAIN
LSW   ALDERSHOT   ASH
A
B
LUDGERSHALL*   OVERTON   Worting Jcn   BASINGSTOKE   Farnham Jcn   Ash Jcn
Five
TIDWORTH   WHITCHURCH   BENTLEY   FARNHAM
Summit
Litchfield Tun.
BULFORD   Tuns.
CAMP   ANDOVER   MICHELDEVER   HOLYBOURNE
ANDOVER   ALTON
GRATELEY   TOWN   Butts Jcn   BORDON
FULLERTON   Watters Ash Tun.   MEDSTEAD &
FOUR MARKS   LONGMOOR   Summit
SALISBURY   Laverstock Jcns   ALRESFORD   DOWNS   HASLEMERE
MILFORD   CHESIL   ROPLEY   LIPHOOK
DEAN   MID-HANTS   LISS
East Grimstead   MOTTISFONT DUNBRIDGE   WINCHESTER   RAILWAY   PETERSFIELD   MIDHURST
ROMSEY   SHAWFORD   LBSC
Buriton Tun
Summit
SOUTHAMPTON   EASTLEIGH   BISHOPS
PARKWAY   WALTHAM   ROWLANDS
SWAYTHLING   CASTLE
ST DENYS   BOTLEY   WARBLINGTON   LAVANT
TOTTON   REDBRIDGE   BITTERNE   HAVANT
MILLBROOK   WOOLSTON   BEDHAMPTON   EMSWORTH   BOSHAM
LYNDHURST RD.   SOUTHAMPTON   SHOLING   BURSLEDON   SOUTHBOURNE
W.E.   NETLEY   SWANWICK   Knowle Jcn   NUTBOURNE   CHICHESTER
MARCHWOOD   DOCKS   HAMBLE   PORTCHESTER   FISHBOURNE   Drayton
BEAULIEU RD.   COSHAM   LBSC
RINGWOOD   FAREHAM   PORTSMOUTH & SOUTHSEA
FAWLEY   GOSPORT   HILSEA   HAYLING   SELSEY LT. RLY
BROCKENHURST   BEDENHAM   FRATTON   ISLAND
Lymington Jcn   SOUTHAMPTON   LEE-ON-THE-
SWAY   WATER   SOLENT
HINTON   LYMINGTON TOWN   Harbour   SELSEY
ADMIRAL   NEW   AMPRESS   PIER   PORTSMOUTH
MILTON   WORKS   COWES   RYDE
CHRISTCHURCH   HALT*   PIER HEAD
POKESDOWN   THE SOLENT   IOW   ESPLANADE
STEAM   Smallbrook   ST JOHNS RD.
RAILWAY   Jcn
WOOTTON   BEMBRIDGE
NEWPORT   HAVEN-
FY & N   STREET   BRADING
ISLE OF WIGHT
FRESHWATER   SANDOWN
LAKE
VENTNOR   SHANKLIN
C
D
E
F
G

GW
MSW
GW
GW
GW
GW
SEC
LSW
LSW
GW
MSW
LSW
MSW
LSW
NS
Quidhampton
LSW
LSW
LSW
LSW
LSW
LSW
LSW
LSW
LSW
LSW
LSW
LMR
LBSC
LBSC
IW
IWC
IWC
IW

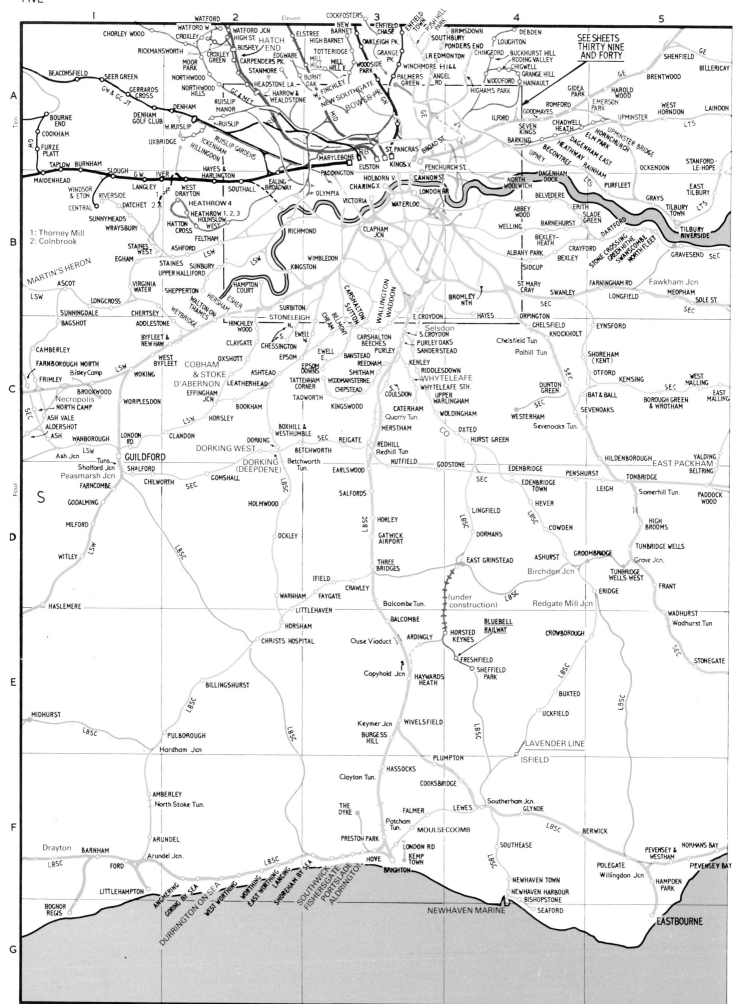

FIVE

SEE SHEETS THIRTY NINE AND FORTY

5   FAMBRIDGE ALTHORNE   4   3   Twelve   2   1

BATTLESBRIDGE   WOODHAM
GE   FERRERS
WICKFORD   GE   HOCKLEY   BURNHAM·ON·CROUCH
                    ROCHFORD
BASILDON   RAYLEIGH
LT&S   PITSEA   LEIGH· CHALKWELL PRITTLEWELL
CORYTON   BENFLEET ON·SEA VICTORIA EAST   THORPE BAY
                    WESTCLIFF   CENTRAL PIGS BAY
                    SOUTHEND·   SHOEBURYNESS
THAMESHAVEN   ON·SEA

A

ALL HALLOWS·
ON·SEA
Cliffe   Kingsnorth   Yantlet   DOCKYARD SHEERNESS
HIGHAM   GRAIN→ PORT ON·SEA
Tunnels   STROOD   VICTORIA QUEENBOROUGH   BIRCHINGTON MARGATE
                    Kingsferry Bridge LEYSDOWN   ON·SEA
ROCHESTER   GILLINGHAM SWALE   CHESTFIELD &   WESTGATE· RAMSGATE BROADSTAIRS
CUXTON   Tunnels CHATHAM HALT   SWALECLIFFE HALT ON·SEA
HALLING   RAINHAM Ridham Dk HERNE   WHITSTABLE &   SE&C   MINSTER   DUMPTON
                    KEMSLEY NEWINGTON   BAY   TANKERTON   PARK
SNODLAND   SITTINGBOURNE TEYNHAM   STURRY   SANDWICH RD   SANDWICH
NEW HYTHE   SE&C   WEST CANTERBURY   Betteshanger Col
AYLESFORD   SITTINGBOURNE   FAVERSHAM   EAST BEKESBOURNE WINGHAM   DEAL
E.MALLING Allington & KEMSLEY RAILWAY SELLING   SE&C ADISHAM   WALMER
BARMING EAST BEARSTED   Selling Tun. CHARTHAM   E.K.LT.R TILMANSTONE
    BARRACKS   CHILHAM   AYLESHAM   COLLIERY
E.FARLEIGH WEST MAIDSTONE HOLLINGBOURNE   SNOWDOWN   SHEPHERDS   MARTIN
WATERINGBURY Tovil HARRIETSHAM   Lydden Tun. WELL   MILL
         LENHAM   WYE   KEARSNEY
         SE&C CHARING   Buckland Jcn   Guston Tun.
MARDEN STAPLEHURST   Hothfield   PRIORY PRIORY
    HEADCORN PLUCKLEY Sevington   WARREN * Abbotscliffe Tun. DOVER
    SE&C   ASHFORD   Martello Tun. *EAST SE&C WESTERN DOCKS
HAWKHURST ROLVENDEN (KENT) SMEETH   *EAST SHAKESPEARE STAFF HALT
    UNDER   TENTERDEN TOWN   SANDLING CENTRAL Shakespeare Tun.
ETCHINGHAM CONSTRUCTION KENT& HAM ST. WESTENHANGER WEST FOLKESTONE
    NORTHIAM EAST SUSSEX   Sandling Tun. HYTHE HARBOUR
    BODIAM RAILWAY APPLEDORE   SANDGATE
ROBERTSBRIDGE WITTERSHAM ROAD   R.H.&D.R   ROMNEY HYTHE
    Mountfield Tun SE&C   DYMCHURCH & DYMCHURCH
MOUNTFIELD   RYE   JEFFERSTONE LANE RAILWAY
    RYE Tramway   NEW
BATTLE WINCHELSEA RYE CAMBER Dungeness ROMNEY
CROWHURST HARBOUR   GREATSTONE·ON·SEA
WEST ST. DOLEHAM   ROMNEY SANDS
LEONARDS THREE OAKS   LADE HALT
BEXHILL Ore Tun.   PILOT HALT
WEST ORE HASTINGS   DUNGENESS
BEXHILL ST. LEONARDS
COLLINGTON WARRIOR SQUARE Galley Hill
COODEN
BEACH

B

C

D

E

F

G

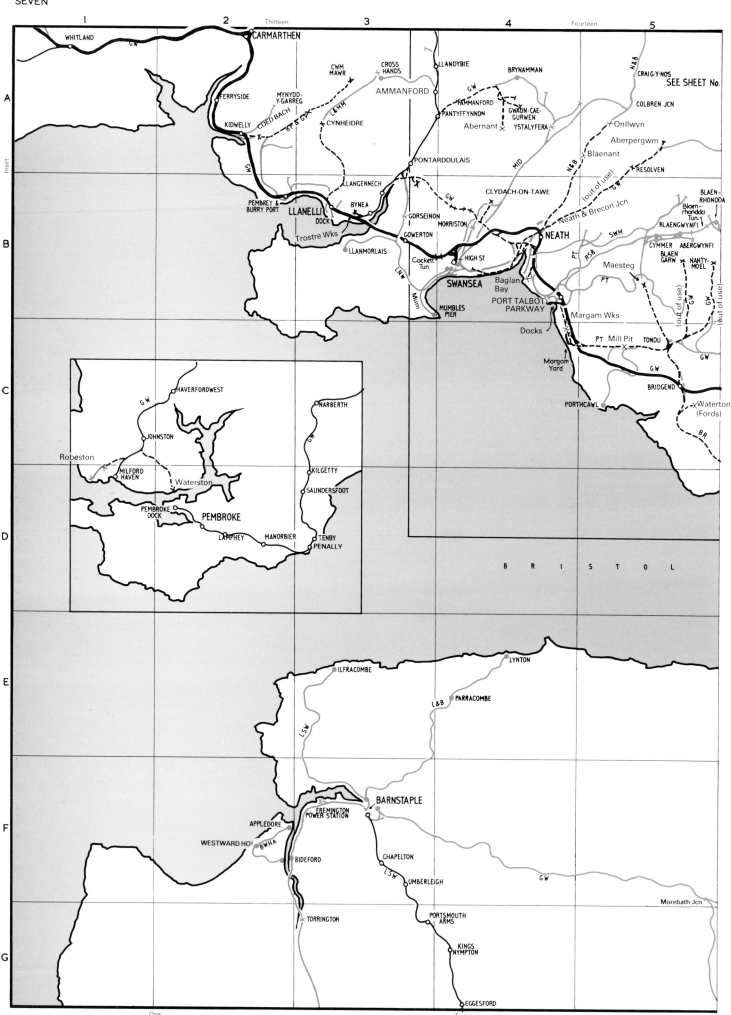

1 2 3 4 5

A B C D E F G

WHITLAND

GW

CARMARTHEN

CWM MAWR

CROSS HANDS

LLANDYBIE

BRYNAMMAN

CRAIG·Y·NOS

N&B

SEE SHEET No.

FERRYSIDE

MYNYDD·Y·GARREG

AMMANFORD

AMMANFORD

GW

COLBREN JCN

KIDWELLY

COED BACH

CYNHEIDRE

PANTYFFYNNON

GWAUN·CAE·GURWEN

Onllwyn

Aberpergwm

BP & GV

L&MM

Abernant

YSTALYFERA

MID

N&B

Blaenant

RESOLVEN

PONTARDDULAIS

GW

(out of use)

GW

PEMBREY & BURRY PORT

LLANGENNECH

CLYDACH-ON-TAWE

BLAEN-RHONDDA

Blaenrhondda Tun.

LLANELLI DOCK

BYNEA

GW

Neath & Brecon Jcn

SWM

BLAENGWYNFI

Trostre Wks

GORSEINON

MORRISTON

NEATH

PT

RSB

CYMMER

ABERGWYNFI

LLANMORLAIS

GOWERTON

NEATH

BLAEN GARW

NANTY-MOEL

LNW

Cockett Tun.

HIGH ST

Maesteg

PT

Mum

SWANSEA

Baglan Bay

PORT TALBOT PARKWAY

Margam Wks

(out of use)

GW

(out of use)

MUMBLES PIER

Docks

PT Mill Pit

TONDU

GW

Margam Yard

GW

BRIDGEND

B R I S T O L

GW

PORTHCAWL

Waterton (Fords)

BR

Inset

HAVERFORDWEST

NARBERTH

GW

GW

JOHNSTON

Robeston

MILFORD HAVEN

Waterston

KILGETTY

SAUNDERSFOOT

PEMBROKE DOCK

PEMBROKE

LAMPHEY

MANORBIER

TENBY

PENALLY

ILFRACOMBE

LYNTON

LSW

L&B

PARRACOMBE

BARNSTAPLE

FREMINGTON POWER STATION

APPLEDORE

WESTWARD HO!

BWHA

BIDEFORD

CHAPELTON

LSW

UMBERLEIGH

GW

Morebath Jcn

TORRINGTON

PORTSMOUTH ARMS

KINGS NYMPTON

EGGESFORD

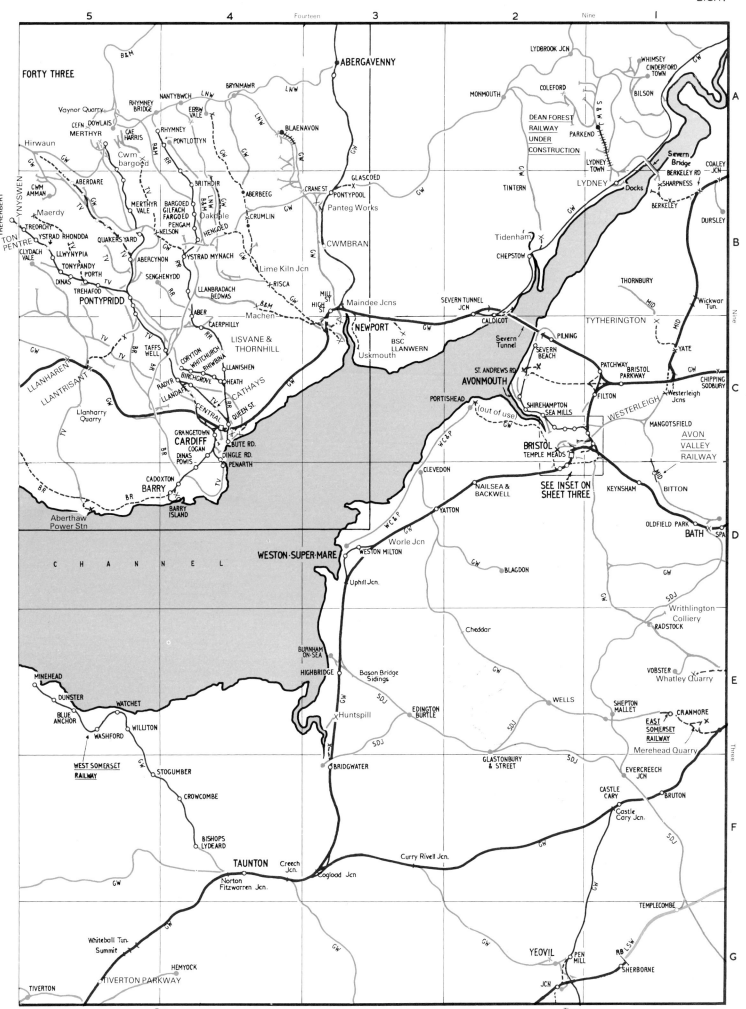

5   4   Fourteen   3   2   Nine   I

FORTY THREE

B&M

WHIMSEY
CINDERFORD
TOWN

LYDBROOK JCN

Vaynor Quarry
CEFN   DOWLAIS
MERTHYR   CAE
HARRIS   RHYMNEY
RHYMNEY
BRIDGE   NANTYBWCH
EBBW
VALE
BRYNMAWR

ABERGAVENNY

MONMOUTH   COLEFORD   BILSON

S&W J

Hirwaun   PONTLOTTYN   LNW   BLAENAVON
CWM   ABERDARE
AMMAN   RHYMNEY

DEAN FOREST
RAILWAY
UNDER
CONSTRUCTION

PARKEND

Cwm
bargoed   BRITHIR   ABERBEEG
MERTHYR
VALE   BARGOED
GILFACH
FARGOED   CRANE ST
Oakdale   GLASCOED
PONTYPOOL

LYDNEY
TOWN   Severn
Bridge
BERKELEY RD   COALEY
JCN
SHARPNESS

Maerdy   PENGAM
NELSON   CRUMLIN
Panteg Works

TINTERN   LYDNEY   Docks

BERKELEY

DURSLEY

TREORCHY
YSTRAD RHONDDA   QUAKERS YARD   HENGOED   CWMBRAN
CLYDACH
VALE   LLWYNYPIA   ABERCYNON   YSTRAD MYNACH
TONYPANDY   Lime Kiln Jcn
PORTH   SENGHENYDD   RISCA
DINAS   LLANBRADACH
TREHAFOD   BEDWAS
PONTYPRIDD   ABER   MILL
ST   HIGH
ST

Tidenham   THORNBURY

CHEPSTOW

TYTHERINGTON

WICKWAR
Tun.

SEVERN TUNNEL
JCN
CALDICOT

Machen   Maindee Jcns
NEWPORT

Severn
Tunnel   PILNING
Severn
Beach

MID

YATE

CAERPHILLY
LISVANE &
THORNHILL
TAFFS
WELL   CORYTON
WHITCHURCH   LLANISHEN
RHIWBINA
BIRCHGROVE   HEATH
RADYR
LLANDAF   CATHAYS

BSC
LLANWERN
Uskmouth

ST. ANDREWS RD
AVONMOUTH   PATCHWAY
BRISTOL
PARKWAY

Westerleigh
Jcns
FILTON   CHIPPING
SODBURY

LLANHAREN
LLANTRISANT

Llanharry
Quarry   CENTRAL
QUEEN ST.
GRANGETOWN
CARDIFF
COGAN
DINAS
POWIS   BUTE RD.
DINGLE RD.
PENARTH

PORTISHEAD   (out of use)   SHIREHAMPTON
SEA MILLS

WESTERLEIGH

MANGOTSFIELD
AVON
VALLEY
RAILWAY

BRISTOL
TEMPLE MEADS
SEE INSET ON
SHEET THREE

KEYNSHAM   BITTON

BARRY
CADOXTON
BARRY
ISLAND   CLEVEDON   MID   OLDFIELD PARK   BATH
SPA

Aberthaw
Power Stn   NAILSEA &
BACKWELL
YATTON

C H A N N E L   WESTON-SUPER-MARE   WESTON MILTON
Worle Jcn   WC&P   BLAGDON   GW
Uphill Jcn.   GW   GW   SDJ
Cheddar   Writhlington
Colliery
RADSTOCK

BURNHAM
ON-SEA   VOBSTER
Whatley Quarry

MINEHEAD   HIGHBRIDGE
Bason Bridge
Sidings   EDINGTON
BURTLE   WELLS   SHEPTON
MALLET   CRANMORE
EAST
SOMERSET
RAILWAY
DUNSTER   WATCHET   SDJ
BLUE
ANCHOR   WILLITON   Huntspill   Merehead Quarry
WASHFORD   GW   SDJ   GLASTONBURY
& STREET   EVERCREECH
JCN
WEST SOMERSET
RAILWAY   STOGUMBER   BRIDGWATER   CASTLE
CARY   BRUTON
CROWCOMBE   Castle
Cary Jcn.

BISHOPS
LYDEARD

TAUNTON   Creech
Jcn.   Curry Rivell Jcn.   GW   SDJ
Cogload Jcn.
Norton
Fitzwarren Jcn.   TEMPLECOMBE

Whiteball Tun.
Summit   GW   GW   YEOVIL   PEN
MILL   RB LSW
HEMYOCK   SHERBORNE
TIVERTON   TIVERTON PARKWAY   JCN

Two   Three

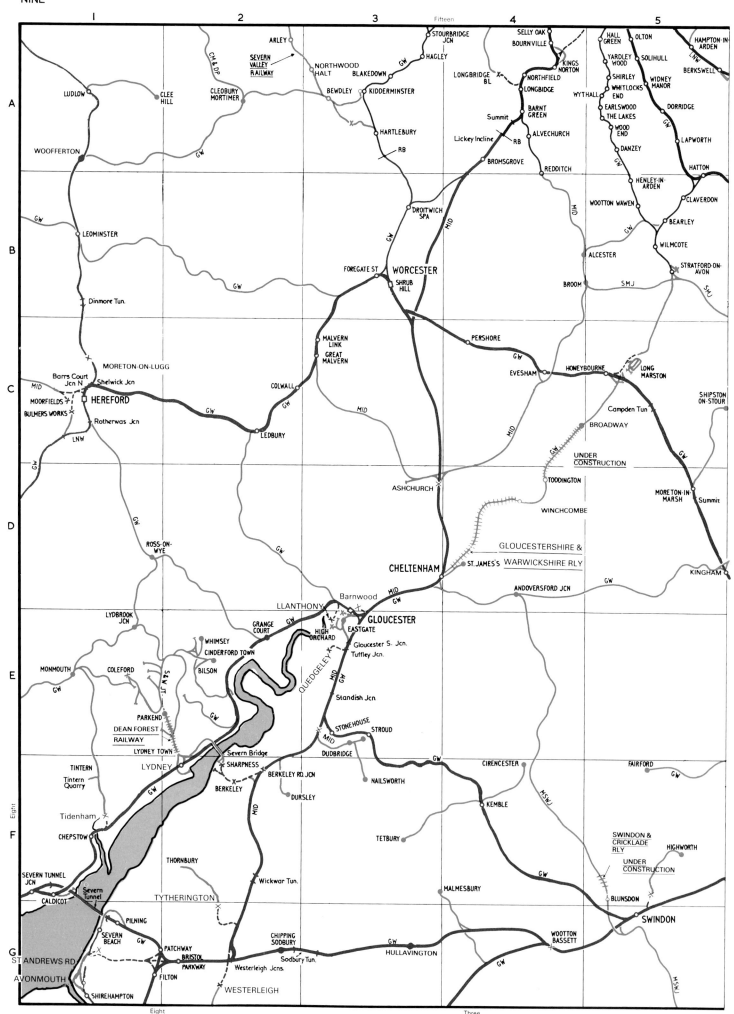

1   2   3   4   5

A

LUDLOW   CLEE HILL   CLEOBURY MORTIMER   ARLEY   SEVERN VALLEY RAILWAY   NORTHWOOD HALT   BLAKEDOWN   HAGLEY   STOURBRIDGE JCN   SELLY OAK   BOURNVILLE   HALL GREEN   OLTON   HAMPTON-IN-ARDEN

CM & DP   BEWDLEY   KIDDERMINSTER   LONGBRIDGE BL   KINGS NORTON   YARDLEY WOOD   SOLIHULL   BERKSWELL

WOOFFERTON   HARTLEBURY   NORTHFIELD   SHIRLEY   WIDNEY MANOR

GW   RB   LONGBRIDGE   WHITLOCKS END   WYTHALL

Summit   BARNT GREEN   EARLSWOOD THE LAKES   DORRIDGE

Lickey Incline   RB   WOOD END   LAPWORTH

ALVECHURCH   DANZEY

BROMSGROVE   REDDITCH   HATTON

B

GW   LEOMINSTER   DROITWICH SPA   MID   HENLEY-IN-ARDEN   CLAVERDON

GW   FOREGATE ST   WORCESTER   WOOTTON WAWEN   BEARLEY

Dinmore Tun.   SHRUB HILL   ALCESTER   WILMCOTE   STRATFORD-ON-AVON

GW   BROOM   SMJ   SMJ

C

MID   Barrs Court Jcn N   MALVERN LINK   PERSHORE   HONEYBOURNE   LONG MARSTON   SHIPSTON-ON-STOUR

MOORFIELDS   Shelwick Jcn   GREAT MALVERN   EVESHAM   GW   Campden Tun.   BROADWAY

BULMERS WORKS   HEREFORD   COLWALL   MID   UNDER CONSTRUCTION

GW   Rotherwas Jcn   GW   MID   TODDINGTON   MORETON-IN-MARSH   Summit

LNW   LEDBURY   ASHCHURCH   GW

D

GW   ROSS-ON-WYE   GW   WINCHCOMBE   KINGHAM

CHELTENHAM   St. JAMES'S   GLOUCESTERSHIRE & WARWICKSHIRE RLY   GW

LYDBROOK JCN   GRANGE COURT   Barnwood   MID   ANDOVERSFORD JCN   GW

E

MONMOUTH   WHIMSEY   LLANTHONY   GLOUCESTER   GW

COLEFORD   CINDERFORD TOWN   HIGH ORCHARD   EASTGATE

GW   BILSON   QUEDGELEY   Gloucester S. Jcn.   Tuffley Jcn.

S & W JT   Standish Jcn.   MID   GW

PARKEND   STONEHOUSE   STROUD   CIRENCESTER   FAIRFORD

DEAN FOREST RAILWAY   GW   MID   GW   GW

LYDNEY TOWN   DUDBRIDGE

F

TINTERN   LYDNEY   Severn Bridge   SHARPNESS   Berkeley Rd. Jcn   NAILSWORTH   KEMBLE   SWINDON & CRICKLADE RLY

Tintern Quarry   GW   Berkeley   DURSLEY   MSWJ   HIGHWORTH

Tidenham   MID   TETBURY   UNDER CONSTRUCTION

CHEPSTOW   THORNBURY   Wickwar Tun.   MALMESBURY   BLUNSDON

G

SEVERN TUNNEL JCN   TYTHERINGTON   CHIPPING SODBURY   GW   WOOTTON BASSETT   SWINDON

CALDICOT   Severn Tunnel   GW   HULLAVINGTON   GW

St ANDREWS RD   PILNING   PATCHWAY   Sodbury Tun.   GW   MSWJ

AVONMOUTH   SEVERN BEACH   GW   BRISTOL PARKWAY   Westerleigh Jcns.

SHIREHAMPTON   FILTON   WESTERLEIGH

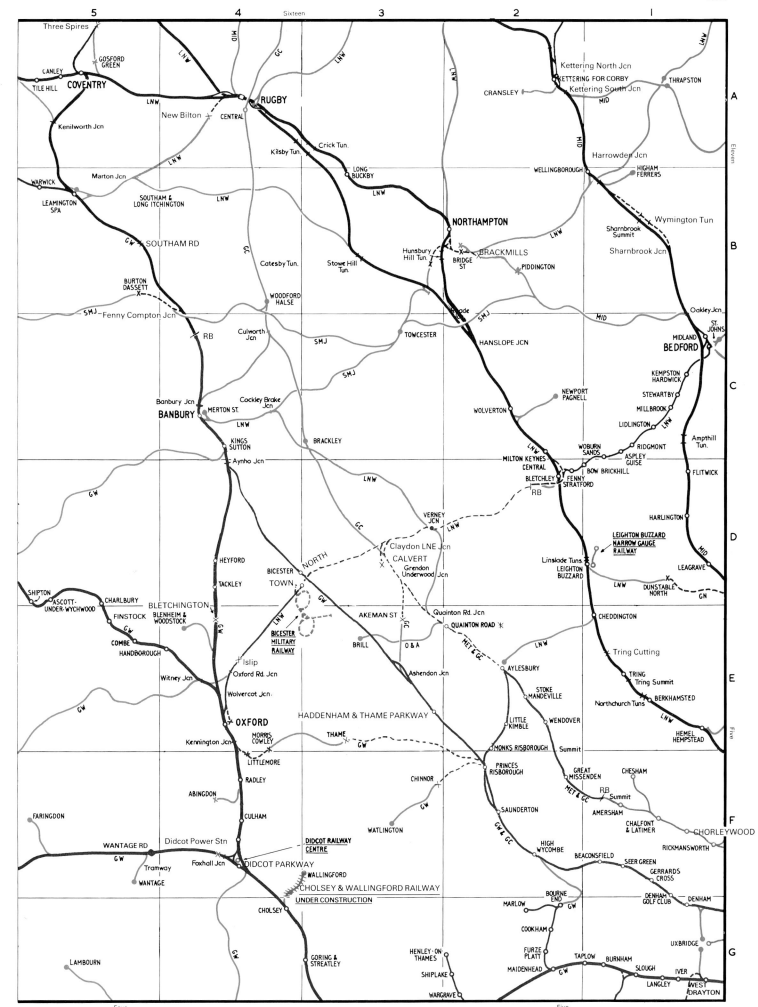

Three Spires
CANLEY
GOSFORD GREEN
COVENTRY
TILE HILL
Kenilworth Jcn
WARWICK
Marton Jcn
LEAMINGTON SPA
SOUTHAM & LONG ITCHINGTON
SOUTHAM RD
BURTON DASSETT
SMJ Fenny Compton Jcn
RB
Culworth Jcn
WOODFORD HALSE
Cockley Brake Jcn
Banbury Jcn
MERTON ST.
BANBURY
KINGS SUTTON
Aynho Jcn
BRACKLEY
HEYFORD
TACKLEY
BLETCHINGTON
SHIPTON
ASCOTT-UNDER-WYCHWOOD
CHARLBURY
FINSTOCK
BLENHEIM & WOODSTOCK
COMBE
HANDBOROUGH
Witney Jcn
Wolvercot Jcn.
BICESTER TOWN
NORTH
BICESTER MILITARY RAILWAY
Islip
Oxford Rd. Jcn
OXFORD
Kennington Jcn.
MORRIS COWLEY
LITTLEMORE
RADLEY
ABINGDON
FARINGDON
WANTAGE RD
Didcot Power Stn
Tramway
WANTAGE
Foxhall Jcn
DIDCOT PARKWAY
DIDCOT RAILWAY CENTRE
WALLINGFORD
CHOLSEY & WALLINGFORD RAILWAY
UNDER CONSTRUCTION
CHOLSEY
LAMBOURN
GORING & STREATLEY

RUGBY
CENTRAL
New Bilton
Kilsby Tun.
Crick Tun.
LONG BUCKBY
Catesby Tun.
Stowe Hill Tun.
NORTHAMPTON
Hunsbury Hill Tun.
BRIDGE ST
BRACKMILLS
PIDDINGTON
Slade
SMJ
TOWCESTER
HANSLOPE JCN
NEWPORT PAGNELL
WOLVERTON
MILTON KEYNES CENTRAL
BLETCHLEY
FENNY STRATFORD
RB
VERNEY JCN
CALVERT
Claydon LNE Jcn
Grendon Underwood Jcn
Quinton Rd. Jcn
QUAINTON ROAD
AKEMAN ST.
BRILL
O & A
Ashendon Jcn
MET & GC
AYLESBURY
HADDENHAM & THAME PARKWAY
THAME
CHINNOR
WATLINGTON
STOKE MANDEVILLE
LITTLE KIMBLE
WENDOVER
MONKS RISBOROUGH
Summit
PRINCES RISBOROUGH
SAUNDERTON
HIGH WYCOMBE
GW & GC
BEACONSFIELD
SEER GREEN
GERRARDS CROSS
BOURNE END
MARLOW
COOKHAM
FURZE PLATT
MAIDENHEAD
SHIPLAKE
HENLEY-ON-THAMES
WARGRAVE
TAPLOW
BURNHAM
SLOUGH
LANGLEY
IVER
WEST DRAYTON
UXBRIDGE

KETTERING NORTH Jcn
KETTERING FOR CORBY
KETTERING SOUTH Jcn
CRANSLEY
THRAPSTON
Harrowden Jcn
HIGHAM FERRERS
WELLINGBOROUGH
Wymington Tun.
Sharnbrook Summit
Sharnbrook Jcn
Oakley Jcn
ST. JOHNS
MIDLAND
BEDFORD
KEMPSTON HARDWICK
STEWARTBY
MILLBROOK
LIDLINGTON
Ampthill Tun.
WOBURN SANDS
RIDGMONT
ASPLEY GUISE
BOW BRICKHILL
FLITWICK
HARLINGTON
LEIGHTON BUZZARD NARROW GAUGE RAILWAY
Linslade Tuns
LEIGHTON BUZZARD
LEAGRAVE
DUNSTABLE NORTH
GN
CHEDDINGTON
Tring Cutting
TRING
Tring Summit
Northchurch Tuns
BERKHAMSTED
HEMEL HEMPSTEAD
GREAT MISSENDEN
CHESHAM
RB
Summit
AMERSHAM
CHALFONT & LATIMER
CHORLEYWOOD
RICKMANSWORTH
DENHAM GOLF CLUB
DENHAM

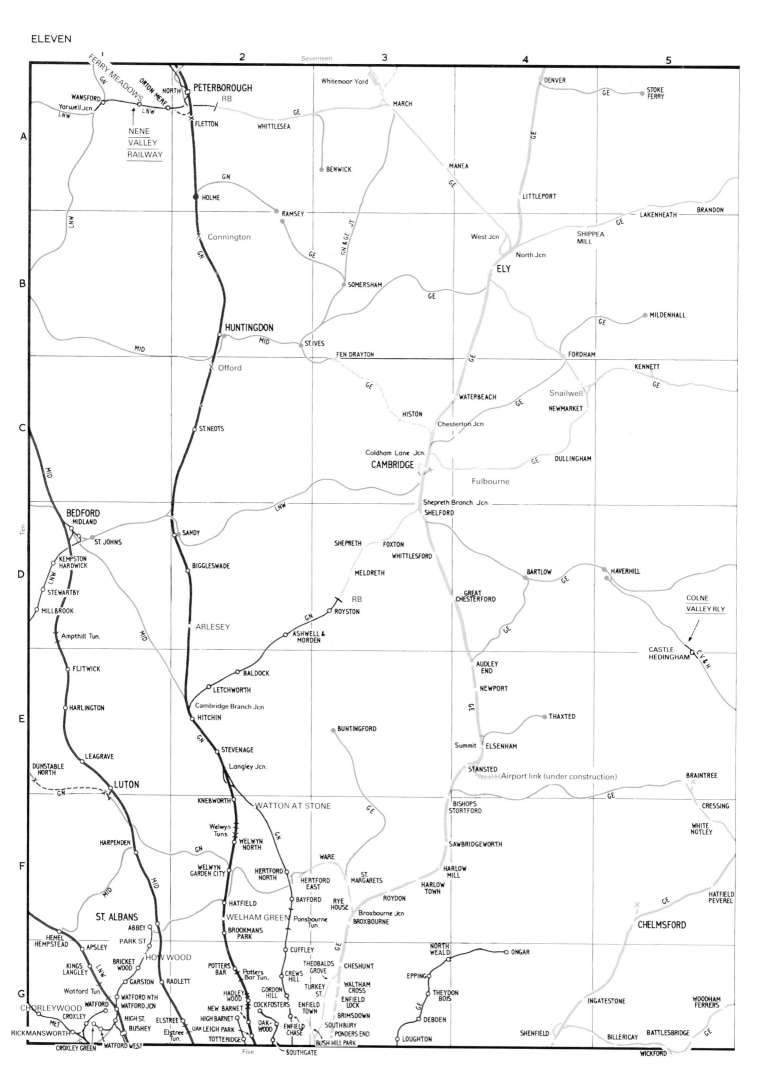

FERRY MEADOWS

ORTON MERE

NENE
VALLEY
RAILWAY

PETERBOROUGH
RB

NORTH
LNW
FLETTON

WANSFORD
Yarwell Jcn
LNW
GN

LNW

Whitemoor Yard

WHITTLESEA

GE

MARCH

DENVER
GE

STOKE
FERRY

GN

BENWICK

MANEA

LITTLEPORT

GE

GE

HOLME

RAMSEY

GE

GN & GE JT

West Jcn

SHIPPEA
MILL

LAKENHEATH

BRANDON

Connington

GN

SOMERSHAM

North Jcn

ELY

GE

MILDENHALL

GE

HUNTINGDON

MID

MID

ST.IVES

FEN DRAYTON

GE

FORDHAM

KENNETT

GE

Offord

GE

HISTON

WATERBEACH

GE

Snailwell

NEWMARKET

GE

ST NEOTS

Chesterton Jcn

ST.JOHNS

Coldham Lane Jcn.

CAMBRIDGE

GE

DULLINGHAM

BEDFORD
MIDLAND

SANDY

Fulbourne

KEMPSTON
HARDWICK

LNW

BIGGLESWADE

LNW

SHEPRETH

FOXTON

WHITTLESFORD

Shepreth Branch Jcn.
SHELFORD

BARTLOW

GE

HAVERHILL

STEWARTBY

MELDRETH

GE

MILLBROOK

Ampthill Tun.

ARLESEY

MID

GREAT
CHESTERFORD

GE

COLNE
VALLEY RLY

FLITWICK

RB
ROYSTON

ASHWELL &
MORDEN

GN

AUDLEY
END

CASTLE
HEDINGHAM

CV&H

HARLINGTON

BALDOCK

NEWPORT

THAXTED

LEAGRAVE

LETCHWORTH

Cambridge Branch Jcn
HITCHIN

GE

Summit

ELSENHAM

DUNSTABLE
NORTH

GN

LUTON

GN

STEVENAGE

Langley Jcn.

BUNTINGFORD

STANSTED
Airport link (under construction)

BRAINTREE

KNEBWORTH

WATTON AT STONE

BISHOPS
STORTFORD

GE

CRESSING

HARPENDEN

GN

Welwyn
Tuns.

WELWYN
NORTH

GN

WARE

SAWBRIDGEWORTH

WHITE
NOTLEY

MID

MID

WELWYN
GARDEN CITY

HERTFORD
NORTH

HERTFORD
EAST

ST.
MARGARETS

HARLOW
MILL

HARLOW
TOWN

ST. ALBANS

HATFIELD

WELHAM GREEN

BAYFORD

Ponsbourne
Tun.

RYE
HOUSE

ROYDON

Broxbourne Jcn.
BROXBOURNE

GE

CHELMSFORD

HATFIELD
PEVEREL

HEMEL
HEMPSTEAD

ABBEY

PARK ST

HOW WOOD

BROOKMANS
PARK

CUFFLEY

THEOBALDS
GROVE

CHESHUNT

NORTH
WEALD

ONGAR

APSLEY

BRICKET
WOOD

POTTERS
BAR

CREWS
HILL

TURKEY
ST.

WALTHAM
CROSS

EPPING

INGATESTONE

WOODHAM
FERRERS

KINGS
LANGLEY

LNW

GARSTON

RADLETT

HADLEY
WOOD

Potters
Bar Tun.

GORDON
HILL

ENFIELD
LOCK

THEYDON
BOIS

Watford Tun.

WATFORD NTH
WATFORD JCN

NEW BARNET

HIGH BARNET

COCKFOSTERS

ENFIELD
TOWN

ENFIELD
CHASE

SOUTHBURY

BRIMSDOWN

DEBDEN

SHENFIELD

BILLERICAY

BATTLESBRIDGE

CHORLEYWOOD

WATFORD

CROXLEY

HIGH ST.
BUSHEY

ELSTREE

Elstree
Tun.

OAKLEIGH PARK

OAK-
WOOD

PONDERS END

BUSH HILL PARK

GE

LOUGHTON

MET

RICKMANSWORTH

CROXLEY GREEN

WATFORD WEST

TOTTERIDGE

SOUTHGATE

WICKFORD

5   4   3   2   1

WYMONDHAM

N & S JT.

HADDISCOE

SPOONER ROW

SOMMERLEYTON

ATTLEBOROUGH

FORNCETT

Swing.
bridge

OULTON BROAD
NORTH

A   LOWESTOFT

ECCLES RD

GE

OULTON BROAD
SOUTH

BECCLES

Roudham Jcn

HARLING RD

TIVETSHALL

GE

BRAMPTON

THETFORD

GE

DISS

HARLESTON

HALESWORTH

SOUTHWOLD

B

SOUTHWOLD Rly

GE

EYE

LAXFIELD

DARSHAM

THURSTON

ELMSWELL

M S L R

FRAMLINGHAM

GE

LEISTON (Sizewell)

C

BURY
ST. EDMUNDS

GE

HAUGHLEY

SAXMUNDHAM

STOWMARKET

SNAPE

ALDEBURGH

NEEDHAM MARKET

WICKHAM
MARKET

BARHAM

MELTON

Claydon

WESTERFIELD

WOODBRIDGE

GLEMSFORD

E. Suffolk Jcn

DERBY RD

D

LONG
MELFORD

HADLEIGH

IPSWICH
Griffen Whf

Lower Yard

GE

GE

SUDBURY

BENTLEY

TRIMLEY

BURES

North FLT

FELIXSTOWE

MANNINGTREE

HARWICH
PARKESTON
QUAY

HARWICH
TOWN

Felixstowe Beach Jcn

South FLT

EAST ANGLIAN
RAILWAY MUSEUM

DOCKS

CV
&H

MISTLEY

GE   WRABNESS

DOVERCOURT

CHAPPEL &
WAKES COLNE

COLCHESTER

E

St. BOTOLPHS

East Gate Jcn

HYTHE

MARKS
TEY

WIVENHOE

ALRESFORD

WEELEY

KIRBY
CROSS

WALTON-ON-
NAZE

GE

GREAT
BENTLEY

THORPE-LE-
SOKEN

FRINTON

KELVEDON

BRIGHTLINGSEA

WITHAM

CLACTON-ON-
SEA

F

MALDON EAST &
HEYBRIDGE

TOLLESBURY

GE

SOUTHMINSTER

G

FAMBRIDGE   ALTHORNE

GE

BURNHAM-ON-CROUCH

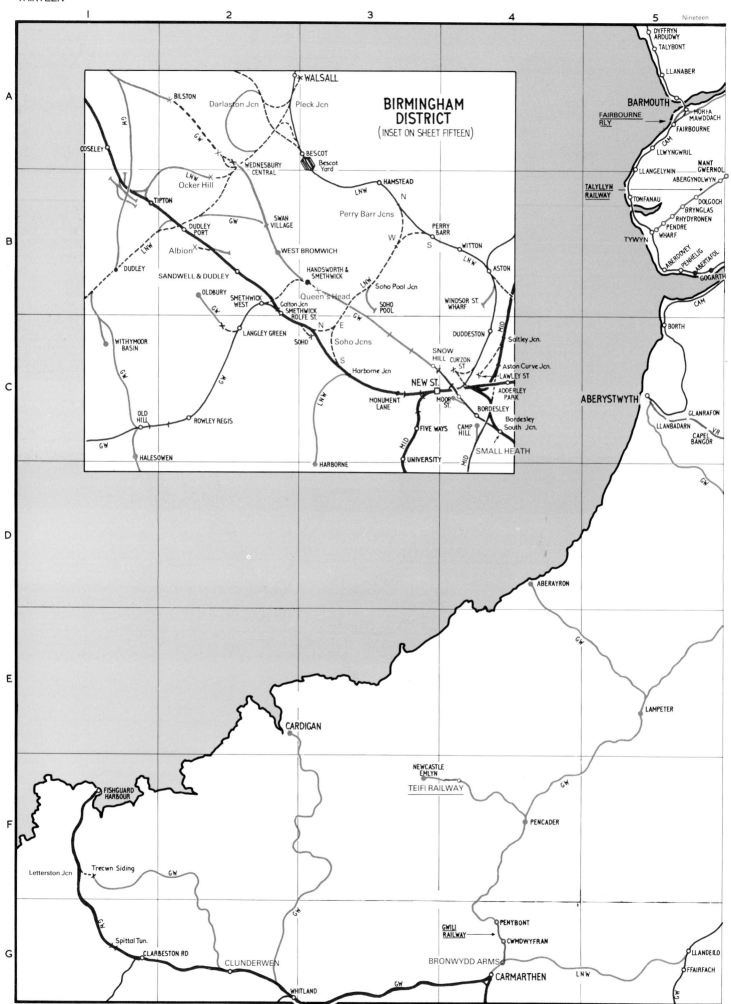

BIRMINGHAM DISTRICT
(INSET ON SHEET FIFTEEN)

WALSALL

Darlaston Jcn   Pleck Jcn

BILSTON

GW

COSELEY

BESCOT
Bescot Yard

WEDNESBURY CENTRAL

LNW
Ocker Hill

HAMSTEAD

LNW

N

TIPTON

GW

DUDLEY PORT

SWAN VILLAGE

Perry Barr Jcns

W

PERRY BARR

LNW

Albion

LNW

DUDLEY

WEST BROMWICH

S

WITTON

LNW

ASTON

SANDWELL & DUDLEY

HANDSWORTH & SMETHWICK

Soho Pool Jcn

Queen's Head

SOHO POOL

OLDBURY

SMETHWICK WEST

Galton Jcn
SMETHWICK ROLFE ST.

WINDSOR ST. WHARF

GW

LANGLEY GREEN

N

E

DUDDESTON

MID

Saltley Jcn.

WITHYMOOR BASIN

SOHO

GW

Soho Jcns

SNOW HILL

CURZON ST

Aston Curve Jcn.

GW

S

Harborne Jcn

LAWLEY ST

GW

NEW ST.

ADDERLEY PARK

OLD HILL

ROWLEY REGIS

LNW

MONUMENT LANE

MOOR ST.

BORDESLEY

Bordesley South Jcn.

GW

FIVE WAYS

CAMP HILL

HALESOWEN

HARBORNE

MID

UNIVERSITY

SMALL HEATH

MID

DYFFRYN ARDUDWY

TALYBONT

LLANABER

BARMOUTH

MORFA MAWDDACH

FAIRBOURNE RLY →

FAIRBOURNE

CAM

LLWYNGWRIL

NANT GWERNOL

LLANGELYNIN

ABERGYNOLWYN

TALYLLYN RAILWAY

DOLGOCH

BRYNGLAS

RHYDYRONEN

PENDRE

TYWYN

WHARF

ABERDOVEY

PENHELIG

ABERTAFOL

GOGARTH

CAM

BORTH

ABERYSTWYTH

GLANRAFON

LLANBADARN

CAPEL BANGOR

VR

GW

ABERAYRON

GW

LAMPETER

CARDIGAN

NEWCASTLE EMLYN

TEIFI RAILWAY

GW

FISHGUARD HARBOUR

PENCADER

Letterston Jcn   Trecwn Siding

GW

GW

Spittal Tun.

PENYBONT

GWILI RAILWAY →

CWMDWYFRAN

CLARBESTON RD

CLUNDERWEN

BRONWYDD ARMS

LLANDEILO

FFAIRFACH

GW

WHITLAND

GW

CARMARTHEN

LNW

GW

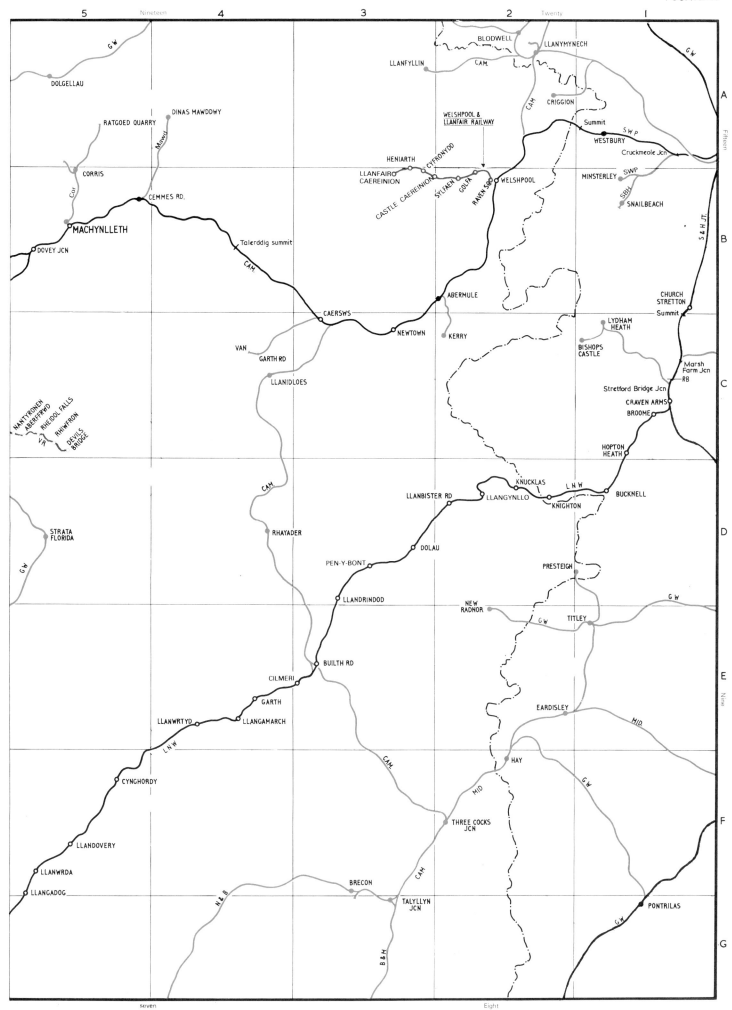

GW

DOLGELLAU

RATGOED QUARRY

DINAS MAWDDWY

Mawd

CORRIS

Cor

CEMMES RD.

MACHYNLLETH

DOVEY JCN

Talerddig summit

CAM.

CAERSWS

NEWTOWN

VAN

GARTH RD

LLANIDLOES

NANTYRONEN
ABERFFRWD
RHEIDOL FALLS
RHIWFRON
VR
DEVILS BRIDGE

CAM

STRATA FLORIDA

GW

RHAYADER

PEN-Y-BONT

LLANDRINDOD

CILMERI

BUILTH RD

GARTH

LLANWRTYD

LLANGAMARCH

LNW

CYNGHORDY

LLANDOVERY

LLANWRDA

LLANGADOG

N & B

CAM

BRECON

TALYLLYN JCN

B & H

LLANFYLLIN

BLODWELL

LLANYMYNECH

CAM.

CRIGGION

CAM

WELSHPOOL &
LLANFAIR RAILWAY

HENIARTH

CYFRONYDD

Summit

SWP

WESTBURY

Cruckmeole Jcn

LLANFAIR
CAEREINION

CASTLE CAEREINION

SYLFAEN

GOLFA

RAVEN SQ

WELSHPOOL

MINSTERLEY

SWP

SBH

SNAILBEACH

ABERMULE

KERRY

CHURCH
STRETTON

Summit

LYDHAM
HEATH

BISHOPS
CASTLE

Marsh
Farm Jcn

RB

Stretford Bridge Jcn

CRAVEN ARMS

BROOME

HOPTON
HEATH

KNUCKLAS

LNW

LLANBISTER RD

LLANGYNLLO

KNIGHTON

BUCKNELL

DOLAU

PRESTEIGN

NEW
RADNOR

GW

TITLEY

GW

GW

EARDISLEY

MID

HAY

MID

GW

THREE COCKS
JCN

CAM

PONTRILAS

GW

S & H JT.

Nine

1   2   3   Twenty one   4   5

Twenty

Fourteen

HOUGH GREEN
WIDNES
WIDNES
Fiddlers Ferry Power Stn
WARRINGTON
LNW
Acton Grange Jcn.
RUNCORN EAST
CLC
DITTON
RUNCORN
Halton Jcn
FRODSHAM
INCE & ELTON
HELSBY
GW &
Weaver Jcn.
Oakleigh Sdgs.
ACTON BRIDGE
MOULDSWORTH
CLC
DELAMERE
CUDDINGTON
HARTFORD
GREENBANK
NORTHWICH
LOSTOCK GRALAM

HALE
ASHLEY
SEE SHEET No. FORTY FIVE
MOBBERLEY
KNUTSFORD
PLUMLEY
CLC
ALDERLEY EDGE
CHELFORD

CHEADLE HULME
HEALD GREEN
STYAL
HANDFORTH
BRAMHALL
POYNTON
WILMSLOW
ADLINGTON
PRESTBURY
BOLLINGTON
LNW
MACCLESFIELD

HAZEL GROVE
MID
MIDDLE-WOOD
STRINES
NEW MILLS CENTRAL
NEW MILLS NEWTOWN
DISLEY
FURNESS VALE
WHALEY BRIDGE
CHINLEY
LNW
HAYFIELD
CHAPEL-EN-LE FRITH
Dove Holes Tun.
DOVE HOLES
PEAK FOREST
BUXTON
TOPLEY PIKE
LADMANLOW
TUNSTEAD
Millers Dale Jcn.

EDALE
Cowburn Tun.
HOPE
MID
BAMFORD
HATHERSAGE
MILLERS DALE
HINDLOW
MID
BAKEWELL
HARTINGTON
LNW (NS)

WINSFORD Jcn.
MIDDLEWICH
WINSFORD & OVER
OVER & WHARTON
WINSFORD
HOLMES CHAPEL
GOOSTREY
NORTH RODE
CONGLETON
NS
LEEK
Leek Brook Jcn
CHEDDLETON
WATERHOUSES
HULME END
HARTINGTON

TATTENHALL JCN
BEESTON CASTLE & TARPORLEY
LNW
SANDBACH
NS
CREWE
NS
RADWAY GREEN
ALSAGER
KIDSGROVE
Bradwell/ Chatterley Valley
NS
LONGPORT
HANLEY
CALDON LOW
(out of Use) NS
ASHBOURNE

NANTWICH
Basford Hall Yard
NS
ETRURIA
STOKE-ON-TRENT
POOL DAM
Trentham
LONGTON
BLYTHE BRIDGE
CHEADLE
OAKAMOOR
ROCESTER
HORNINGLOW WHARF

WRENBURY
GW
Madeley Chord
Whitmore Summit
TRENTHAM PARK
WEDGWOOD
BARLASTON
CRESSWELL
NS

WHITCHURCH
CAM
MARKET DRAYTON
STONE
NS
BURTON-ON-TRENT
SHOBNALL WHARF
Drakelow Power Stn
Stretton Jcn.

PREES
WEM
YORTON
LNW
GW
NORTON BRIDGE
NS
UTTOXETER
EGGINGTON JCN
STRETTON JCN
BURTON-ON-TRENT (See inset above)
GN

1: Holditch Col
2: Silverdale Col
3: Round Oak
4: Brierley Hill
5: Pensnett

STAFFORD COMMON
STAFFORD
Shugborough Tun.
COLWICH JCN
RUGELEY
Lea Hall Colliery/ Power Station
Wichnor Jcn.
Branston Jcn.
MID

SHREWSBURY
GENERAL
ABBEY
S&H
ALSCOTT
GW & LNW JT
Market Drayton Jcn.
NEWPORT
DONNINGTON
Bushbury Jcn.
Stafford Rd Jcn.
LL
VICTORIA BASIN
WOLVERHAMPTON H.L.
Portobello Jcn.
Steel Term.
MONMORE GREEN
PRIESTFIELD
PENKRIDGE
Littleton Col
Trent Valley Jcn.
RUGELEY TOWN
MIDCANNOCK
LNW
LICHFIELD TV
HL
CITY

Bayston Hill
GW
WELLINGTON TELFORD WEST
OAKENGATES
TELFORD CENTRAL
Madeley Jcn.
SHIFNAL
COSFORD
ALBRIGHTON
CODSALL
Four Ashes
MNT
LNW
Anglesea
SHENSTONE
TAMWORTH LL
HL

CHURCH STRETTON
GW
BUILDWAS
COALPORT
Oxley Jcn
Bushbury Jcn
BILBROOK
Oxley Sdgs
WOLVERHAMPTON (See inset above)
WALSALL
Sutton Park
MID
BLAKE ST.
BUTLERS LANE
FOUR OAKS
SUTTON COLDFIELD
WYLDE GREEN
CHESTER RD
WATER ORTON
ERDINGTON
COLESHILL
WILNECOTE
Kingsbury Branch Jcn
Daw Mill Col

DITTON PRIORS
BRIDGNORTH
EARDINGTON
HAMPTON LOADE
SEVERN VALLEY RAILWAY
SEE INSET ON SHEET No. THIRTEEN
COSELEY
TIPTON
DUDLEY
BESCOT
GW
WEST BROMWICH
PERRY BARR
ASTON
SALTLEY
BIRMINGHAM

HIGHLEY
ARLEY
CML&DP
GW
Baggeridge Jcn
Kingswinford Jcn.
STOURBRIDGE TOWN
STOURBRIDGE JCN
CRADLEY HEATH
OLD HILL
ROWLEY REGIS
LYE
HALESOWEN
DUDLEY PORT
SMETHWICK WEST
ROLFE ST.
SNOW HILL
SOHO
HOCKLEY
STECHFORD
LEA HALL
MARSTON GREEN
BIRMINGHAM INTERNATIONAL
HAMPTON-IN-ARDEN
NEW ST.
MOOR ST.
SPRING RD
SELLY OAK
HARBORNE
SMALL HEATH
TYSELEY
ACOCKS GREEN
OLTON
MID
GW

Nine

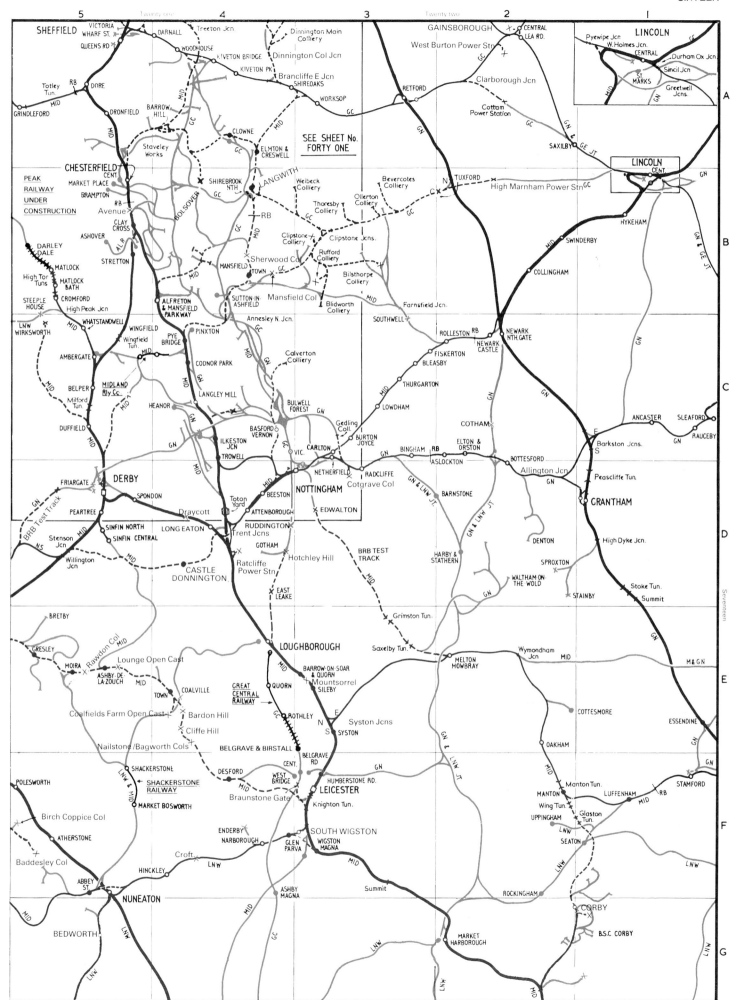

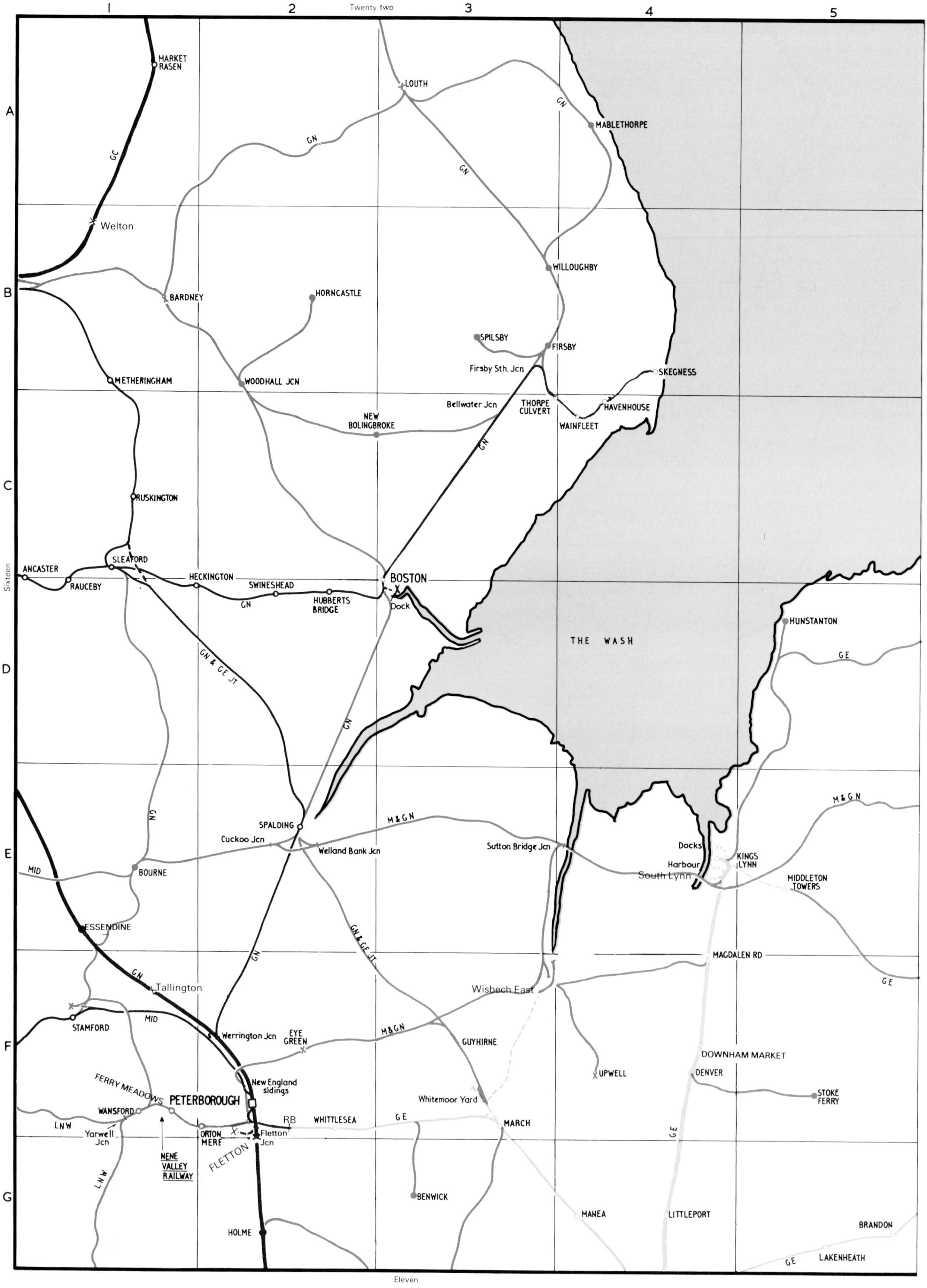

MARKET
RASEN

GC

LOUTH

GN

GN

MABLETHORPE

GN

Welton

WILLOUGHBY

BARDNEY

HORNCASTLE

SPILSBY   FIRSBY

METHERINGHAM   WOODHALL JCN   Firsby Sth. Jcn   SKEGNESS

Bellwater Jcn   THORPE   HAVENHOUSE
CULVERT

NEW   WAINFLEET
BOLINGBROKE

GN

RUSKINGTON

ANCASTER   SLEAFORD   HECKINGTON   SWINESHEAD   BOSTON   THE WASH   HUNSTANTON

RAUCEBY   HUBBERTS   Dock   GE
GN   BRIDGE

GN & GE JT

GN

MID   SPALDING   M&GN   M&GN

Cuckoo Jcn   Welland Bank Jcn   Sutton Bridge Jcn   Docks   KINGS
LYNN
BOURNE   Harbour   MIDDLETON
South Lynn   TOWERS

GN

ESSENDINE   MAGDALEN RD

GN & GE JT

GN

Tallington   Wisbech East   GE

STAMFORD   MID   M&GN

Werrington Jcn   EYE   GUYHIRNE
GREEN   DOWNHAM MARKET

FERRY MEADOWS   UPWELL   DENVER

PETERBOROUGH   New England
sidings   Whitemoor Yard   STOKE
FERRY
WANSFORD   RB   WHITTLESEA   GE

LNW   ORTON   Fletton   MARCH
Yarwell   MERE   Jcn   GE
Jcn   NENE
VALLEY   FLETTON
LNW   RAILWAY

BENWICK

MANEA   LITTLEPORT   BRANDON

HOLME   GE   LAKENHEATH

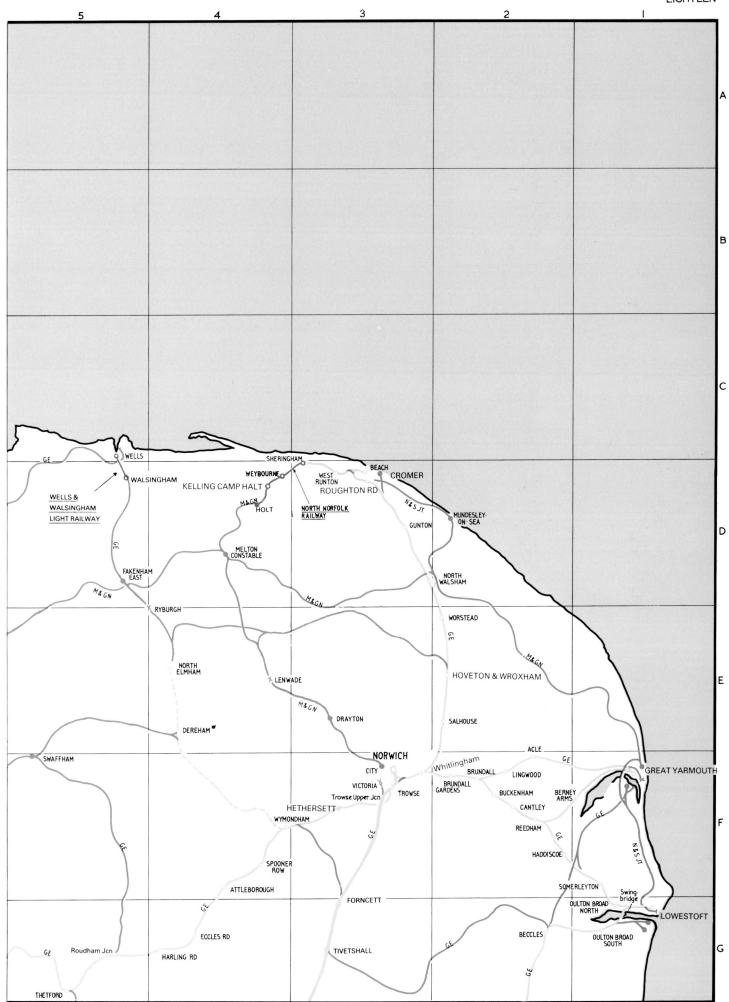

1   2   3   4   5

A

HOLYHEAD

Holy Island

VALLEY

LNW

B

RHOSNEIGR

Inset

C

AMLWCH

Rhosgoch

GREAT ORME TRAMWAY

GREAT ORME

HALF WAY

LLANDUDNO

REDWHARF BAY
& BENLLECH

DEGANWY

COLWYN
BAY

RHYL

PRESTATYN

RHOSNEIGR

DYSERTH

TY CROES

CONWY
PENMAENMAWR

LLANDUDNO JCN

GLAN
CONWY

Penmaenrhos
Tun.

LNW

ABERGELE &
PENSARN

D

BODORGAN

Tuns.

LNW

GAERWEN

LLANFAIRPWLL

BANGOR

Belmont
Tun.

Bangor Tun.

LLANFAIRFECHAN

TAL-Y-CAFN

DENBIGH

LNW

BETHESDA

Britannia
Tubular Bridge

DOLGARROG

CAERNARVON

LLANBERIS LAKE
RAILWAY

LLANRWST

LNW

E

CEI LLYDAN

GILFACH DDU

LLANBERIS

DINAS
JCN

HEBRON

HALFWAY

SNOWDON MOUNTAIN
RLY

BETWS-Y-COED

BRYNGWYN

NW N G (WH)

CLOGWYN

SNOWDON
SUMMIT

PONT-Y-PANT

NANTLLE

SOUTH
SNOWDON

ROMAN
BRIDGE

DOLWYDDELAN

BEDDGELERT

Ffestiniog Tun.

BLAENAU FFESTINIOG CENTRAL

TANYGRISIAU

HM

CROESOR
R.

GW

CORWEN

TAN-Y-BWLCH

DDUALLT

F

PORTHMADOG

FR

PENRHYN

Maentwrog Rd

GW

CRICCIETH

MINFFORDD

PENRHYNDEUDRAETH

AFONWEN

PORTHMADOG

LLANDEGWYN

ABERERCH

BOSTON LODGE

FFESTINIOG
RAILWAY

TALSARNAU

TRAWSFYNYDD

PWLLHELI

PENYCHAIN

TYGWYN

Bala Lake

BALA

LLANGOWER

C.M.H.

HARLECH

LLANDANWG

G

PENSARN

LLANUWCHLLYN

BALA LAKE
RAILWAY

LLANBEDR

LLANGYNOG

DYFFRYN
ARDUDWY

GW

CAM

TALYBONT

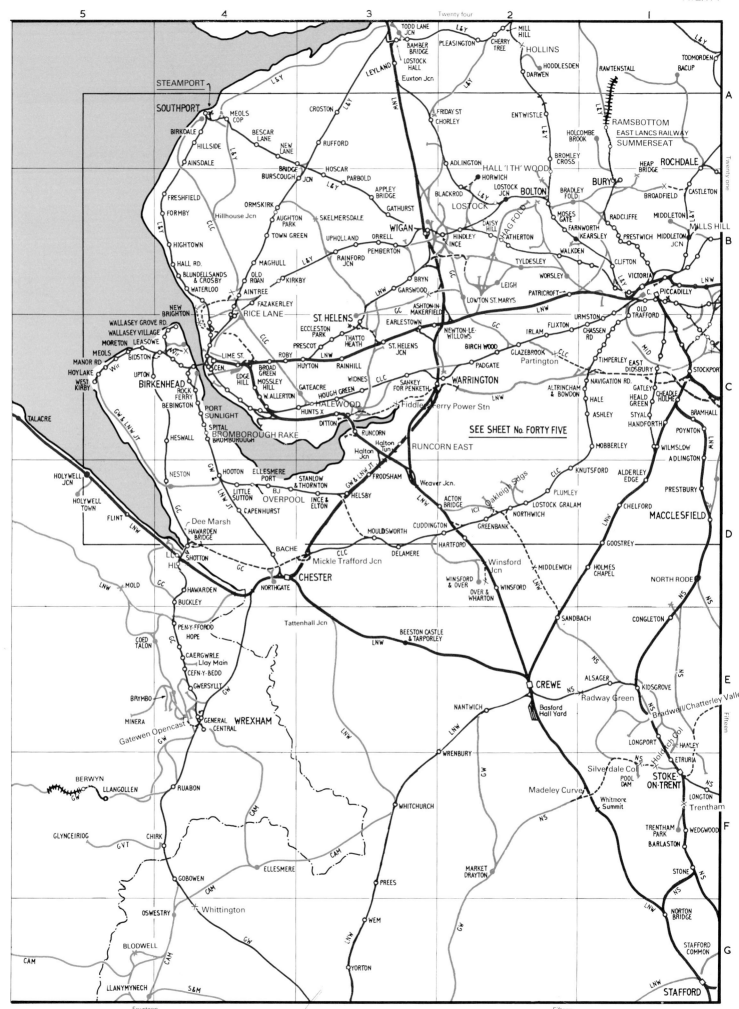

1 2 3 Twenty eight 4 5

Twenty four

Inset

Twenty

Insets and labels

REDMIRE
NE
NE
MASHAM
NE
NORTHALLERTON
NE
THIRSK
NE

Ashton Moss Jcn. ASHTON UNDER-LYNE
L&Y GC LNW
DROYLSDEN
GC LNW STALYBRIDGE
GC GUIDE BRIDGE
Denton Jcn. GC

Poppleton Jcn Bootham Jcn
ROWNTREE WORKS
Burton La. Jcn.
YORK LAYERTHORPE
Holgate Bridge Jcn FOSS ISLANDS
QVL
NE

THORNTON-IN-CRAVEN
BARNOLDSWICK
EARBY
MID
COLNE
L&Y NELSON

MELMERBY
NE
PILMOOR
NE
EASINGWOLD
NE
ALNE
NE

LOFTHOUSE-IN-NIDDERDALE
NV
PATELEY BRIDGE
NE

LEEDS
WELLINGTON ST.
CENTRAL
NE
MID CITY
GN HUNSLET LANE
LNW WHITEHALL
LNW MID
Farnley N. Jcn.
YORKSHIRE DALES RAILWAY

GRASSINGTON & THRESHFIELD
RYLSTONE
MID
GARGRAVE
Embsay Jcn
EMBSAY
SKIPTON
RB
CONONLEY
MID
EARBY

KNARESBOROUGH
STARBECK
HARROGATE
Crimple Jcn
PANNAL
NE
WEETON
WETHERBY
NE
CATTAL HAMMERTON
NE
POPPLETON
Bootham Jcn
YORK LAYERTHORPE
FOSS ISLANDS
BR
NE
GILLING
NE
NE

ILKLEY BEN RHYDDING
G&I BURLEY-IN-WHARFEDALE
MID
MENSTON
GUISELEY
NE
HORSFORTH
Bramhope Tun.
ULLESKELF
NE
COLTON JCN
NE
BR
SELBY
CAWOOD
CLIFF COMMON
NE
NE

KEIGHLEY & WORTH VALLEY RAILWAY
DERKER L&Y
OLDHAM MUMPS
CENTRAL LNW
WERNETH GC
KEIGHLEY
INGROW
DAMEMS
OAKWORTH
HAWORTH
OXENHOPE
CROSSFLATTS
BINGLEY BAILDON
SHIPLEY
FRIZINGHALL
BRADFORD
QUEENSBURY
NEW PUDSEY
LOW MOOR
DUDLEY HILL
GN
GN
MID

SEE SHEET No. FORTY TWO

CHURCH FENTON
Hambleton Jcns
NE W N E S
SOUTH MILFORD
Gasoigne Wood Jcn
BR
WRESSLE
BARLOW
DRAX
NE

L&Y
RB
HEBDEN BRIDGE
MYTHOLMROYD
TODMORDEN
ST. PAULS
SOWERBY BRIDGE
HALIFAX
SPEN VALLEY RAILWAY
BIRSTALL
BATLEY
DEWSBURY
WESTGATE
WAKEFIELD
Healey Mills Yd
KIRKGATE
MIRFIELD
DEIGHTON
HUDDERSFIELD
HILLHOUSE
RAVENSTHORPE
STAINLAND
RISHWORTH
SLAITHWAITE
SUMMIT TUNS
LITTLEBOROUGH
SMITHY BRIDGE
ROCHDALE
MILNROW
NEW HEY
SHAW
ROYTON
MUMPS
CEN.
OLDHAM
MOSSLEY
GREENFIELD
DROYLSDEN
ASHTON-UNDER-LYME
STALYBRIDGE
GUIDE BR.
NEWTON FOR HYDE
NTH HYDE
DENTON
HYDE CENT.
GODLEY
DINTING
GLOSSOP
HADFIELD
BROADBOTTOM
HATTERSLEY
GODLEY EAST
WOODLEY
BREDBURY
ROMILEY
MARPLE
HAZEL GROVE
ROSE HILL
WOODHEAD
Woodhead Tun.
PENISTONE
DUNFORD BRIDGE
SILKSTONE COMMON
HOLMFIRTH
SHEPLEY
DENBY DALE
SILKSTONE
BARNSLEY
CLAYTON WEST
DARTON
STOCKSMOOR
BROCKHOLES
HONLEY
KIRKBURTON
MELTHAM
MARSDEN
Standedge Tun.
Diggle Tun
DELPH

HEADINGLEY
BRAMLEY
BURLEY PARK
LEEDS
CROSS GATES
HUNSLET
MIDDLETON RAILWAY
COTTINGLEY
MORLEY
Morley Tun.
ARDSLEY
OUTWOOD
GARFORTH
EAST GARFORTH
MICKLEFIELD
WOODLESFORD
Methley Jcn.
ALTOFTS
Goose Hill Jcn.
Altofts Jcn.
NORMANTON
CASTLEFORD
PONTEFRACT MONKHILL
FERRYBRIDGE
KNOTTINGLEY
Temple Hurst Jcn.
HENSALL
SNAITH
WHITLEY BRIDGE
PONTEFRACT BAGHILL
FITZWILLIAM
SANDALL & AGBRIGG
MOORTHORPE
GRIMETHORPE COL
THURNSCOE
GOLDTHORPE
GOLDTHORPE COL
BOLTON-ON-DEARNE
WOMBWELL
ELSECAR
ELSECAR EAST
Smithywood
DEEPCAR
CHAPELTOWN
ECCLESFIELD WEST
ROTHERHAM CENTRAL WESTGATE
BRIGHTSIDE
ATTERCLIFFE
VICTORIA
DARNALL
SHEFFIELD
MIDLAND
RAWCLIFFE
HECK
ASKERN
Shaftholme Jcn
Thorpe Marsh Power Station
THORNE NORTH
THORNE SOUTH
STAINFORTH & HATFIELD
Thorne Jcn.
Brodsworth Col
YORK RD
Kirk Sandall Jcn.
MARSHGATE
DONCASTER
Conisbrough
MEXBOROUGH
Silverwood Col
Firbeck Jcns
Rossington Main Colliery
MISSON
BAWTRY
Harworth Col
Dinnington Main Colliery
Thurcroft Col
Treeton Jcns
TINSLEY YARD
Silverwood Col

Sixteen

DONCASTER
YORK RD
Bentley Colliery
Kirk Sandall Jcn.
MARSHGATE
Markham Main Colliery
GC & H&B
Low Ellers Jcn.
Black Carr Jcn.
Potteric Carr
Hexthorpe Jcn.
St Catherines Jcn
Rossington Main Colliery

1: BRINNINGTON
2: FLOWERY FIELD

Fifteen

5   Twenty eight   4   3   2   1

LEVISHAM

NORTH YORKSHIRE
MOORS RAILWAY →

NE

PICKERING

NE

MARISHES RD.

NE

MALTON

Burdale Tun.

NE

NE

NE

NE

NE

HOWDEN

EASTRINGTON

GILBER-
DYKE NE

BROOMFLEET

H&B

MARKET
WEIGHTON

NE

NE

SCARBOROUGH

SEAMER
Seamer Jcn

FILEY

FILEY
HOLIDAY CAMP

HUNMANBY

BEMPTON

BRIDLINGTON

NAFFERTON
DRIFFIELD

HUTTON
CRANSWICK

ARRAM

Beverley Jcn
BEVERLEY

COTTINGHAM

HORNSEA

WITHERNSEA

NE

Cottingham
Jcn.

Calvert Lane

BOOTHFERRY
PARK

HULL NEW
YARD

HESSLE

SCULCOATES

CANNON
ST.
PARAGON

NEPTUNE ST.

ENGLISH ST.

CENTRAL

Dairycoates

Sweet Dews

King George Dock

DRY-
POOL

VICTORIA
DOCK

ALEXANDRA
DOCK

Saltend

HULL

A

B

C

D

E

F

G

GOOLE

Swing
Bridge

SALTMARSHE

Docks

Marshland Jcn.

LY & NE JT

FOCKERBY

GC

NORMANDY PARK

KEADBY

CROWLE

ALTHORPE

HATFIELD
MOOR

Keadby Lift
Bridge

SCUNTHORPE

BSC

GC
Foreign
Ore
Terminal

ELSHAM

BARNETBY
Wrawby Jcn

BRIGG

LY & NE JT

Kirton Tun.
KIRTON
LINDSEY

HAXEY
JCN

GC

GN & GE JT

GAINSBOROUGH
CENTRAL

GAINSBOROUGH
LEA RD.

Sixteen

MELTON HALT*

BROUGH

FERRIBY

WHITTON

HESSLE

PIER

NEW HOLLAND

BARTON-
ON-HUMBER

BARROW
HAVEN

GOXHILL

THORNTON
ABBEY

ULCEBY

BROCKLESBY

GC

GC

HABROUGH

STALLINGBOROUGH

HEALING

GREAT
COATES

HULL

KILLINGHOLME

2
3

1

GC

4

IMMINGHAM
DOCK

Docks
W E

DOCK

TOWN
GRIMSBY PASTURE
ST

MARKET
RASEN

GC

GN

LOUTH

NEW
CLEE

CLEETHORPES

GN

1: Humber Oil Refinery
2: Lindsey Oil Refinery
3: Iron Ore and Coal Import Terminal
4: Export Coal Terminal

Seventeen

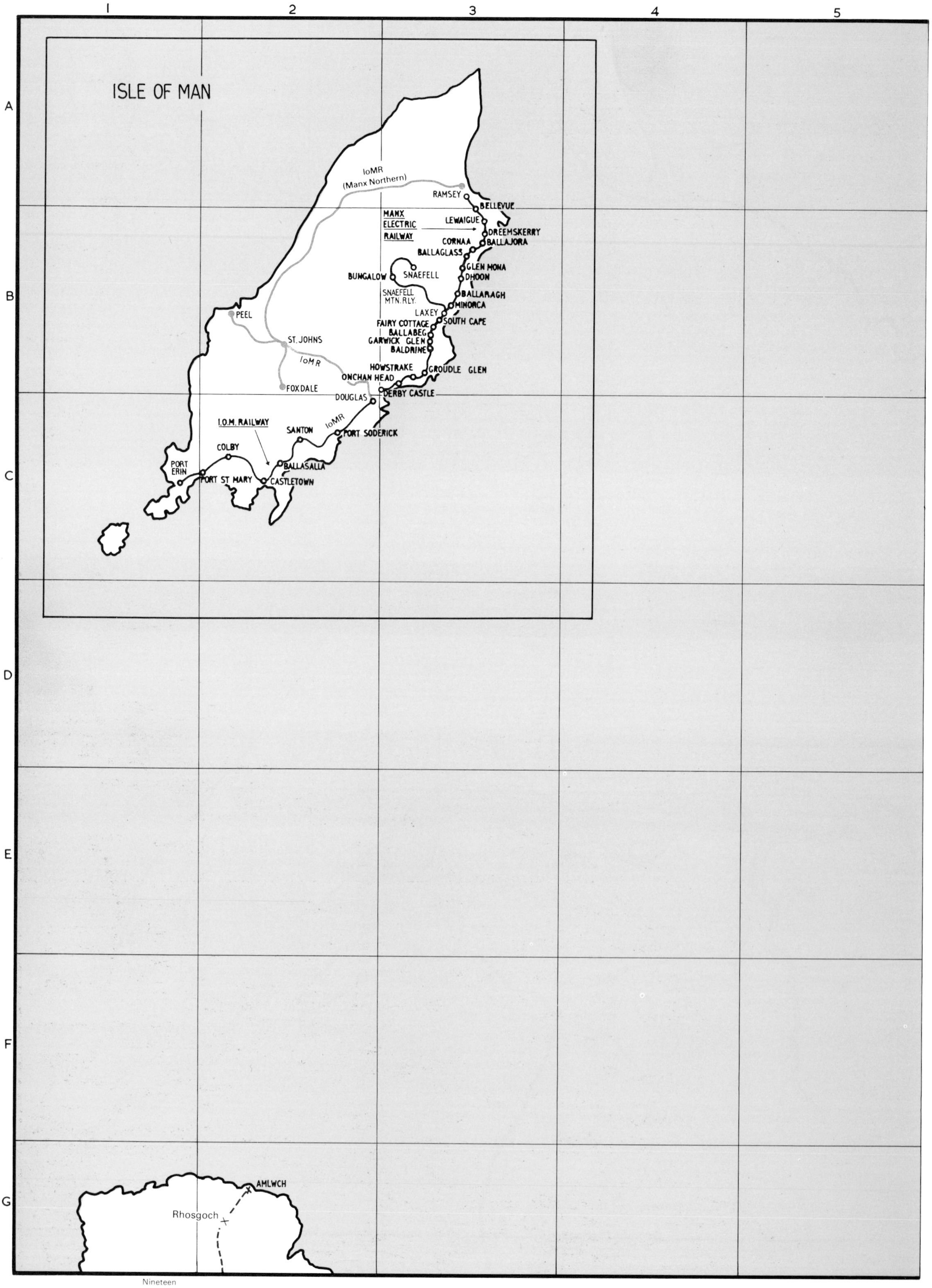

ISLE OF MAN

IoMR
(Manx Northern)

RAMSEY
BELLEVUE
MANX
ELECTRIC LEWAIGUE
RAILWAY DREEMSKERRY
CORNAA BALLAJORA
BALLAGLASS
GLEN MONA
BUNGALOW SNAEFELL DHOON
BALLARAGH
SNAEFELL MINORCA
MTN. RLY.
LAXEY
PEEL FAIRY COTTAGE SOUTH CAPE
BALLABEG
ST. JOHNS GARWICK GLEN
BALDRINE
IoMR
HOWSTRAKE GROUDLE GLEN
FOXDALE ONCHAN HEAD
DOUGLAS DERBY CASTLE

I.O.M. RAILWAY
SANTON
IoMR
COLBY PORT SODERICK
PORT
ERIN
BALLASALLA
PORT ST MARY CASTLETOWN

AMLWCH
Rhosgoch

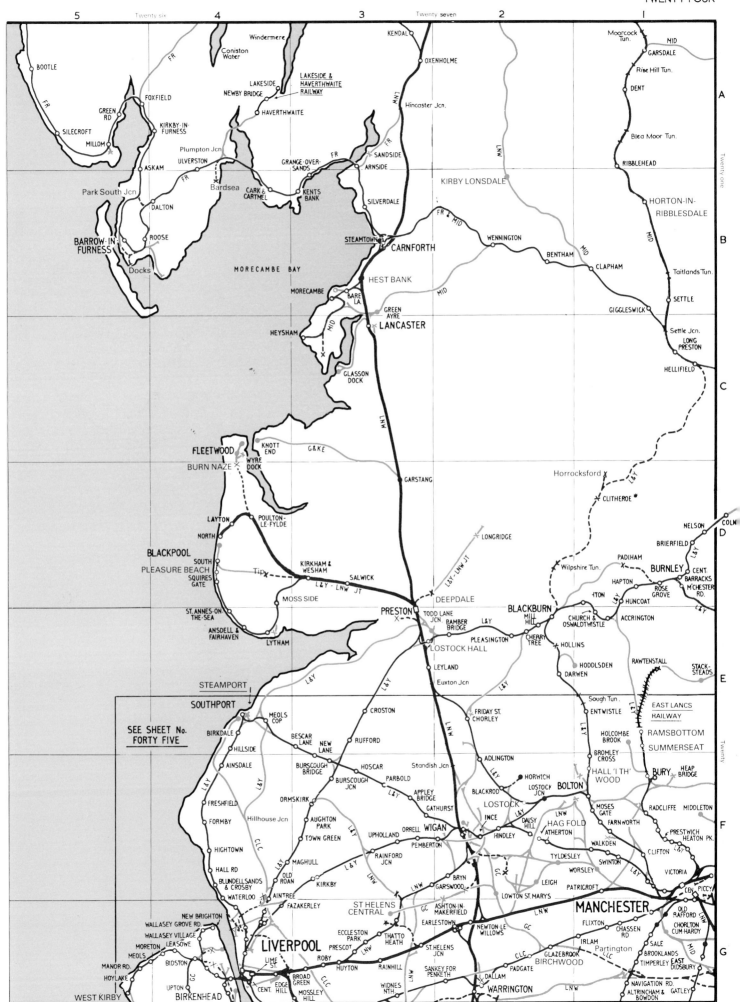

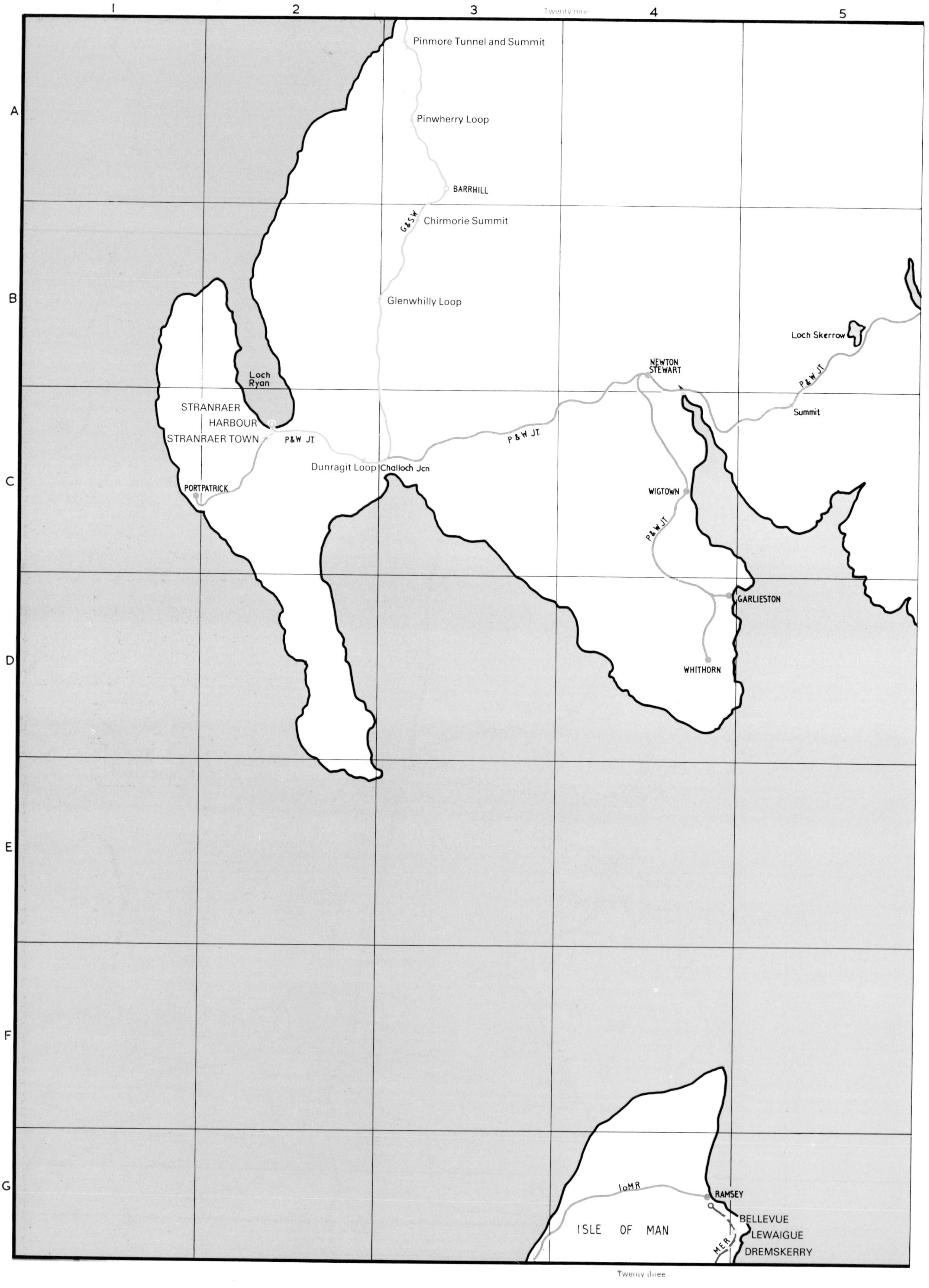

1
2
3
Twenty nine
4
5
A
B
C
D
E
F
G
Pinmore Tunnel and Summit
Pinwherry Loop
BARRHILL
G&SW
Chirmorie Summit
Glenwhilly Loop
Loch Skerrow
NEWTON STEWART
P&W JT.
Summit
Loch Ryan
STRANRAER
HARBOUR
STRANRAER TOWN
P&W JT.
P&W JT.
Dunragit Loop
Challoch Jcn
PORTPATRICK
WIGTOWN
P&W JT.
GARLIESTON
WHITHORN
IoMR
RAMSEY
ISLE OF MAN
BELLEVUE
LEWAIGUE
DREMSKERRY
MER
Twenty three

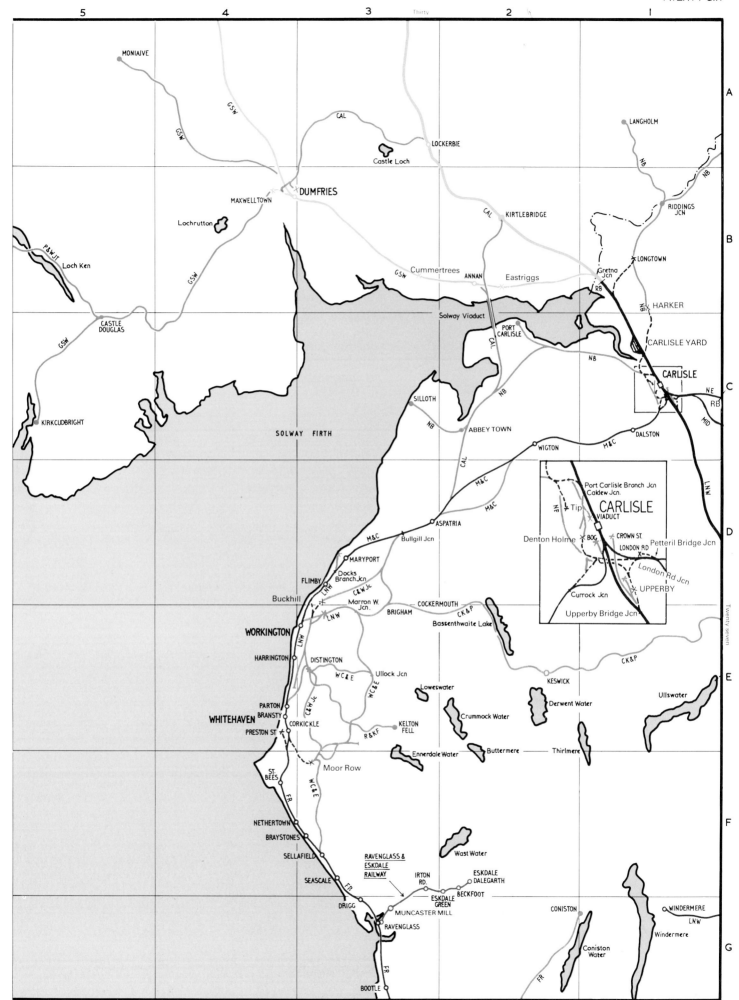

MONIAIVE

GSW

GSW

CAL

LOCKERBIE

Castle Loch

LANGHOLM

NB

NB

RIDDINGS JCN

MAXWELLTOWN

DUMFRIES

Lochrutton

CAL

KIRTLEBRIDGE

LONGTOWN

Gretna Jcn

NB

HARKER

P&WJT

Loch Ken

GSW

Cummertrees

ANNAN

Eastriggs

RB

CARLISLE YARD

Solway Viaduct

PORT CARLISLE

CAL

NB

CARLISLE

NE

RB

CASTLE DOUGLAS

GSW

SILLOTH

NB

ABBEY TOWN

NB

WIGTON

M&C

DALSTON

MID

LNW

KIRKCUDBRIGHT

SOLWAY FIRTH

CAL

M&C

ASPATRIA

M&C

Bullgill Jcn

Port Carlisle Branch Jcn

Caldew Jcn.

CARLISLE

NE

Tip

VIADUCT

Denton Holme

BOG

CROWN ST.

LONDON RD.

Petteril Bridge Jcn

MARYPORT

Docks Branch Jcn

London Rd Jcn

FLIMBY

LNW

C&WJc

Buckhill

Marron W. Jcn.

COCKERMOUTH

CK&P

London Rd Jcn

UPPERBY

Currock Jcn

BRIGHAM

Bassenthwaite Lake

Upperby Bridge Jcn

WORKINGTON

LNW

LNW

HARRINGTON

DISTINGTON

Ullock Jcn

WC&E

KESWICK

CK&P

WC&E

Loweswater

Derwent Water

Ullswater

PARTON

BRANSTY

C&WJc

WHITEHAVEN

CORKICKLE

PRESTON ST

Crummock Water

Buttermere

Thirlmere

R&KF

KELTON FELL

Ennerdale Water

ST. BEES

WC&E

Moor Row

FR

NETHERTOWN

BRAYSTONES

Wast Water

SELLAFIELD

RAVENGLASS & ESKDALE RAILWAY

IRTON RD.

ESKDALE DALEGARTH

SEASCALE

ESKDALE GREEN

BECKFOOT

CONISTON

WINDERMERE

LNW

DRIGG

MUNCASTER MILL

FR

RAVENGLASS

Coniston Water

Windermere

FR

BOOTLE

Twenty seven

NB

NEWCASTLETON

WIDDRINGTON

Butterwell ✕

PEGSWOOD

ASHINGTON

NB

MORPETH

NE

BEDLINGTON

A

NB

SCOTSGAP

NB

NB

REEDSMOUTH

NB

CRAMLINGTON

NE

CALLERTON ICI

1: KINGSTON PK
2: LONG BENTON
3: FOUR LANE ENDS
4: BENTON

BANKFOOT

REGENT CENTRE

B

DARRAS HALL FAWDON

WANSBECK RD

SOUTH GOSFORTH

JESMOND

Scotswood

CENTRAL

BRAMPTON TOWN

BRAMPTON

NE

HALTWHISTLE

BARDON MILL

HAYDON BRIDGE

HEXHAM

CORBRIDGE

PRUDHOE

WYLAM

Haltwhistle Tun.

NE

NE

Corbridge Tun.

RIDING MILL

STOCKSFIELD

NE

NEWCASTLE

SEE MAP No TWENTY-EIGHT

WETHERALL

NE

ALLENDALE

NE

BLACKHILL

ANNFIELD PLAIN

CHESTER-LE-STREET

C

SLAGGYFORD

GILDERDALE

CONSETT

ROWLEY

NE

ARMATHWAITE

Armathwaite Tun.

ALSTON

SOUTH TYNEDALE RAILWAY

BLANCHLAND

DURHAM

Baron Wood Tuns.

WATERHOUSES

Relly Mill Jcn

LAZONBY & KIRKOSWALD

Lazonby Tun.

Long Meg

MID

WEARHEAD

EASTGATE

STANHOPE*

NE

CROOK

NE

D

LNW

LANGWATHBY

Waste Bank Tun.

Culgaith Tun.

PENRITH

Eamont Bridge Jcn.

Eden Valley Jcn.

NEWBIGGIN

NE

Etherley

BISHOP AUCKLAND

SHILDON

NEWTON AYCLIFFE

E

MIDDLETON-IN-TEESDALE

NE

HEIGHINGTON

APPLEBY

NE

WARCOP

BARNARD CASTLE

NE

Forcett Jcn

Merrybent Jcn

Helm Tun.

SHAP

Shap Summit 916ft

LNW

NE

Stainmore Summit

NE

FORCETT

BARTON

F

EAST KIRKBY STEPHEN

Birkett Tun.

TEBAY

NE

NE

RICHMOND

STAVELEY

BURNESIDE

LOW GILL

LNW

LNW

LNW

Ais Gill Summit 1,166ft

Shotlock Hill Tunnel

Moorcock Tun.

MID

REDMIRE ✕

NE

G

KENDAL

OXENHOLME

GARSDALE

NE

NE

Rise Hill Tun.

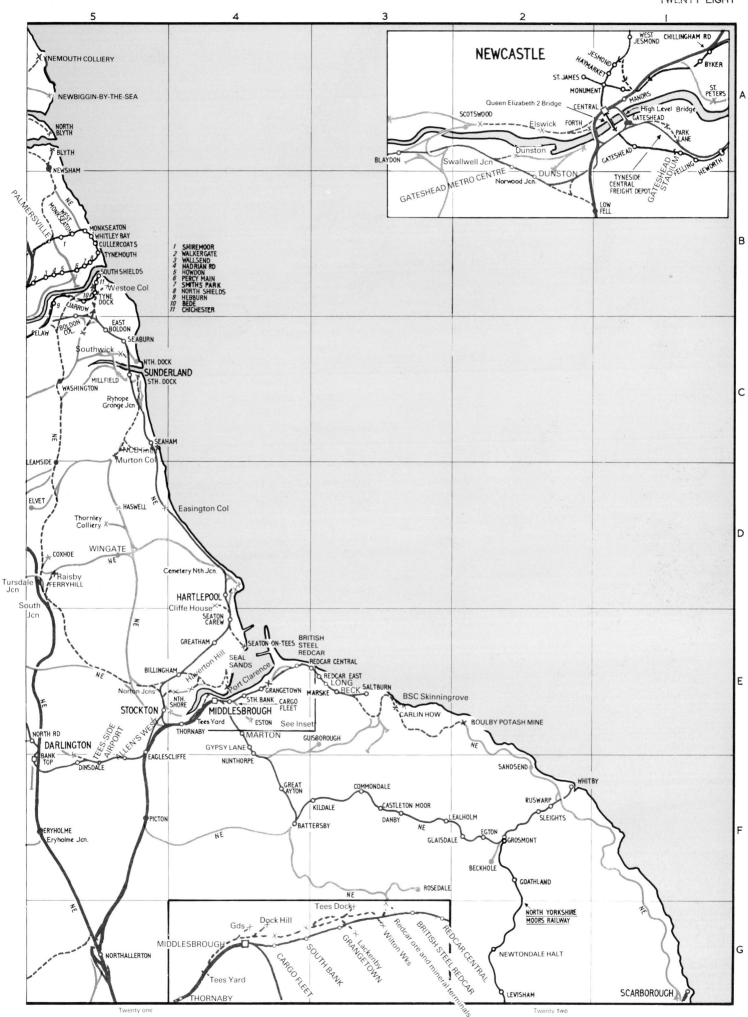

5 4 3 2 1

NEWCASTLE

WEST JESMOND CHILLINGHAM RD
JESMOND HAYMARKET BYKER
ST. JAMES MONUMENT ST. PETERS
Queen Elizabeth 2 Bridge MANORS High Level Bridge A
SCOTSWOOD CENTRAL GATESHEAD
Elswick FORTH GATESHEAD PARK LANE
Dunston GATESHEAD STADIUM
BLAYDON Swallwell Jcn GATESHEAD HEWORTH
GATESHEAD METRO CENTRE Norwood Jcn DUNSTON TYNESIDE CENTRAL FREIGHT DEPOT FELLING
LOW FELL

TYNEMOUTH COLLIERY

NEWBIGGIN-BY-THE-SEA

NORTH BLYTH

BLYTH

NEWSHAM

PALMERSVILLE
NE
WEST MONKSEATON
MONKSEATON
WHITLEY BAY
CULLERCOATS
TYNEMOUTH
SOUTH SHIELDS
Westoe Col
TYNE DOCK
JARROW
PELAW
BOLDON COL.
EAST BOLDON
SEABURN

1 SHIREMOOR
2 WALKERGATE
3 WALLSEND
4 HADRIAN RD
5 HOWDON
6 PERCY MAIN
7 SMITHS PARK
8 NORTH SHIELDS
9 HEBBURN
10 BEDE
11 CHICHESTER

Southwick NTH. DOCK
MILLFIELD **SUNDERLAND**
WASHINGTON STH. DOCK
Ryhope Grange Jcn
SEAHAM
NCB lines
LEAMSIDE Murton Col
ELVET HASWELL Easington Col
Thornley Colliery
COXHOE WINGATE
NE
Tursdale Jcn Raisby Cemetery Nth Jcn.
FERRYHILL
South Jcn **HARTLEPOOL**
Cliffe House
SEATON CAREW
GREATHAM SEATON-ON-TEES BRITISH STEEL REDCAR
SEAL SANDS REDCAR CENTRAL
Haverton Hill REDCAR EAST
BILLINGHAM Port Clarence LONG BECK SALTBURN
Norton Jcns GRANGETOWN MARSKE BSC Skinningrove
NTH. SHORE STH. BANK CARGO FLEET
STOCKTON Tees Yard CARLIN HOW BOULBY POTASH MINE
NORTH RD **MIDDLESBROUGH** ESTON See Inset
DARLINGTON THORNABY MARTON
BANK TOP EAGLESCLIFFE GUISBOROUGH
DINSDALE GYPSY LANE SANDSEND
TEES-SIDE AIRPORT ALLEN'S WEST NUNTHORPE WHITBY
GREAT AYTON COMMONDALE RUSWARP
ERYHOLME KILDALE CASTLETON MOOR SLEIGHTS
Eryholme Jcn. BATTERSBY DANBY LEALHOLM GROSMONT
PICTON NE GLAISDALE EGTON
NE BECKHOLE
GOATHLAND
ROSEDALE
NORTH YORKSHIRE MOORS RAILWAY
NEWTONDALE HALT
NE

Tees Dock
Gds Dock Hill
MIDDLESBROUGH Redcar ore and mineral terminals
Tees Yard SOUTH BANK Lackenby Wilton Wks REDCAR CENTRAL
NORTHALLERTON CARGO FLEET GRANGETOWN BRITISH STEEL REDCAR **SCARBOROUGH**
THORNABY LEVISHAM

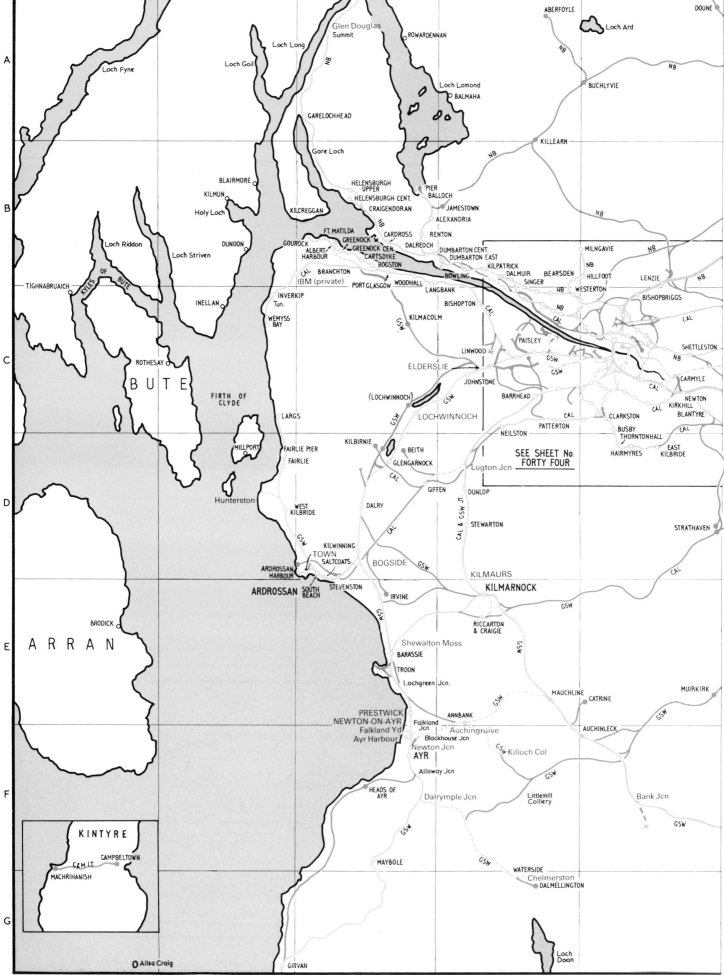

1 2 3 4 5

Loch Fyne

Loch Long
Loch Goil
Glen Douglas
Summit
ROWARDENNAN
Loch Ard
ABERFOYLE
DOUNE
NB
NB

A

GARELOCHHEAD
Loch Lomond
BALMAHA
BUCHLYVIE

Gare Loch
NB
KILLEARN

BLAIRMORE
KILMUN
HELENSBURGH
UPPER
PIER
BALLOCH
NB
NB

Holy Loch
KILCREGGAN
HELENSBURGH CENT.
CRAIGENDORAN
JAMESTOWN
NB
MILNGAVIE
NB
LENZIE
NB

B

Loch Riddon
DUNOON
FT. MATILDA
CARDROSS
ALEXANDRIA
NB
HILLFOOT
NB

Loch Striven
GOUROCK
GREENOCK W.
GREENOCK CEN.
DALREOCH
RENTON
DUMBARTON CENT.
KILPATRICK
DALMUIR
BEARSDEN
WESTERTON
BISHOPBRIGGS

KYLES OF BUTE
ALBERT
HARBOUR
CARTSDYKE
BOGSTON
DUMBARTON EAST
SINGER
HILLFOOT
CAL
NB

TIGHNABRUAICH
CAL
BRANCHTON
IBM (private)
PORT GLASGOW
BOWLING
CAL
NB
CAL
CAL

INELLAN
WOODHALL
LANGBANK
NB
CAL

INVERKIP
Tun.
KILMACOLM
BISHOPTON
CAL
GSW

WEMYSS
BAY
GSW
LINWOOD
PAISLEY
GSW
SHETTLESTON
NB

C

ROTHESAY
ELDERSLIE
GSW
CARMYLE

B U T E
FIRTH OF
CLYDE
JOHNSTONE
BARRHEAD
NEWTON
KIRKHILL
BLANTYRE

LARGS
(LOCHWINNOCH)
LOCHWINNOCH
CLARKSTON
CAL

MILLPORT
GSW
NEILSTON
PATTERTON
BUSBY
THORNTONHALL
CAL

FAIRLIE PIER
FAIRLIE
KILBIRNIE
BEITH
GLENGARNOCK
Lugton Jcn.
HAIRMYRES
EAST
KILBRIDE

Hunterston
CAL
GIFFEN
DUNLOP
SEE SHEET No.
FORTY FOUR

D

WEST
KILBRIDE
DALRY
CAL & GSW JT.
STEWARTON
STRATHAVEN

GSW
KILWINNING
TOWN
SALTCOATS
CAL
CAL

ARDROSSAN
HARBOUR
BOGSIDE
GSW
KILMAURS
CAL

ARDROSSAN
SOUTH
BEACH
STEVENSTON
KILMARNOCK

BRODICK
IRVINE
RICCARTON
& CRAIGIE
GSW

E

A R R A N
Shewalton Moss
BARASSIE
GSW

TROON
Lochgreen Jcn.
MAUCHLINE
CATRINE
MUIRKIRK
GSW

PRESTWICK
NEWTON-ON-AYR
Falkland Yd
Ayr Harbour
Falkland
Jcn
ANNBANK
Auchingruive
GSW
GSW
AUCHINLECK

Blackhouse Jcn
Newton Jcn
GSW Killoch Col
AYR

F

Alloway Jcn
HEADS OF
AYR
Dalrymple Jcn
Littlemill
Colliery
Bank Jcn
GSW

GSW

MAYBOLE
GSW
WATERSIDE
Chelmerston
DALMELLINGTON

G

Ailsa Craig
Loch
Doon

KINTYRE
CAMPBELTOWN
C&M LT.
MACHRIHANISH

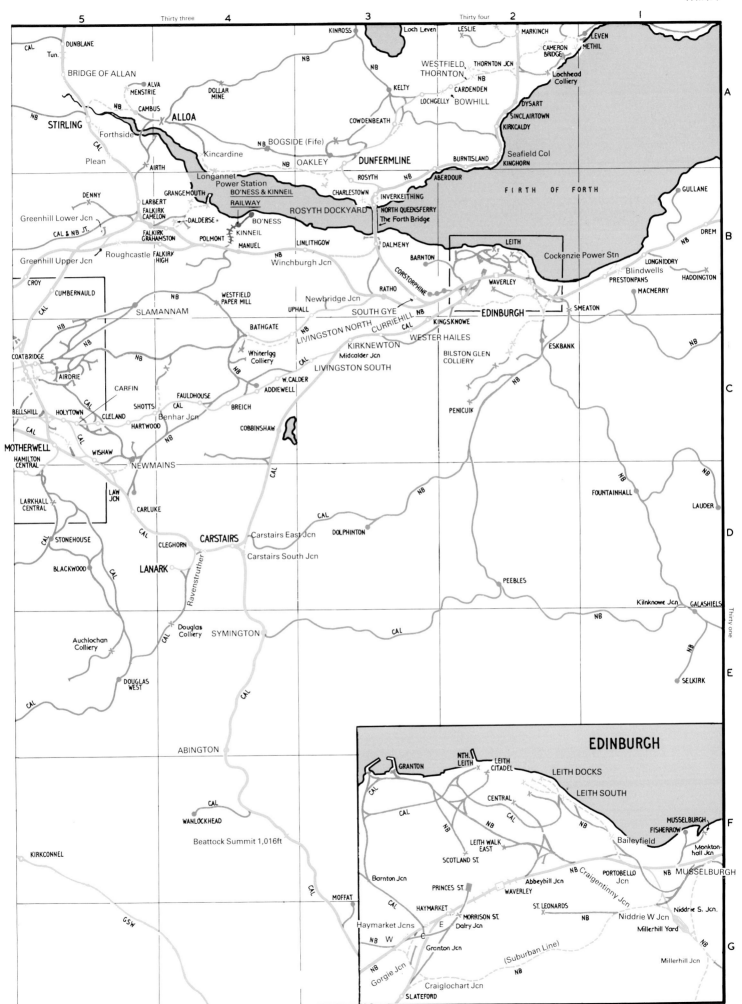

CAL   DUNBLANE
Tun.
BRIDGE OF ALLAN
ALVA
MENSTRIE
CAMBUS
NB
STIRLING   ALLOA
Forthside
Plean
AIRTH
CAL
DOLLAR
MINE

KINROSS   Loch Leven   LESLIE   MARKINCH
NB   CAMERON   LEVEN
BRIDGE   METHIL
WESTFIELD   THORNTON JCN
NB   THORNTON   Lochhead
KELTY   CARDENDEN   Colliery
LOCHGELLY   BOWHILL   DYSART
COWDENBEATH   SINCLAIRTOWN
KIRKCALDY
NB BOGSIDE (Fife)
Kincardine   OAKLEY   DUNFERMLINE   Seafield Col
NB OAKLEY   BURNTISLAND   KINGHORN
Longannet   ROSYTH   NB   ABERDOUR
Power Station   CHARLESTOWN   INVERKEITHING   FIRTH OF FORTH   GULLANE
GRANGEMOUTH   BO'NESS & KINNEIL
LARBERT   RAILWAY   ROSYTH DOCKYARD   NORTH QUEENSFERRY   DREM
FALKIRK   DALDERSE   The Forth Bridge   LEITH   NB
CAMELON   BO'NESS   DALMENY   Cockenzie Power Stn   LONGNIDDRY
DENNY   KINNEIL   BARNTON   Blindwells
Greenhill Lower Jcn   FALKIRK   POLMONT   LINLITHGOW   PRESTONPANS   HADDINGTON
CAL & NB JT.   GRAHAMSTON   MANUEL   CORSTORPHINE   WAVERLEY   MACMERRY
Greenhill Upper Jcn   FALKIRK   NB   RATHO   SMEATON
Roughcastle   HIGH   Winchburgh Jcn   EDINBURGH
CROY   Newbridge Jcn   ESKBANK
CUMBERNAULD   WESTFIELD   NB   SOUTH GYE
CAL   PAPER MILL   UPHALL   CURRIEHILL NB
SLAMANNAM   LIVINGSTON NORTH   KINGSKNOWE   NB
NB   BATHGATE   CAL   WESTER HAILES
COATBRIDGE   Whiterigg   KIRKNEWTON   NB
AIRDRIE   Colliery   Midcalder Jcn   BILSTON GLEN
CARFIN   NB   LIVINGSTON SOUTH   COLLIERY
BELLSHILL   CAL   W. CALDER   FOUNTAINHALL
HOLYTOWN   FAULDHOUSE   ADDIEWELL   PENICUIK   LAUDER
CLELAND   SHOTTS   CAL   BREICH
CAL   Benhar Jcn   NB
MOTHERWELL   HARTWOOD
WISHAW   COBBINSHAW   NB
HAMILTON   NEWMAINS   FOUNTAINHALL
CENTRAL   CAL   LAUDER
LARKHALL   LAW   CARLUKE   CAL   Kilnknowe Jcn   GALASHIELS
CENTRAL   JCN   DOLPHINTON   PEEBLES   NB
CAL   CARSTAIRS   Carstairs East Jcn
STONEHOUSE   CLEGHORN   CARSTAIRS   CAL   SELKIRK
BLACKWOOD   CAL   LANARK   Carstairs South Jcn
Ravenstruther
Auchlochan   Douglas   CAL
Colliery   CAL   Colliery   SYMINGTON   CAL
Douglas
West   CAL
CAL   ABINGTON
KIRKCONNEL   CAL
WANLOCKHEAD
Beattock Summit 1,016ft
CAL
MOFFAT
GSW

EDINBURGH

GRANTON   NTH.   LEITH
CAL   LEITH   CITADEL   LEITH DOCKS
CAL   LEITH SOUTH
NB   CAL   NB   MUSSELBURGH
CENTRAL   FISHERROW
Barnton Jcn   LEITH WALK   NB   Baileyfield
EAST   Monkton-
SCOTLAND ST   hall Jcn
CAL   Abbeyhill Jcn   NB   MUSSELBURGH
PRINCES ST.   Craigentinny Jcn
WAVERLEY   PORTOBELLO   NB
ST. LEONARDS   Jcn   Niddrie S. Jcn.
HAYMARKET   Niddrie W Jcn
CAL   MORRISON ST.   NB   Millerhill Yard
Haymarket Jcns   E   Dalry Jcn
NB   W   C   Craiglochart Jcn   Millerhill Jcn
NB   Granton Jcn   (Suburban Line)   NB
Gorgie Jcn
SLATEFORD

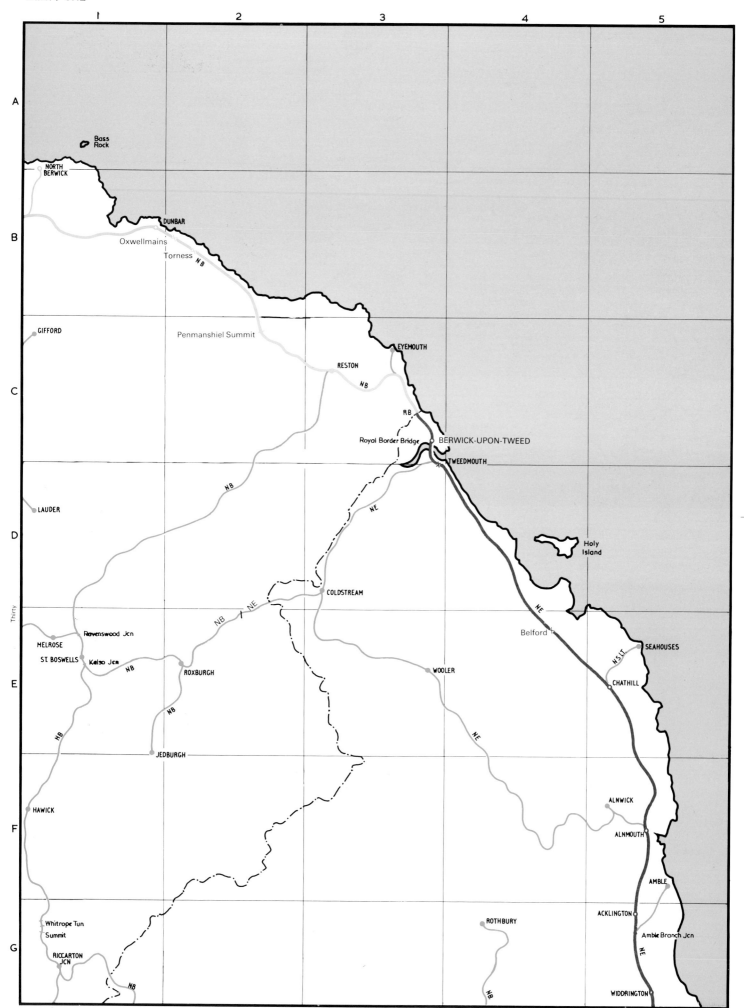

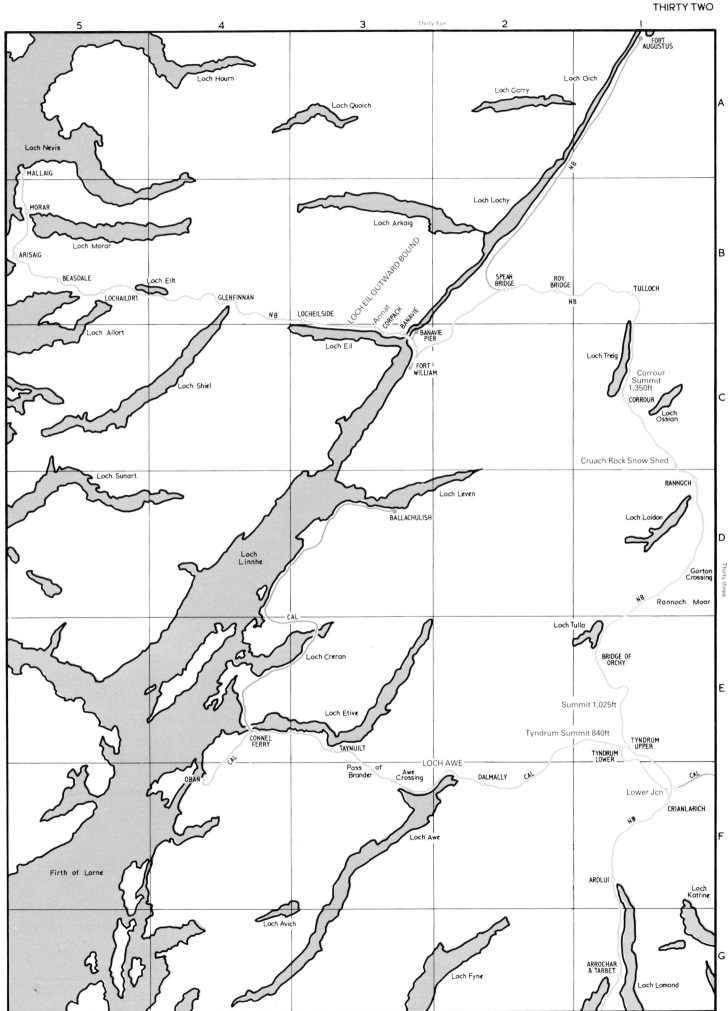

5   4   3   2   1

FORT
AUGUSTUS

Loch Oich

Loch Garry

Loch Hourn

Loch Quoich

A

NB

Loch Nevis

Loch Lochy

MALLAIG

MORAR

Loch Arkaig

B

Loch Morar

SPEAN
BRIDGE

ROY
BRIDGE

TULLOCH

ARISAIG

NB

BEASDALE

Loch Eilt

LOCH EIL OUTWARD BOUND

LOCHAILORT

GLENFINNAN

Annat

CORPACH

BANAVIE

Loch Ailort

NB

LOCHEILSIDE

BANAVIE
PIER

Loch Treig

Loch Eil

FORT
WILLIAM

Corrour
Summit
1,350ft

C

Loch Shiel

CORROUR

Loch
Ossian

Cruach Rock Snow Shed

Loch Sunart

RANNOCH

Loch Leven

Loch Laidon

BALLACHULISH

D

Loch
Linnhe

Gorton
Crossing

NB

Rannoch Moor

Thirty three

CAL

Loch Tulla

Loch Creran

BRIDGE OF
ORCHY

E

Loch Etive

Summit 1,025ft

Tyndrum Summit 840ft

TYNDRUM
UPPER

CONNEL
FERRY

TAYNUILT

TYNDRUM
LOWER

LOCH AWE

CAL

Pass   of
Brander

Awe
Crossing

DALMALLY

CAL

CAL

OBAN

Lower Jcn

CAL

CRIANLARICH

Loch Awe

NB

Firth of Lorne

ARDLUI

Loch
Katrine

F

Loch Avich

G

ARROCHAR
& TARBET

Loch Fyne

Loch Lomond

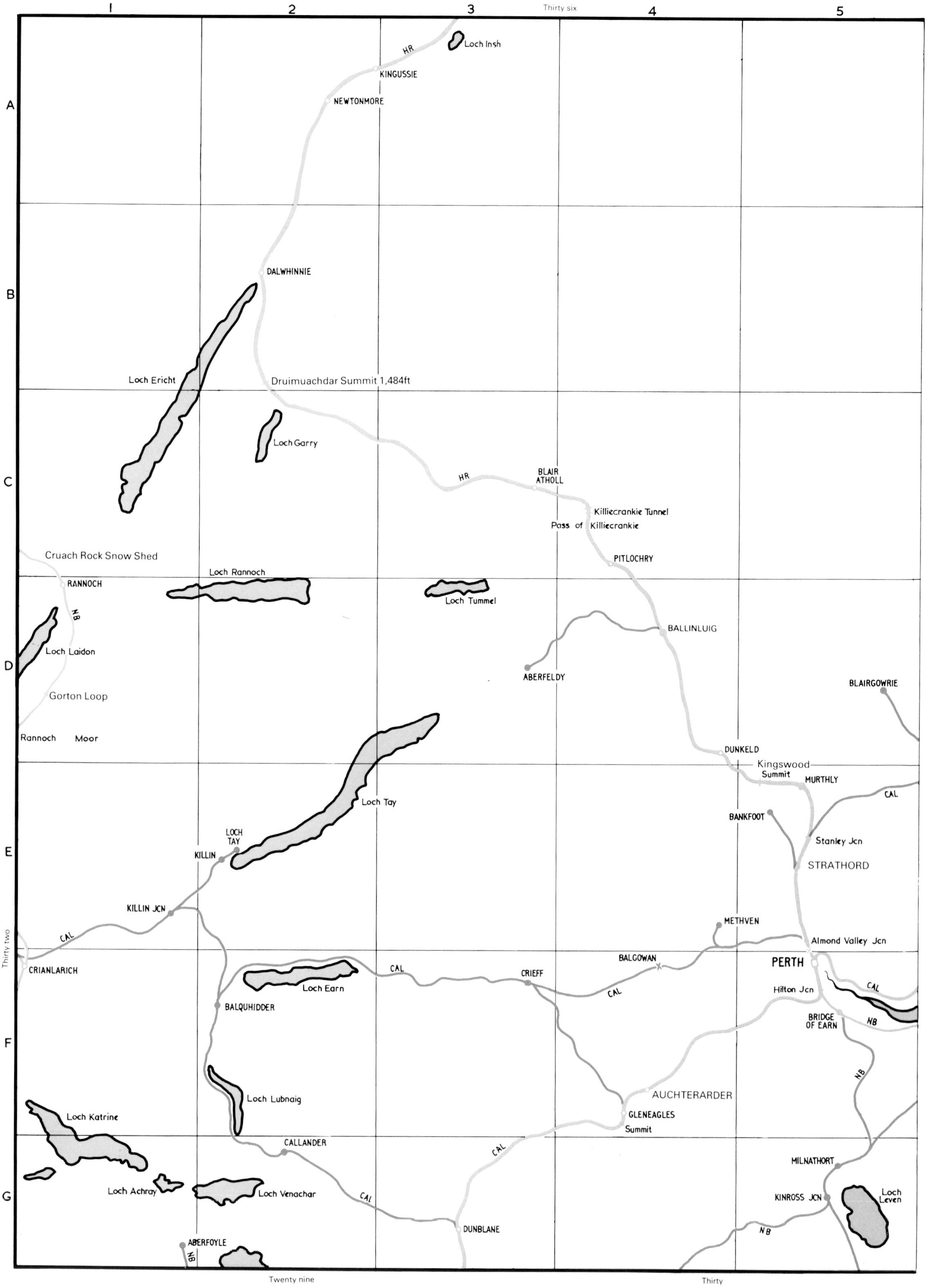

1   2   3   Thirty six   4   5

Loch Insh

HR

KINGUSSIE

A   NEWTONMORE

B   DALWHINNIE

Druimuachdar Summit 1,484ft

Loch Ericht

Loch Garry

BLAIR
ATHOLL

C   HR

Killiecrankie Tunnel

Pass of Killiecrankie

PITLOCHRY

Cruach Rock Snow Shed

Loch Rannoch

RANNOCH

BALLINLUIG

NB

Loch Tummel

Loch Laidon

ABERFELDY

D

BLAIRGOWRIE

Gorton Loop

DUNKELD

Kingswood
Summit

Rannoch   Moor

MURTHLY

CAL

Loch Tay

BANKFOOT

LOCH
TAY

Stanley Jcn

KILLIN

E

STRATHORD

KILLIN JCN

Thirty two

METHVEN

CAL

Almond Valley Jcn

CRIANLARICH

BALGOWAN

PERTH

Loch Earn

CAL

CRIEFF

Hilton Jcn

CAL

BALQUHIDDER

CAL

NB

BRIDGE
OF EARN

F

NB

Loch Lubnaig

AUCHTERARDER

Loch Katrine

GLENEAGLES

Summit

CALLANDER

MILNATHORT

CAL

Loch Achray

Loch Venachar

CAL

KINROSS JCN

Loch
Leven

G

ABERFOYLE

NB

DUNBLANE

NB

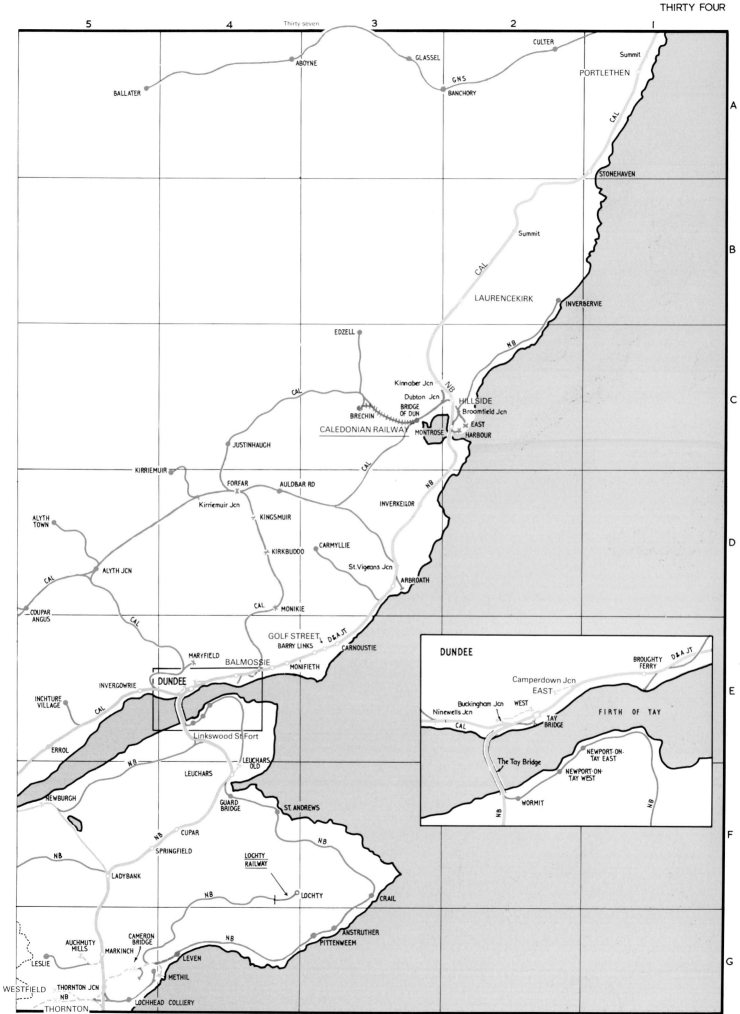

5   4   3   2   1

A
B
C
D
E
F
G

PORTLETHEN
Summit
CAL
STONEHAVEN

CULTER
GLASSEL
ABOYNE
GNS
BANCHORY
BALLATER

Summit
CAL
LAURENCEKIRK
INVERBERVIE
NB

EDZELL

Kinnaber Jcn
NB
Dubton Jcn
BRIDGE OF DUN
HILLSIDE
Broomfield Jcn
CAL
BRECHIN
EAST HARBOUR
CALEDONIAN RAILWAY
MONTROSE

JUSTINHAUGH
CAL
KIRRIEMUIR
FORFAR
AULDBAR RD
Kirriemuir Jcn
INVERKEILOR
NB
KINGSMUIR
ALYTH TOWN
CARMYLLIE
CAL
KIRKBUDDO
St. Vigeans Jcn
ALYTH JCN
ARBROATH
COUPAR ANGUS
CAL
MONIKIE
CAL

GOLF STREET   D&AJT
BARRY LINKS
MARYFIELD   CARNOUSTIE
BALMOSSIE
DUNDEE   MONIFIETH
INVERGOWRIE
INCHTURE VILLAGE   Linkswood St Fort
CAL
ERROL
NB
LEUCHARS OLD
LEUCHARS
NEWBURGH
GUARD BRIDGE
ST. ANDREWS
CUPAR
SPRINGFIELD
NB
NB
LOCHTY RAILWAY
LADYBANK
NB
NB
LOCHTY
CRAIL
ANSTRUTHER
NB
PITTENWEEM
AUCHMUTY MILLS
CAMERON BRIDGE
MARKINCH
LEVEN
LESLIE
METHIL
WESTFIELD
THORNTON JCN
NB
LOCHHEAD COLLIERY
THORNTON

DUNDEE
Camperdown Jcn
EAST
Buckingham Jcn
WEST
Ninewells Jcn
CAL
TAY BRIDGE
The Tay Bridge
NB
WORMIT
BROUGHTY FERRY
D&A JT
FIRTH OF TAY
NEWPORT-ON-TAY EAST
NEWPORT-ON-TAY WEST
NB

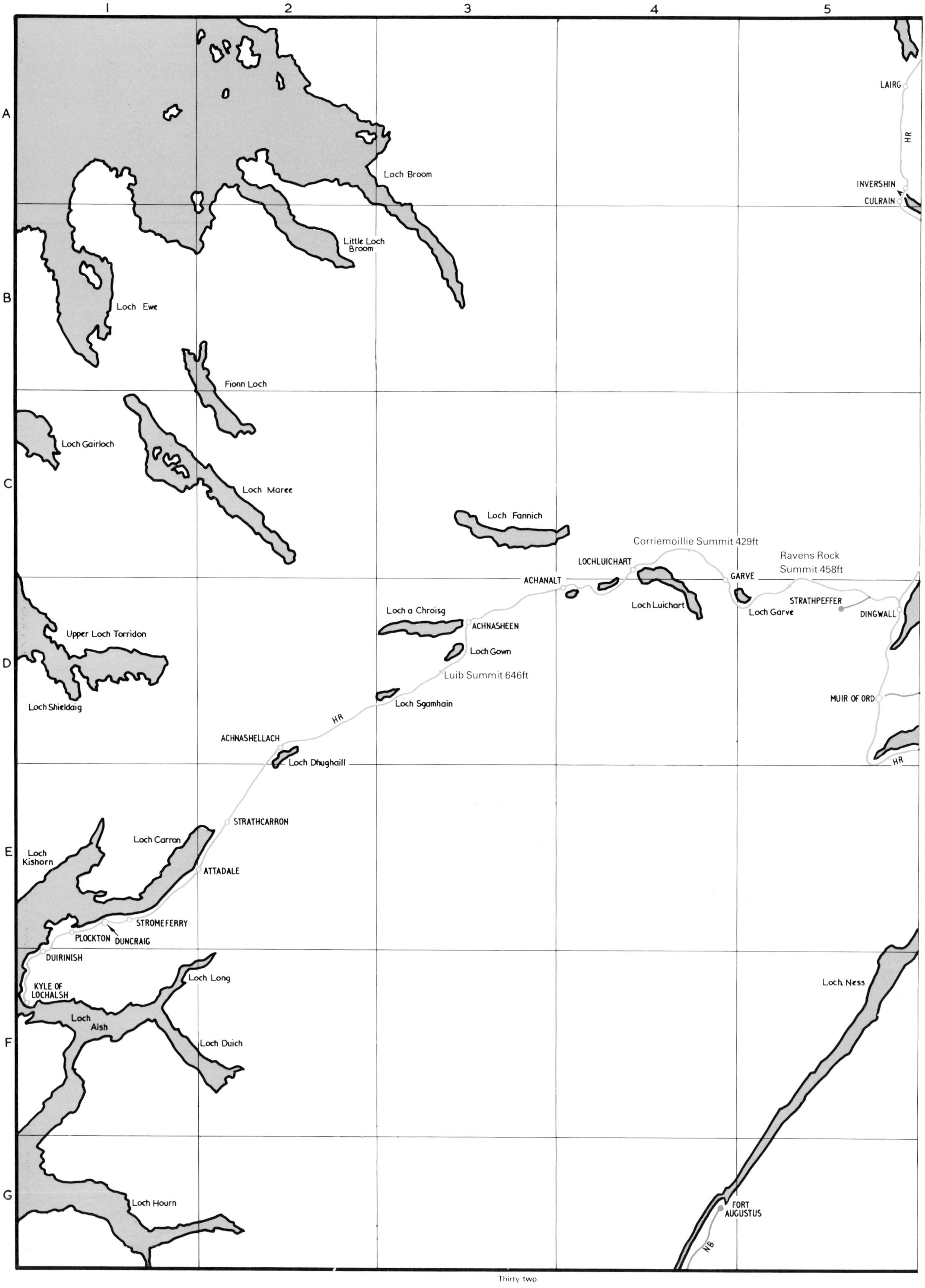

1
2
3
4
5
A
B
C
D
E
F
G
LAIRG
HR
INVERSHIN
CULRAIN
Loch Broom
Little Loch Broom
Loch Ewe
Fionn Loch
Loch Gairloch
Loch Maree
Loch Fannich
Corriemoillie Summit 429ft
Ravens Rock Summit 458ft
LOCHLUICHART
ACHANALT
GARVE
Loch Luichart
STRATHPEFFER
Loch Garve
DINGWALL
Loch a Chroisg
ACHNASHEEN
Upper Loch Torridon
Loch Gown
Luib Summit 646ft
Loch Sgamhain
Loch Shieldaig
MUIR OF ORD
HR
ACHNASHELLACH
Loch Dhughaill
HR
STRATHCARRON
Loch Carron
Loch Kishorn
ATTADALE
STROMEFERRY
PLOCKTON
DUNCRAIG
DUIRINISH
Loch Long
KYLE OF LOCHALSH
Loch Ness
Loch Alsh
Loch Duich
Loch Hourn
FORT AUGUSTUS
NB

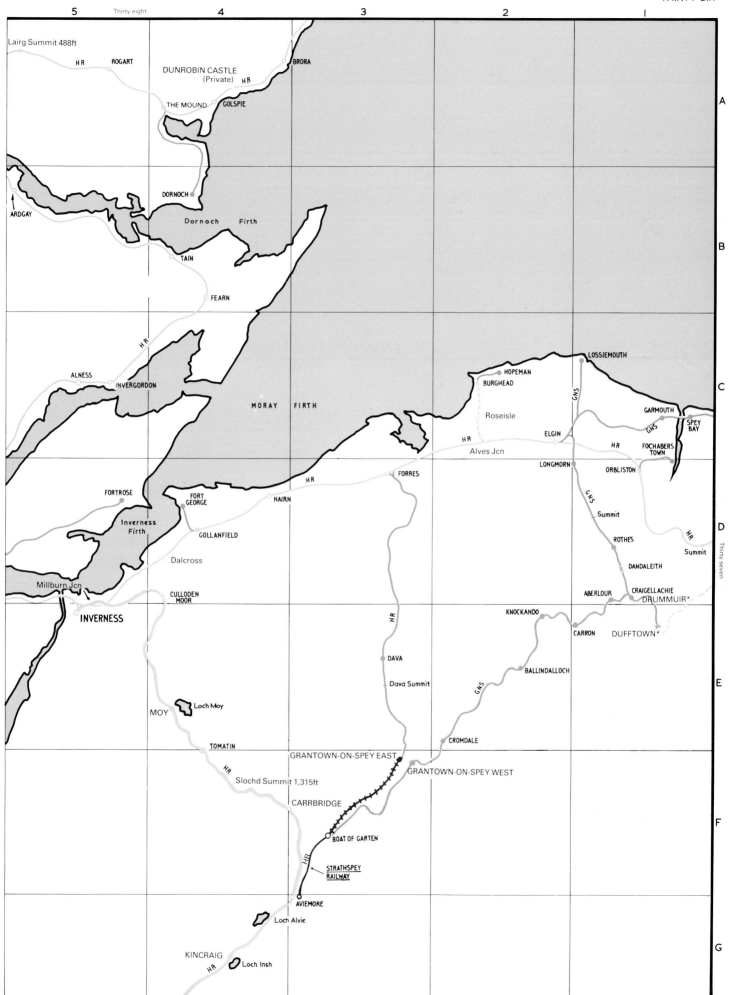

5   Thirty eight   4   3   2   1

Lairg Summit 488ft

HR   ROGART

DUNROBIN CASTLE
(Private)   HR

BRORA

THE MOUND   GOLSPIE

A

ARDGAY

DORNOCH

Dornoch Firth

TAIN

B

FEARN

LOSSIEMOUTH

HOPEMAN
BURGHEAD

Roseisle

GARMOUTH

GNS

SPEY
BAY

C

ALNESS

INVERGORDON

MORAY FIRTH

ELGIN

GNS

HR   FOCHABERS
TOWN

HR

Alves Jcn

LONGMORN

ORBLISTON

FORTROSE

FORT
GEORGE

NAIRN

FORRES

HR

GNS

Summit

D

Inverness
Firth

GOLLANFIELD

Dalcross

ROTHES

Summit

Thirty seven

DANDALEITH

Millburn Jcn

CULLODEN
MOOR

ABERLOUR

CRAIGELLACHIE
DRUMMUIR*

INVERNESS

KNOCKANDO

E

HR

CARRON

DUFFTOWN*

MOY   Loch Moy

DAVA

BALLINDALLOCH

GNS

Dava Summit

TOMATIN

CROMDALE

HR

GRANTOWN-ON-SPEY EAST

Slochd Summit 1,315ft

GRANTOWN-ON-SPEY WEST

CARRBRIDGE

F

HR

BOAT OF GARTEN

STRATHSPEY
RAILWAY

AVIEMORE

Loch Alvie

G

KINCRAIG

HR   Loch Insh

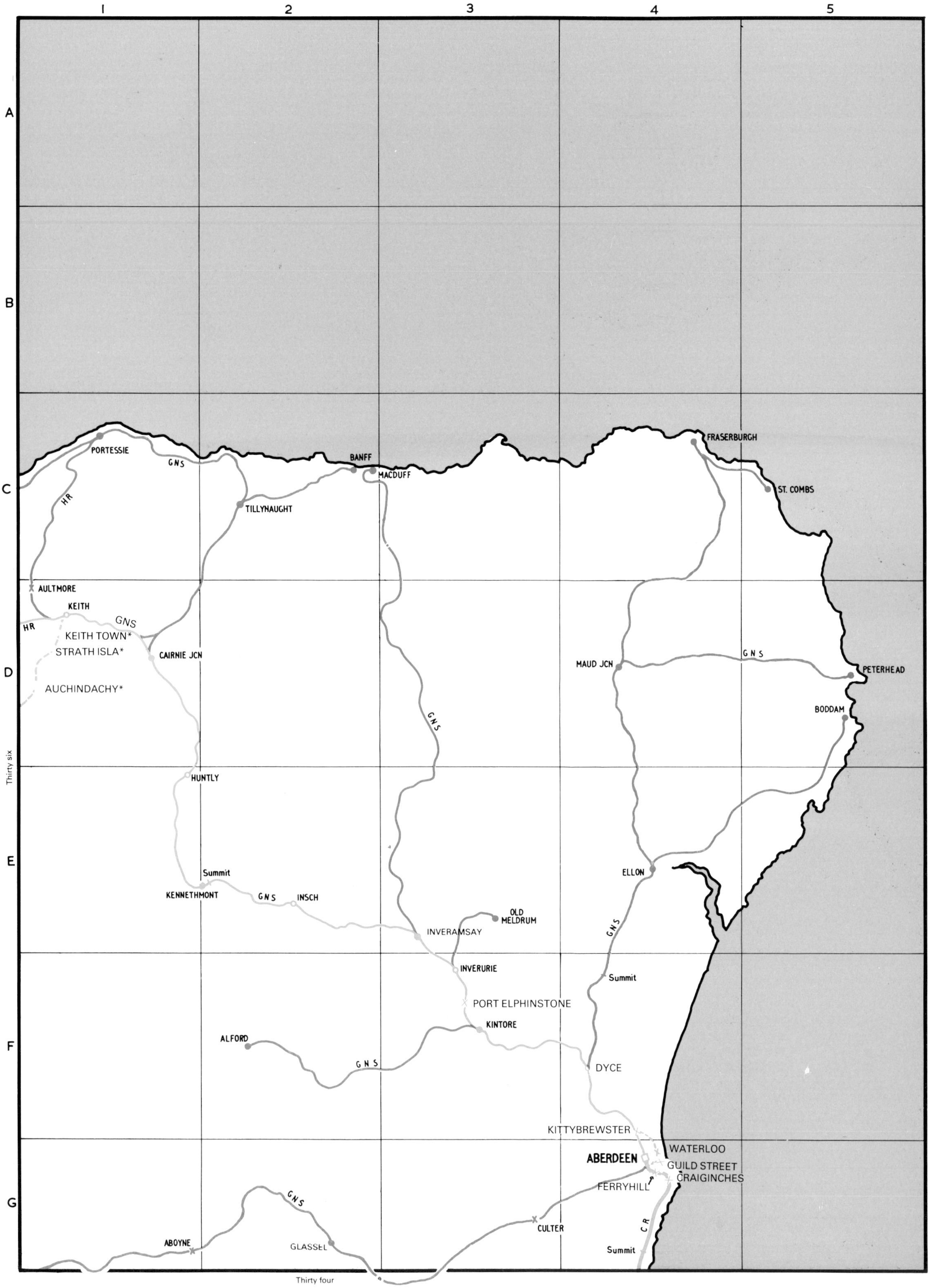

1 2 3 4 5

A

B

PORTESSIE

GNS

HR

C BANFF
MACDUFF

FRASERBURGH

ST. COMBS

TILLYNAUGHT

AULTMORE

KEITH

HR GNS

KEITH TOWN*

STRATH ISLA* CAIRNIE JCN

D MAUD JCN GNS PETERHEAD

AUCHINDACHY*

BODDAM

GNS

HUNTLY

Thirty six

E Summit ELLON

KENNETHMONT GNS INSCH

GNS

OLD
MELDRUM

INVERAMSAY

Summit

INVERURIE

PORT ELPHINSTONE

KINTORE

F ALFORD

GNS DYCE

KITTYBREWSTER

WATERLOO

ABERDEEN GUILD STREET
CRAIGINCHES

FERRYHILL

G GNS CR

CULTER

ABOYNE GLASSEL Summit

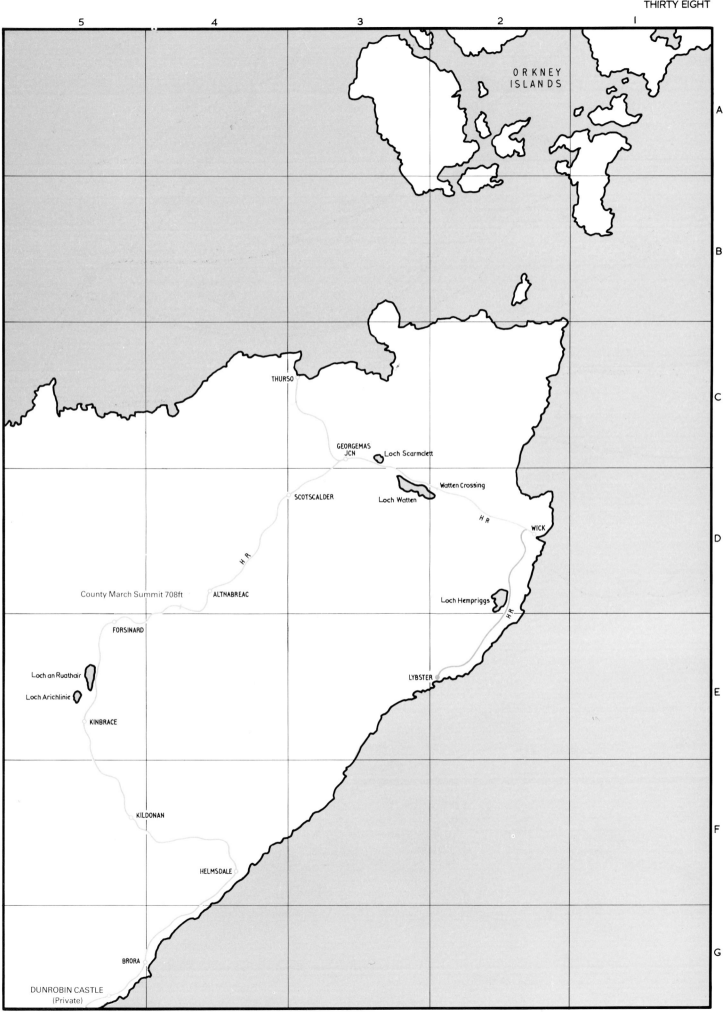

5   4   3   2   I

ORKNEY
ISLANDS

A

B

C

THURSO

GEORGEMAS
JCN   Loch Scarmclett

Watten Crossing
SCOTSCALDER
Loch Watten
H R
WICK

D

County March Summit 708ft   ALTNABREAC
H R
Loch Hempriggs
H R

FORSINARD

Loch an Ruathair
LYBSTER
Loch Arichlinie
KINBRACE

E

KILDONAN

F

HELMSDALE

BRORA

G

DUNROBIN CASTLE
(Private)

1   2   3   4   5

A

HEADSTONE LANE
PINNER
NORTH HARROW
MET & GC JT.
LNW
LNW
HARROW & WEALDSTONE
KENTON
HARROW-ON-THE-HILL
NORTHWICK PARK
RB
STH. KENTON
PRESTON RD
QUEENSBURY
KINGSBURY
COLINDALE
HENDON
HENDON CENTRAL
BRENT CROSS
GN
FINCHLEY CENTRAL
EAST FINCHLEY
GN
GN
Northern Line to Morden
GOLDERS GREEN

B

RAYNERS LANE
MET
WEST HARROW
EASTCOTE
SOUTH HARROW
RUISLIP GARDENS
GW & GC JT.
SOUTH RUISLIP
GC
NORTHOLT
GREENFORD
NORTHOLT PARK
SUDBURY HILL
SUDBURY HILL (HARROW)
SUDBURY & HARROW RD.
SUDBURY TOWN
NORTH WEMBLEY
GC
MET
WEMBLEY PARK
WEMBLEY STADIUM
WEMBLEY STADIUM
WEMBLEY CENTRAL
GC
STONEBRIDGE PARK
Willesden Yard
NEASDEN
RB
Neasden Jcn.
DOLLIS HILL
WILLESDEN GREEN
MID
Brent/Cricklewood Sdgs
Brent Curve Jcn
Dudding Hill Jcn
Brent Jcn.
CRICKLEWOOD
WEST HAMPSTEAD THAMESLINK
WEST HAMPSTEAD
KILBURN
BRONDESBURY PARK
BRONDESBURY
LNW
KENSAL RISE
QUEENS PARK
KILBURN HIGH RD
WEST HAMPSTEAD
Haverstock Hill Tun.
FINCHLEY RD & FROGNAL
LNW
FINCHLEY RD.
HAMPSTEAD HEATH
GOSPEL OAK
Tun.
PRIMROSE HILL
CAMDEN
STH HAMPSTEAD
Primrose Hill Tun.
Lords Tun.
GC
MET
GT. PORTLAND ST.
Jubilee Line to Charing X

C

Portobello Jcn.
ROYAL OAK
GW
WESTBOURNE PARK
PADDINGTON
CRIMEA YARD
CASTLE BAR PARK
DRAYTON GREEN
GW
S. GREENFORD
PERIVALE
HANGER LANE
PARK ROYAL
PARK ROYAL
NORTH EALING
Acton Yard
ACTON MAIN LINE
W. ACTON
NORTH ACTON
EAST ACTON
Acton Canal Wharf Jcn
Old Oak Jcn.
Acton Wells Jcn.
H.L.
LNW
Old Oak Common West Jcn.
GW
N. Pole Jcn.
Mitre Bridge Jcn.
MITRE BRIDGE
RB
WESTBOURNE PARK
ROYAL OAK
PADDINGTON
KENSAL GREEN
Kensal Green Tuns.
LADBROKE GROVE
LATIMER RD.
SHEPHERDS BUSH
WHITE CITY
BAYSWATER
NOTTING HILL GATE
EDGWARE RD.
MET
HIGH ST. KENSINGTON
GLOUCESTER RD
SLOANE SQUARE
VICTORIA
SOUTH KENSINGTON
MET-DIST
MARYLEBONE
BAKER ST.
WILLESDEN JCN.
LNW
KENSAL GREEN
HARLESDEN
ALPERTON
MET-DIST
EALING BROADWAY
HANWELL
WEST EALING
GW
EALING COMMON
ACTON CENTRAL
N & SW JCN
SOUTH ACTON
Central Line to Ongar
Bakerloo Line to Elephant & Castle

D

SOUTHALL
NORTHFIELDS
MET-DIST
SOUTH EALING
ACTON TOWN
GW
BOSTON MANOR
OSTERLEY
SYON LANE
BRENTFORD TOWN
HATTON CROSS
HOUNSLOW WEST
HOUNSLOW CENTRAL
HOUNSLOW EAST
ISLEWORTH
LSW
BRENTFORD
Old Jcn.
New Jcn.
N & SW JCN
RB
CHISWICK PARK
GUNNERSBURY
TURNHAM GREEN
STAMFORD BROOK
RAVENSCOURT PARK
HAMMERSMITH & CHISWICK
Studland Rd. Jcn.
GOLDHAWK RD.
HAMMERSMITH
WEST KENSINGTON
BARONS COURT
WARWICK RD.
KENSINGTON OLYMPIA
EARLS COURT
WEST BROMPTON
W.L.E.JT.
Lillie Bridge
Piccadilly Line to Cockfosters
FULHAM BROADWAY
PARSONS GREEN
PUTNEY BRIDGE
RB
CHELSEA BASIN
Latchmere Jcns.
BATTERSEA PARK
KEW BRIDGE
CHISWICK
BARNES BRIDGE
KEW GARDENS
RICHMOND
NORTH SHEEN
MORTLAKE
BARNES
LSW
PUTNEY
WANDSWORTH TOWN
CLAPHAM JCN

E

FELTHAM JCN.
Feltham Jcn
LSW
Feltham Yard
HOUNSLOW
Hounslow Jcn.
WHITTON
Whitton Jcn.
ST. MARGARETS
TWICKENHAM
LSW
STRAWBERRY HILL
FULWELL
KEMPTON PARK*
LSW
W.L.E JT
Ludgate Jcn.
CLAPHAM JCN
LSW
LSW
NEW WANDSWORTH
Latchmere Jcn.
Pouparts Jcn
FALCON LANE
Culvert Rd Jcn
LBSC
Longhedge Jcn
Battersea Pier Jcn
BATTERSEA PARK
QUEENSTOWN RD BATTERSEA
SEC
Stewarts Lane Jcn.
SOUTH LAMBETH
MID
Factory Jcn
LSW
STEWARTS LANE
WANDSWORTH RD
CLAPHAM
Voltaire Rd Jcn
LBSC
SEC
East PUTNEY
Point Pleasant Jcn.
SOUTHFIELDS
WANDSWORTH COMMON
EARLSFIELD
BALHAM
LBSC
WIMBLEDON PARK
Carriage sidings
HAYDONS RD.
WIMBLEDON
Northern line to High Barnet, Edgware and Mill Hill East

F

HAMPTON
TEDDINGTON
HAMPTON WICK
KINGSTON
LSW
NORBITON
RAYNES PARK
WIMBLEDON CHASE
MERTON PARK
TOOTING
LBSC & LSW JT
LBSC
MORDEN RD
MORDEN PARK
MITCHAM

G

HAMPTON COURT
THAMES DITTON
SURBITON
Hampton Court Jcn
NORBITON
MALDEN MANOR
NEW MALDEN
BERRYLANDS
MOTSPUR PARK
LSW
WORCESTER PARK
SOUTH MERTON
MORDEN
MORDEN SOUTH
ST. HELIER
SUTTON COMMON
MITCHAM JCN.
HACKBRIDGE
HERSHAM
ESHER
TOLWORTH
LSW

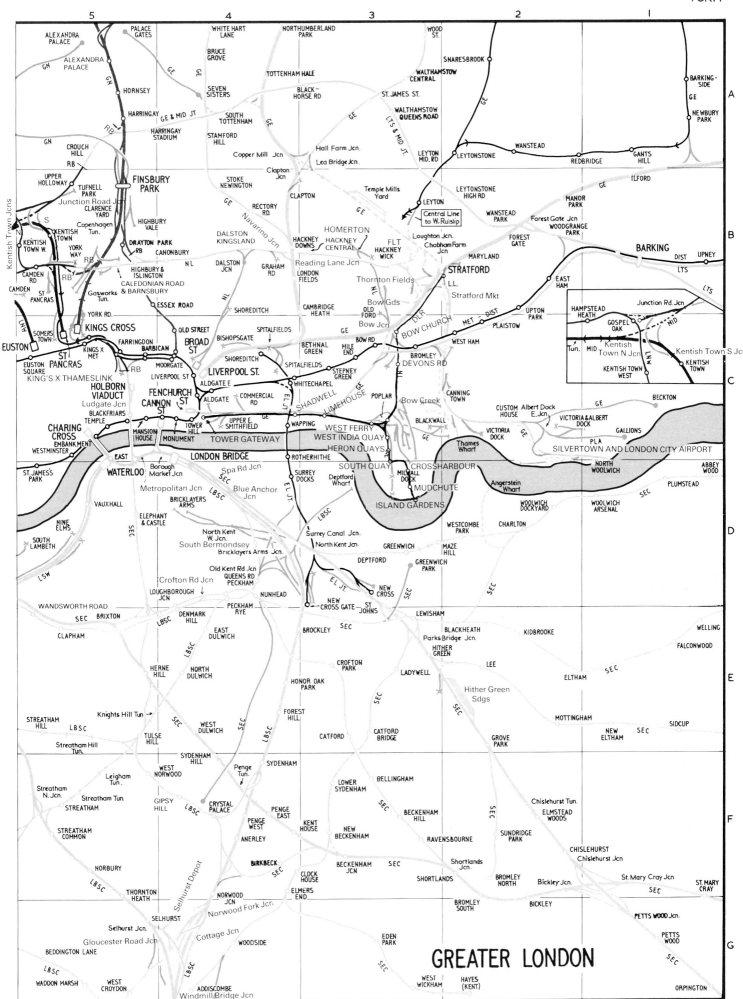

GREATER LONDON

DERBY AND NOTTINGHAM TO SHEFFIELD

VICTORIA PARK
WHARF ST
QUEENS RD.
SHEFFIELD
NUNNERY
DARNALL
WOODHOUSE
Treeton Jcns
Dinnington Main Col
Dinnington Col Jcn
BEIGHTON
KIVETON BRIDGE
KIVETON PARK
Brancliffe E Jcn
SHIREOAKS
GC
WORKSOP
RB
DORE
Bradway Tun.
WEST KILLAMARSH
UPPERTHORPE & KILLAMARSH
CENT.
GC
MID
Totley Tun.
GRINDLEFORD
DRONFIELD
Renishaw Pk Col
RENISHAW CENTRAL
SPINK HILL
MID
GC
BARROW HILL
Broomhouse Tun.
Foxlow Jcn
CLOWNE
Whitwell
GC
STAVELEY CENTRAL
MID
GC
Staveley Works
Oxcroft Col
ELMTON & CRESWELL
Seymour Jcn
Tapton Jcn.
CHESTERFIELD
MARKET PLACE
BRAMPTON
Markham Staveley Col
Creswell Col
RB
GC
ARKWRIGHT TOWN
BOLSOVER
SHIREBROOK NORTH
LANGWITH
Warsop Main Col
Welbeck Colliery
Wellbeck Coll Jcn
Thoresby Colliery
GC
Avenue
Shirebrook Col
RB
EDWINSTOWE
GC
Clipstone Jcns
W E S
Clay Cross S Jcn
GN
PLEASLEY
Clipstone Colliery
Rufford Colliery Jcn.
Clay Cross Tun.
ASHOVER
Silverhill Col
Sherwood Col
GC
Rufford Colliery
Bilsthorpe Colliery
ALR STRETTON
PILSLEY
Sutton Col
MID
MANSFIELD TOWN
Mansfield Col
RB
MATLOCK
High Tor Tuns.
MATLOCK BATH
MID
Willersley Tun.
CROMFORD
MID
Tibshelf
Blackwell
SUTTON-IN-ASHFIELD
SUTTON JCN
Blidworth Colliery
MID Farnsfield Jcn.
Lea Wood Tun.
High Peak Jcn.
ALFRETON & MANSFIELD PARKWAY
Alfreton Tun.
Bentinck Col
KIRKBY-IN-ASHFIELD
GC
LNW
WIRKSWORTH
Tun.
WHATSTANDWELL
Wingfield Tun.
PINXTON
MID
Annesley N. Jcn.
NEWSTEAD
DERBY AND NOTTINGHAM TO SHEFFIELD
PYE BRIDGE
HAMMERSMITH
BUTTERLEY
MIDLAND RAILWAY
AMBERGATE
MID
GN
MID
HUCKNALL
Calverton Colliery
BELPER
Marehay Crossing
Denby Open Cast
Bestwood Pk Jcn
Milford Tun.
DUFFIELD
MID
LANGLEY MILL
Bennerley Open Cast
BULWELL FOREST
Bestwood Jcn
GN
GN
MID
HEANOR
MID
BASFORD VERNON
Bagthorpe Jcn.
GN
Gedling Colliery
BURTON JOYCE
Little Eaton Jcn.
ILKESTON N.
TOWN
ILKESTON JCN
Radford Jcn
Tun.
VICTORIA
CARLTON
MID
NETHERFIELD
MID
GN
TROWELL
MID
MIDLAND
Cotgrave Col
DERBY
ST. MARYS
Chaddesden Sidings
Spondon Jcn.
NOTTINGHAM
BEESTON
MIDLAND
GN
PEAR TREE
SPONDON
MID
Toton Yard
ATTENBOROUGH
MID
BRB Test Track
BRB Test Track
GN

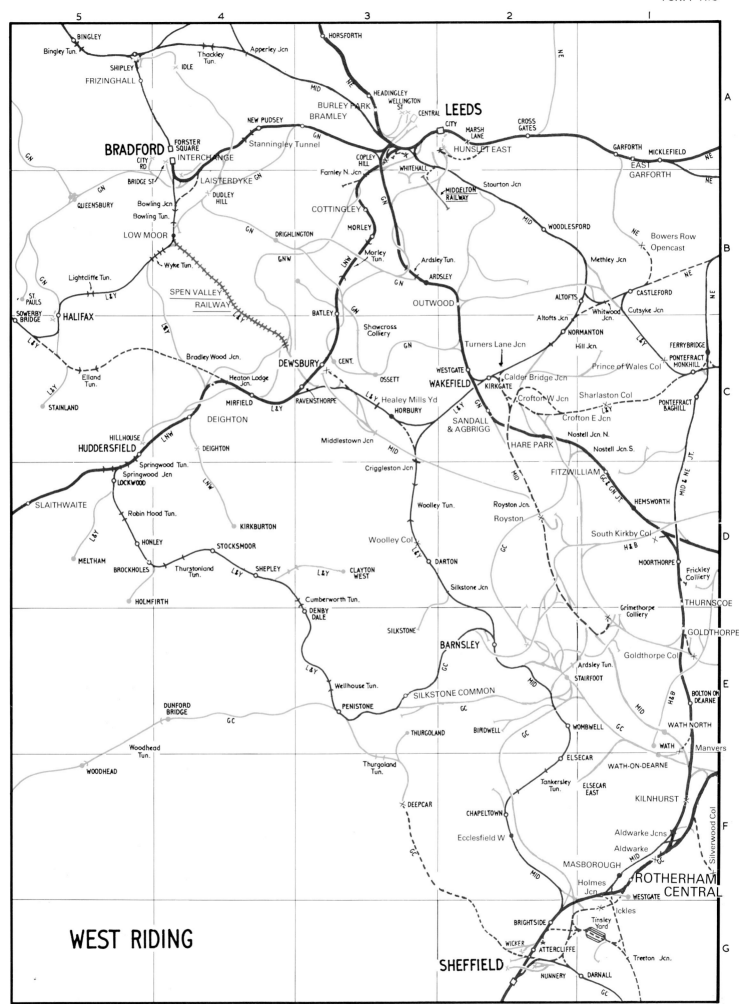

5   4   3   2   1

WEST RIDING

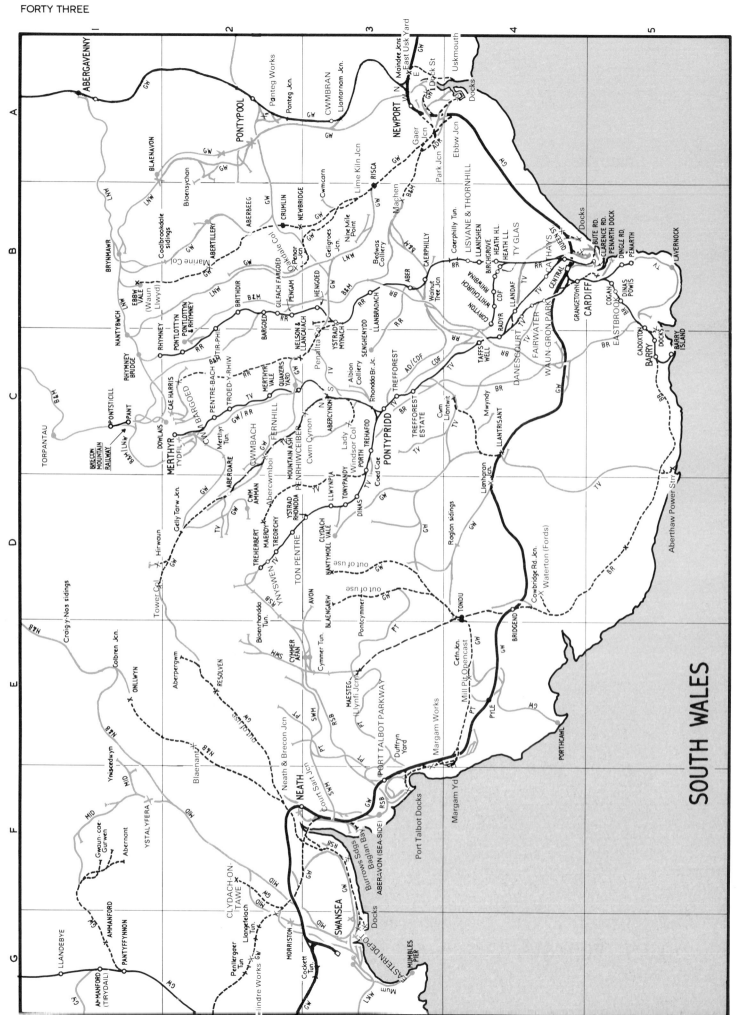

SOUTH WALES

GLASGOW DISTRICT

5 · 4 · 3 · 2 · 1

A · B · C · D · E · F · G

WHITERIGG
SPRINGBANK
CLARKSTON
MOFFAT MILLS
CUMBERNAULD
BN
CHAPEL HALL
CAL
CLELAND
CAL
NEWMAINS
CAL
DALSERF
R. Clyde
CAL
LARKHALL CENTRAL
CAL
AIRDRIE
NB
NB
COATDYKE
CAL
HOLYTOWN
CARFIN HALT
WISHAW
CAL
Garriongill Jcn
WISHAW SOUTH
Shieldmuir Jcn
Dalzell Jcn
Merryton Jcn
CAL
NB
CAL
SUNNYSIDE
CALDER
MOSSEND YARD
Mossend Jcns
BELLSHILL
RAVENSCRAIG
S E CAL
Braidhurst
MOTHERWELL
Ross Jcn
Garnqueen N. Jcn
Garnqueen S. Jcn
GUNNIE
NB
CENTRAL
COATBRIDGE
Langloan Jcn
Whifflet S Jcn
NB
View Park
Lesmahagow Jcn
HAMILTON CENTRAL
WEST
BEDLAY COLLIERY
GARTSHERRIE
(Coatbridge CB¹)
NB
CAL
UDDINGSTON
NB
BOTHWELL
NB
CAL
BLANTYRE
HAMILTON
CAL
GARTSHORE
Waterside Jcn
Bridgend Jcn
NB
Gartosh
Gartosh Jcn
CAL
EASTERHOUSE
GARROWHILL
CAL
NB
NEWTON
R. Clyde
CAMBUSLANG
Hunthill Jcn
HIGH BLANTYRE
LENZIE
Cadder
CAL
SHETTLESTON
CARNTYNE
CAL
CARMYLE
Rutherglen Jcn
RUTHERGLEN
CAL
KIRKHILL
CAL
EAST KILBRIDE
KIRKINTILLOCH
NB
BISHOPBRIGGS
Bishopbriggs OT
St Rollox
BARNHILL
ALEXANDRA PARADE
DUKE ST
BELLGROVE
BRIDGETON
DALMARNOCK
CROFTFOOT
BURNSIDE
KINGS PARK
CAL
THORNTONHALL
HAIRMYRES
TORRANCE
NB
Cowlairs Jcn
SPRINGBURN
N E
SIGHTHILL
HIGH ST
BUCHANAN ST.
CENTRAL
ST ENOCH
GUSHETFAULDS
CROSSHILL
MOUNT FLORIDA
QUEENS PK.
E.
CATHCART
MUREND
BUSBY
CLARKSTON
MILNGAVIE
HILLFOOT
BEARSDEN
NB
Milngavie Jcn
WESTERTON
Jordan Hill
WHITEINCH
ANNIESLAND
HYNDLAND
PARTICK
CHARING CROSS
QUEEN ST.
EXHIBITION CENTRE
PRINCES DOCK
POLLOKSHIELDS WEST
SHAWLANDS
E.
LANGSIDE
Busby Jcn
POLLOK-SHAWS E.
GIFFNOCK
THORNLIEBANK
WILLIAMWOOD
WHITECRAIGS
CAL
PATTERTON
NB
NB
BRIDGETON
GSW
GSW
ANDERSTON
ARGYLE HIGH ST
CENTRAL
STREET COLLEGE
ST ENOCH
GUSHETFAULDS
CAL
CAL
DRUMCHAPEL
GARSCADDEN
SCOTSTOUNHILL
CAL
GOVAN
CORKERHILL
MAXWELL PARK
POLLOKSHAWS WEST
KENNISHEAD
NITSHILL
SINGER
DRUMRY
YOKER
CLYDEBANK
NB
CARDONALD
CROOKSTON
GSW
HILLINGTON EAST
HILLINGTON WEST
DEANSIDE
SPIERSBRIDGE
CAL
Bridge St Jcn
CAL
Terminus Jcn
GENERAL TERMINUS
KINNING PARK
Lyon Cross Jcn
BARRHEAD
Rothesay Dock
WHARF
RENFREW
GSW
EAST
HAWKHEAD
GILMOUR ST.
CANAL
POTTERHILL
CAL
GSW
Longside S. Jcn
POLLOKSHIELDS EAST
QUEENS PARK
Muirhouse Jcns
GSW
Shields Jcn
CAL
POLLOKSHIELDS WEST
CAL
CROSSMYLOOF
KILPATRICK
NB
CAL
DALMUIR RIVERSIDE
DALMUIR
OLD KILPATRICK
Blackstone Jcn.
ST JAMES
WEST
PAISLEY
UNDERWOOD
GSW
LINWOOD
ELDERSLIE
CAL
NEILSTON
GSW
CAL
CAL

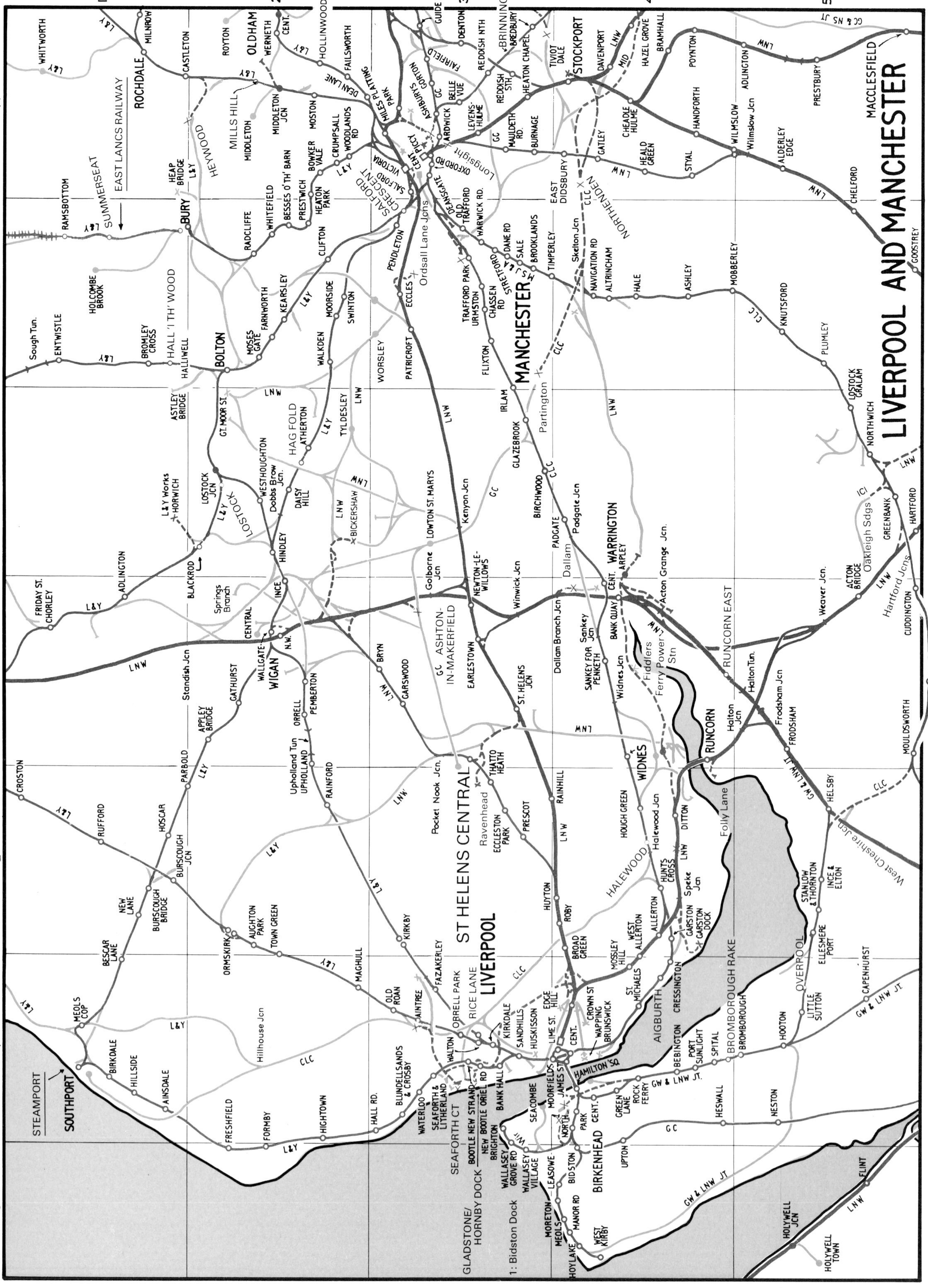

LIVERPOOL AND MANCHESTER

Grid references across top: 1 2 3 4 5
Grid references down left: A B C D E F G

WHITWORTH
MILNROW
ROCHDALE
CASTLETON
ROYTON
OLDHAM
WERNETH
HOLLINWOOD
GUIDE BRIDGE
DENTON
BRINNINGTON
REDDISH NTH
BREDBURY
STOCKPORT
DAVENPORT
MID
HAZEL GROVE
BRAMHALL
POYNTON
ADLINGTON
PRESTBURY
LNW
MACCLESFIELD

MILLS HILL
MIDDLETON
MIDDLETON JCN
MOSTON
BOWKER VALE
CRUMPSALL
WOODLANDS RD
MILES PLATTING
PARK
ASHBURYS
FAIRFIELD
GC
DEAN LANE
FAILSWORTH
ASHTON JCN
ARDWICK
BELLE VUE
LEVENS-HULME
REDDISH STH
HEATON CHAPEL
HEATON NTH
TIVIOT DALE
CHEADLE HULME
HANDFORTH
WILMSLOW JCN
HEALD GREEN
STYAL
WILMSLOW
ALDERLEY EDGE
CHELFORD
GOOSTREY
GC & NS JT

WHITWORTH
EAST LANCS RAILWAY
SUMMERSEAT
RAMSBOTTOM
HEAP BRIDGE
HEYWOOD
L&Y
BURY
BESSES O'TH' BARN
PRESTWICH
HEATON PARK
SALFORD CRESCENT
SALFORD
VICTORIA
OXFORD RD
DEANSGATE
Ordsall Lane Jcns
CENT PECY
LONGSIGHT
GC
MAULDETH RD
BURNAGE
EAST DIDSBURY
GATLEY
STYAL
HANDFORTH

HOLCOMBE BROOK
WHITEFIELD
RADCLIFFE
CLIFTON
PENDLETON
PENDLEBURY
ECCLES
TRAFFORD PARK
OLD TRAFFORD
WARWICK RD
MANCHESTER
DANE RD
SALE
BROOKLANDS
TIMPERLEY
SKELTON JCN
NAVIGATION RD
ALTRINCHAM
HALE
ASHLEY
MOBBERLEY
KNUTSFORD
CLC
PLUMLEY
LOSTOCK GRALAM
NORTHWICH
HARTFORD

ENTWISTLE
Sough Tun.
BROMLEY CROSS
HALL 'I TH' WOOD
HALLIWELL
ASTLEY BRIDGE
BOLTON
MOSES GATE
FARNWORTH
KEARSLEY
MOORSIDE
SWINTON
WALKDEN
WORSLEY
PATRICROFT
FLIXTON
IRLAM
GLAZEBROOK
BIRCHWOOD
PADGATE
PADGATE JCN
WARRINGTON
ARPLEY
Dallam
Acton Grange Jcn
WEAVER JCN
ACTON BRIDGE
Hartford Jcns
CUDDINGTON
DELAMERE

GT. MOOR ST.
L&Y Works
HORWICH
LOSTOCK JCN
LOSTOCK
WESTHOUGHTON
DOBBS BROW JCN.
DAISY HILL
HAG FOLD
ATHERTON
TYLDESLEY
BICKERSHAW
LNW
LOWTON ST. MARYS
KENYON JCN
GC
DALLAM BRANCH JCN
CENT
SANKEY JCN
BANK QUAY
RUNCORN EAST
RUNCORN
HALTON JCN
HALTON TUN.
FRODSHAM JCN
FRODSHAM
HELSBY
MOULDSWORTH
GW & LNW JT
West Cheshire Jcn

FRIDAY ST.
CHORLEY
ADLINGTON
L&Y
Standish Jcn.
WALLGATE
WIGAN
N.W.
CATHURST
APPLEY BRIDGE
ORRELL
PEMBERTON
INCE
Springs Branch
BLACKROD
HINDLEY
BRYN
GARSWOOD
GOLBORNE JCN
NEWTON-LE-WILLOWS
WINWICK JCN
EARLESTOWN
ST. HELENS JCN
SANKEY FOR PENKETH
WIDNES
WIDNES JCN
Ferry Power Stn
Fiddlers
RUNCORN
STANLOW & THORNTON
INCE & ELTON
Oakleigh Sdgs
GREENBANK
ICI
HARTFORD

CROSTON
RUFFORD
HOSCAR
BURSCOUGH JCN
PARBOLD
APPLEY BRIDGE
UPHOLLAND
UPHOLLAND TUN
RAINFORD
Pocket Nook Jcn
Ravenhead
ST HELENS CENTRAL
ECCLESTON PARK
THATTO HEATH
PRESCOT
RAINHILL
HUYTON
ROBY
HOUGH GREEN
DITTON
HUNTS CROSS
SPEKE JCN
ALLERTON
HALEWOOD JCN
HALEWOOD
STANLOW
FOLLY LANE
OVERPOOL
ELLESMERE PORT
LITTLE SUTTON
CAPENHURST

NEW LANE
BURSCOUGH BRIDGE
BESCAR LANE
ORMSKIRK
AUGHTON PARK
TOWN GREEN
MAGHULL
Hillhouse Jcn
KIRKBY
FAZAKERLEY
RICE LANE
ORRELL PARK
LIVERPOOL
BROAD GREEN
MOSSLEY HILL
WEST ALLERTON
ST. MICHAELS
AIGBURTH
CRESSINGTON
BEBINGTON
PORT SUNLIGHT
SPITAL
BROMBOROUGH
BROMBOROUGH RAKE
HOOTON
HESWALL
NESTON
HOLYWELL JCN
HOLYWELL TOWN
FLINT
LNW

SOUTHPORT
STEAMPORT
BIRKDALE
HILLSIDE
AINSDALE
FRESHFIELD
FORMBY
HIGHTOWN
HALL RD.
BLUNDELLSANDS & CROSBY
WATERLOO
SEAFORTH & LITHERLAND
SEAFORTH CT.
BOOTLE NEW STRAND
NEW BOOTLE ORIEL RD
BRIGHTON
BANK HALL
SANDHILLS
KIRKDALE
HUSKISSON
LIME ST.
CENT.
CROWN ST
WAPPING
BRUNSWICK
EDGE HILL
GARSTON
GARSTON DOCK
ALLERTON

GLADSTONE/HORNBY DOCK
1: Bidston Dock
MOORFIELDS
JAMES ST.
HAMILTON SQ.
SEACOMBE
WALLASEY GROVE RD
WALLASEY VILLAGE
MORETON
LEASOWE
MEOLS
MANOR RD
HOYLAKE
WEST KIRBY
BIDSTON
BIRKENHEAD
NORTH
PARK
CENT.
ROCK FERRY
GREEN LANE
GW & LNW JT.
GC
UPTON
GW & LNW JT

Abbreviations on lines: L&Y, LNW, GC, CLC, MN?, MID, ICI, NS

MANCHESTER (large label)
LIVERPOOL (large label)
ST HELENS CENTRAL (large label)
BIRKENHEAD (large label)
WIDNES (large label)
RUNCORN (large label)
WARRINGTON (large label)
WIGAN (large label)
BOLTON (large label)
BURY (large label)
ROCHDALE (large label)
OLDHAM (large label)
STOCKPORT (large label)
MACCLESFIELD (large label)
SOUTHPORT (large label)

Station	Region	Pre Group	Map Ref.
Kensal Rise	LM	LNW	39, B4
Kensington (Olympia)	S	WL (H & C/ LBSC/ LSW)	5, B3; 39, D4
Kensington High Street	LUL	Dist	39, D5
Kent House	S	SEC	40, F4
Kentish Town	LM	Mid (LTS/ GE) & LNW (NL)	40, B5 and Inset C1
Kenton Bankfoot	TWM	NE	27, B5
Kenton (Middx)	LM	LNW	39, A2
Kents Bank	LM	Fur	24, B3
Kerry	W	Cam	14, C2
Keswick	LM	CKP	26, E2
Kettering	LM	Mid	10, A2
Kew Bridge	S	LSW	39, D3
Kew Gardens (London)	S	LSW	39, D3
Keyham (Devonport)	W	GW	1, D5 and Inset
Keynsham	W	GW	3, A3; 8, D1
Kidbrooke	S	SEC	40, E2
Kidderminster	LM & SVR	GW	9, A3
Kidsgrove (Central)	LM	NS	15, C3; 20, E1
Kidsgrove (Liverpool Road)	LM	NS	15, C3; 20, E1
Kidwelly	W	GW	7, A2
Kilbirnie	Sc	Cal & G & SW	29, D3
Kilburn	LUL	Met	39, B4
Kilburn High Road	LM	LNW	39, B5
Kildale Halt	E	NE	28, F3
Kildonan	Sc	HR	38, F5
Killearn	Sc	NB	29, A4
Kilgetty	W	GW	7, D3
Killin	Sc	Cal	33, E2
Killingholme	E		22, E3
Killin Jcn	Sc	Cal	33, E1
Killoch Colliery	Sc	GSW	29, F4
Kilmacolm	Sc	G & SW	29, C3
Kilmarnock	Sc	G & SW & GBK	29, E4
Kilmaurs	Sc	Cal & GSW Jt	29, D4
Kilnhurst	E	Mid	42, F1
Kilpatrick	Sc	NB	29, B4; 44, G5
Kilwinning	Sc	G & SW & Cal	29, D3
Kinbrace	Sc	HR	38, E5
Kincardine	Sc	NB	30, A4
Kincraig	Sc	HR	36, G4
Kingham	W	GW	9, D5
Kinghorn	Sc	NB	30, A2
Kinross Junction	Sc	NB	30, A3; 33, G5
Kingsbridge		GW	2, E4
Kingsbury	LM	Mid	15, F5; 39, A3
Kings Cross	E	GN	5, A3; 40, C5
King's Cross Thameslink	E	Met	40, C5
Kingsferry Bridge	S	SEC	6, B4
Kingsknowe	Sc	Cal	30, C3
King's Langley	LM	LNW	11, G1
King's Lynn	A	GE	17, E4
Kingsmuir	Sc	Cal	34, D4
Kingsnorth	S	SEC	6, B5
King's Norton	LM	Mid	9, A4
King's Nympton	W	LSW	7, G4
King's Park	Sc	Cal	44, D3
King's Sutton	W	GW	10, C4
Kingston (Surrey)	S	LSW	5, B2; 39, F2
Kingston Park	TWM		27, B5
Kingswear	DVR	GW	2, D3
Kingswood	S	SEC	5, C3
Kingussie	Sc	HR	33, A2
Kinneil	B & K	NB	30, B4
Kinning Park	Sc	Cal	44 Inset
Kintbury	W	GW	4, A4
Kintore	Sc	GNS	37, F3
Kirby Cross	A	GE	12, E3
Kirby Lonsdale	LM	LNW	24, B2
Kirkbuddo	Sc	Cal	34, D4
Kirkburton	E	LNW	21, E2; 42, D4
Kirkby (Merseyside)	LM	LY	20, B4; 42, F3; 45, E3
Kirkby in Ashfield East	LM	Mid & GC	41, E4
Kirkby-in-Furness	LM	Fur	24, A4
Kirkby Stephen	LM	NE	27, F2
Kirkcaldy	Sc	NB	30, A2
Kirkconnel	Sc	G & SW	30, F5
Kirkcudbright	Sc	G & SW	26, C5
Kirkdale	LM	LY	45, F3
Kirkham & Wesham	LM	PWY	24, D3
Kirkhill	Sc	Cal	29, C5; 44, D3
Kirkintilloch	Sc	NB	44, C5
Kirknewton (Midcalder)	Sc	Cal	30, C3
Kirriemuir	Sc	Cal	34, D4
Kirtlebridge	Sc	Cal	26, B2
Kirton Lindsey	E	GC	22, F4
Kittybrewster (Aberdeen)	Sc	GNS	37, F4
Kiveton Bridge	E		16, A4; 41, A3
Kiveton Park	E	GC	16, A4; 41, A4
Knaresborough	E	NE	21, C3
Knebworth	E	GN	11, F2
Knighton	W	LNW	14, D2
Knockando	Sc	GNS	36, E2
Knockholt	S	SEC	5, C4
Knott End	LM	G & KE	24, C3
Knottingley	E	L Y & GN Jt	21, E4
Knucklas	W	LNW	14, D2
Knutsford	LM	CLC	15, A2; 20, D2; 45, B5
Kyle of Lochalsh	Sc	HR	35, F1
Lackenby	E	NE	28, Inset
Ladbroke Grove	LUL	H&C	39, C4
Ladmanlow		LNW	15, B4
Ladybank	Sc	NB	34, F5
Ladywell	S	SEC	40, E3
Lady Windsor Colliery	W	TV	43, C3
Laindon	A	LTS	5, A5
Lairg	Sc	HR	35, A5
Lake	S	IoW	4, F3
Lakenheath	A	GE	11, A5; 17, G5
Lakeside	L & HR	Fur	24, A4
Lambourn		GW	4, A4; 10, G5
Lamington	Sc	Cal	30, E4
Lampeter	W	GW	13, E5
Lamphey	W	GW	7, D2
Lanark	Sc	Cal	30, D4
Lancaster	LM	LNW	24, C3
Lancaster Green Ayre	LM	Mid	24, C3
Lancing	S	LBSC	5, F2
Langbank	Sc	Cal	29, B3
Langholm	Sc	NB	26, A1
Langley (Bucks)	W	GW	5, B1
Langley Green	LM	GW	13, C2; 15, G4
Langley Mill	LM	Mid & GN	41, F3
Langloan	Sc	Cal	44, B3
Langside & Newlands	Sc	Cal	44, E3
Langwathby	LM	Mid	27, D1
Langwith	E	Mid	41, C4 and 16, B4
Lansdown	W	Mid/GW	9, D4
Lanthony	W	GW	9, E3
Lapford	W	LSW	2, A4
Lapworth	LM	GW	9, A5
Larbert	Sc	Cal	30, B5
Largs	Sc	G & SW	29, C2
Larkhall (Cen)	Sc	Cal	30, D5; 44, B1
Latimer Road	LUL	H & C	39, C4
Lauder	Sc	NB	30, D1; 31, D1
Launceston		LSW & GW	1, B4
Laurencekirk	Sc	Cal	34, B2
Lavant		LBSC	4, E1
Lavernock	W	TV	43, B5
Lawrence Hill	W	GW	3, Inset
Laxey (IoM)	ME		23, B3
Laxfield		MSLR	12, B3
Layerthorpe	DVL		21, Inset A5
Layton (Lancs)	LM	L & Y/ LNW	24, D4
Lazonby & Kirkoswald	LM	Mid	27, D1
Lea Bridge	A	GE	40, B3
Leagrave	LM	Mid	10, D1; 11, E1
Lea Hall	LM	LNW	15, G5
Lealholm	E	NE	28, F3
Leamington Spa	LM	GWR	10, B5
Leamside	E	NE	28, D5
Leasowe	LM	Wir	20, C5; 45, G4
Leatherhead	S	LSW & LBSC	5, C2
Ledbury	W	GW	9, C2
Lee	S	SEC	40, E2
Lee-on-the-Solent		LSW	4, E3
Leeds Central	E	GN	21, Inset B2; 42, A2/3
Leeds	E	Mid NE LNW	21, Inset B2; 42, A2/3
Leek	LM	NS	15, C4
Leicester (Central)	LM	GC	16, F3
Leicester	LM	Mid	16, F3
Leigh	S	SEC	5, D5
Leigh (Lancs)	LM	LNW	20, B2; 24, F2; 45, C3
Leigh on Sea	A	LTS	6, A5
Leighton Buzzard	LM & LBNG	LNW	10, D1
Leiston	A	GE	12, C1
Leith Central	Sc	NB	30, Inset
Leith Citadel	Sc	NB	30, Inset
Leith Docks	SC	NB	30, Inset
Leith North	Sc	Cal	30, Inset
Leith South	Sc	NB	30, Inset
Lelant	W	GW	1, E4 Inset
Lelant Saltings	W	GW	1, Inset E4
Lenham	S	SEC	6, C4
Lenwade	A	M & GN	18, E4
Lenzie Jcn	Sc	NB	29, B5; 44, D5
Leominster	W	S & H	9, B1
Leslie	Sc	NB	30, A2; 34, G5
Leuchars Jcn	Sc	NB	34, F4
Leven	Sc	NB	30, A1; 34, G4
Levenshulme North	LM	LNW	45, A3
Levisham	NYMR	NE	22, A5; 28, G2
Lewes	S	LBSC	5, F4
Lewisham	S	SEC	40, E3
Leyland	LM	NU	20, A3; 24, E3
Leysdown	S	SE	6, B3
Leyton	LUL	GE	40, B3
Leyton (Midland Road)	A	TFG	40, B3
Leytonstone	LUL	GE	40, A2
Leytonstone (High Road)	A	TFG	40, B2
Lichfield (City)	LM	LNW	15, E5
Lichfield (Trent Valley)	LM	LNW	15, E5
Lidlington	LM	LNW	10, C1
Lillie Bridge	LUL		39, D4
Limehouse	A	GE	40, C3
	DLR		40, C3
Lincoln Central	E	GN	16, B1 and Inset
Lincoln St Marks	E	Mid	16, B1 and Inset
Lindsey Oil Refinery	E	GC	22, E3
Lingfield	S	LBSC	5, D4
Lingwood	A	GE	18, F2
Linkswood St Fort	Sc	NB	34, E4
Linlithgow	Sc	NB	30, B4
Linwood	Sc	Cal	44, G3
Liphook	S	LSW	4, D1
Liskeard	W	GW & LL	1, D4
Liss	S	LSW & LMR	4, D1
Lisvane & Thornhill	W	RR	8, C4 and 43, B4
Littleborough	LM	LY	21, E1
Littlehampton	S	LBSC	5, G1
Littlehaven	S	LBSC	5, E2
Little Kimble	W	GW & GC Jt	10, E2
Littlemore	W	GW	10, F4
Littleport	A	GE	11, A4; 17, G4
Little Sutton	LM	BJ	20, D4; 45, F5
Littleton Colliery	LM	LNW	15, E4
Liverpool Central	LM	CLC & Mer	20, C4; 24, G4; 45, F4
Liverpool James Street	LM	Mer	45, F4
Liverpool Lime Street	LM	LNW	20, C4; 24, G4; 45, F4
Liverpool Mossfields	LM		40, F4
Liverpool St (London)	A	GE	5, A3; 40, C4
Livingston North	Sc	NB	30, C4
Livingston South	Sc	Cal	30, C3
Llanaber	LM	Cam	13, A5
Llanbadarn	LM	VR	13, C5
Llanbedr	LM	Cam	19, G2
Llanberis	LM SMR LNW Ind		19, E2
Llanbister Rd	W	LNW	14, D2
Llanbradach	W	Rhy	8, B4; 43, B3
Llandaff	W	TV	8, C4; 43, B4
Llandanwg	LM	Cam	19, G2
Llandecwyn	LM	Cam	19, F2
Llandeilo	W	GW & LNW	13, G5
Llanelli	W	GW	7, B3
Llanidloes		Cam	14, C4
Llandovery	W	LNW	14, F5
Llandrindod Wells	W	LNW	14, D3
Llandudno	LM	LNW	19, C3
Llandudno Jcn	LM	LNW	19, D4
Llandybie	W	GW	7, A4; 43, G1
Llanfairpwll	LM	LNW	19, D2
Llanfair Caereinion	W & L		14, B3
Llanfairfechan	LM	LNW	19, D3
Llanfyllin		Cam	14, A3
Llangadog	W	LNW	14, F5
Llangammarch Wells	W	LNW	14, E4
Llangelynin	LM	Cam	13, A5
Llangennech	W	GW	7, B3
Llangollen		GW	20, F5
Llangower	Ind		19, F4
Llangynllo	W	LNW	14, D2
Llangynog	W	Cam	19, G5
Llanharan	W	GW	8, C5
Llanharan Jcn	W	GW	43, D4; 8, C5
Llanishen	W	Rhy	8, C4; 43, B4
Llanmorlais		LNW	7, B3
Llanrwst	LM	LNW	19, E4
Llantrisant	W	GW	43, C4 and 8, C5
Llanuwchllyn	Ind	GW	19, G4
Llanwrda	W	LNW	14, F5
Llanwrtyd Wells	W	LNW	14, E4
Llanymynech	LM	Cam & S & M	14, A2; 20, G4
Llwyngwril	LM	Cam	13, A5
Llwynypia	W	TV	8, B5; 43, D3
Lochailort	Sc	NB	32, B5
Loch Awe	Sc	Cal	32, F2
Loch Eil Outward Bound	Sc	NB	32, C3
Locheilside	Sc	NB	32, B3
Lochgelly	Sc	NB	30, A3
Lochluichart	Sc	HR	35, C4
Lochty	Ind	NB	34, F3
Lochwinnoch	Sc	G & SW	29, C3
Lockerbie	Sc	Cal	26, A3
Lockwood	E	LY	42, D5
Lofthouse-in-Midderdale		NV	21, B2
London Bridge	S	LBSC & SEC	5, B3; 40, D4
London Fields	A	GE	49, B4
London Road (Brighton)	S	LBSC	5, F3
London Road (Guildford)	S	LSW	5, C1
Longannet Power Stn	Sc	NB	30, A4
Longbeck	E	NE	28, E3
Longbenton	TWM		27, B5
Longbridge	LM	Mid	9, A4
Long Buckby	LM	LNW	10, B3
Longcross	S		5, B1
Long Eaton	LM	Mid	16, D4
Longfield	S		5, B5
Long Marston	W	GW	9, C5
Long Meg	LM	Mid	27, D1
Long Melford		GE	12, D5
Longmoor Downs		LMR	4, C1

Station	Region	Pre Group	Map Ref.
Neilston High	Sc	GBK & Cal	29, C4; 44, G2
Nelson (Lancs)	LM	LY	21, Inset B1; 24, D1
Nelson & Llancaiach	W	GW	8, B4; 43, C3
Neston	LM	GC	20, D4; 45, F5
Netherfield & Colwick	LM	GN	16, C3; 41, F5
Nethertown	LM	Fur	26, F3
Netley	S	LSW	4, E3
Newark (Castle)	E	Mid	16, C2
Newark (Northgate)	E	GN	16, C2
New Barnet	E	GN	5, A3; 11, G2
New Beckenham	S	SEC	40, F3
Newbiggin	LM	Mid	27, E2
Newbiggin-by-the-Sea	E	NE	28, A5
New Bolingbroke	E	GN	17, C3
New Brighton	LM	Wir	20, C4; 24, G4; 45, F3
Newbury	W	GW	4, A3
Newbury Park	LUL	GE	40, A1
Newbury Racecourse	W	GW	4, A3
Newby Bridge	L & HR		24, A4
Newcastle Emlyn	WR	GW	13, F3
Newcastle-on-Tyne Central	E	NE	27, B5 & C5; 28, Inset
Newcastleton	Sc	NB	27, A1
New Clee	E	GC	22, F2
New Cross	LUL	SEC	40, D3
New Cross Gate	LUL	LBSC	40, D3
New Eltham	S	SEC	40, E1
Newham	W	GW	1, E1
Newhaven Harbour (Sussex)	S	LBSC	5, F4
Newhaven Marine (Sussex)	S	LBSC	5, F4
Newhaven Town (Sussex)	S	LBSC	5, F4
New Hadley	LM		15, E2
New Hay	LM	L&Y	21, F1
New Holland	E	GC	22, E3
New Hythe	S		6, C5
Newington (Kent)	S	SEC	6, B4
New Lane	LM	LY	20, A4; 24, F3; 45, E1
Newmains	Sc	NB	30, C5 and 44, A2
New Malden	S	LSW	39, F3
Newmarket	A	GE	11, C4
New Mills Central (Derbys)	LM	Mid	15, A4
New Mills New Town (Derbys)	LM	LNW	15, A4
New Milton	S	LSW	4, F5
Newport Dock St	W	GW	43, A3
Newport (Essex)	A	GE	11, E4
Newport (I of W)		IWC	4, F3
Newport (High St) (Gwent)	W	GW	8, B3; 43, A3
Newport (Mill St) (Gwent)	W	GW	8, B3; 43, A3
Newport (Salop)		LNW	15, E2
Newport-on-Tay East	Sc	NB	34, E4 Inset
Newport-on-Tay West	Sc	NB	34, E4 Inset
Newport Pagnell	LM	LNW	10, C2
New Pudsey	E	GN	21, D2; 42, A4
Newquay	W	GW	1, D1
New Radnor	W	GW	14, E2
New Romney	S & RHD	SEC	6, E3
Newsham	E	NE	28, A5
New Southgate	E	GN	5, A3
Newstead	LM	Mid & GN	41, E4
Newton (for Hyde)	LM		21, G1
Newton Abbot	W	GW	2, C3
Newton Aycliffe	E	NE	27, E5
Newton (Lanarks)	Sc	Cal	29, C5; 44, C3
Newtondale	NYMR		28, G2
Newton-le-Willows	LM	LNW	20, C3; 24, G2; 45, D3
Newtonmore	Sc	HR	33, A2
Newton-on-Ayr	Sc	G & SW	29, F3
Newton St Cyres	W	LSW	2, B3
Newton Stewart	Sc	P & W	25, B4
Newtown (Powys)	LM	Cam	14, C3
New Wandsworth	S	LBSC	39, Inset
Ninian Park	W		43, B4
Nitshill	Sc	GBK	44, F3
Norbiton	S	LSW	39, F3
Norbury (London)	S	LBSC	40, F5
Normanby Park	E	GC	22, E4
Norman's Bay	S	LBSC	5, F5
Normanton (Yorks)	E	Mid	21, E3; 42, C2
North Acton	LUL		39, C3
Northallerton	E	NE	21, A3; 28, G5
Northampton Bridge St	LM	LNW	10, B2
Northampton Castle	LM	LNW	10, B2
North Berwick	Sc	NB	31, A1
North Blyth	E	NE	28, A5
North Camp	S	SEC	4, B1; 5, C1
North Dulwich	S	LBSC	40, E4
North Ealing	LUL	Dist	39, C3
North Elmham	A	GE	18, E4
Northenden	LM	CLC	45, A4
Northfield	LM	Mid	9, A4
Northfields	LUL	Dist	39, D2
Northfleet	S	SEC	5, B5
North Harrow	LUL	Met & GC Jt	39, A1
Northolt	W	GW & GC Jt	39, B1
Northolt Park	W	GC	39, B1
North Queensferry	Sc	NB	30, B3
North Rode	LM	NS	15, B3; 20, D1
North Sheen	S	LSW	39, E3
North Shields	TWM	NE	28, B5
Northumberland Park	A	GE	40, A4
North Walsham	A	GE	18, D2
North Weald	LUL	GE	11, G3
North Wembley	LM	LNW	39, B2
Northwich	LM	CLC	15, A2; 20, D2; 45, C5
Northwick Park	LUL	LNW	39, A2
Northwood		SVR	9, A3
Northwood (Middx)	LM & LUL	Met & GC Jt	5, A2
Northwood Hills	LM & LUL		5, A2
North Woolwich	A	GE	5, B4; 40, D1
Norton Bridge	LM	LNW & NS	15, D3; 20, G1
Norwich (Thorpe)	A	GE	18, F3
Norwich (City)		MGN	18, F3
Norwich (Trouse)		GE	18, F3
Norwood Jcn	S	LBSC	40, G4
Nottingham London Road	LM	GN	16, D3; 41, G4/5
Nottingham	LM	Mid	16, D3; 41, G4/5
Nottingham Victoria	LM	GC	16, C4; 41, F4
Notting Hill Gate	LUL	Dist	39, C5
Nuneaton (Abbey Street)	LM	Mid	16, F5
Nuneaton (Trent Valley)	LM	LNW	16, F5
Nunhead	S	SEC	40, D4
Nunthorpe	E	NE	28, F4
Nutbourne	S	LBSC	4, E1
Nutfield	S	SEC	5, D3
Oakamoor	LM	NS	15, C4
Oakdale Col	W	GW	8, B4 and 43, B2
Oakengates	LM	GW & LNW	15, E2
Oakham	LM	Mid	16, E2
Oakleigh Park	E	GN	5, A3; 11, G2
Oakleigh Sidings	LM	CLC	15, A2; 20, D2 and 45, C5
Oakley	Sc	NB	30, A3
Oakwood	LUL		11, G2
Okehampton	W	LSW	2, B5
Oban	Sc	Cal	32, F4
Ockendon	A	LTS	5, A5
Ocker Hill	LM	LNW	13, B2
Ockley	S	LBSC	5, D2
Offord	E	GN	11, C2
Oldfield Park	W		3, A3; 8, D1
Old Fold	TWM		28, Inset
Oldham (Central)	LM	OAGB	21, F1 and Inset D1; 45, A2
Oldham (Mumps)	LM	OAGB	21, F1 and Inset D1; 45, A2
Oldham (Werneth)	LM	OAGB	21, F1 and Inset D1; 45, A2
Old Hill	LM	GW	13, C1; 15, G4
Old Kilpatrick	Sc	Cal	44, G5
Old Meldrum	Sc	GNS	37, D5
Old Roan	LM	LY	20, B4; 24, F4; 45, F3
Old Street	E		40, C4
Old Trafford	LM	MSJA	20, B1; 24, G1; 45, B3
Ollerton Col	E	GC	16, B3
Olton	LM	GW	9, A5; 15, G5
Olympia	LUL		5, B3; 39, D4
Ongar	LUL	GE	11, G4
Onllwyn	W	N & B	43, E1 and 7, A5
Orbliston	Sc	HR	36, D1
Ore	S	SEC	6, F5
Ormskirk	LM	LY	20, B4; 24, F3; 45, E2
Orpington	S	SEC	5, B4; 40, G1
Orrell	LM	LY	20, B3; 24, F2; 45, D2
Orrell Park	LM	LY	45, F3
Orton Mere	NVR	LNW	11, A2; 17, F2
Ossett	E	GN	42, C3
Oswestry	LM	GW & Cam	20, G4
Otford	S	SEC	5, C5
Oulton Broad, North	A	GE	12, A1; 18, G1
Oulton Broad, South	A	GE	12, A1; 18, G1
Outwood	E	GN	21, E3; 42, B2
Over & Wharton	LM	LNW	20, D2
Overpool	LM	BJ	20, D4; 45, F5
Overton (Hants)	S	LSW	4, B3
Oxcroft Colliery	E	Mid	41, B4
Oxenholme	LM	LNW	24, A3; 27, G1
Oxenhope	KWV	Mid	21, D1
Oxford	W	GW & LNW	10, E4
Oxley Sidings	LM	GW	15, F3
Oxshott	S	LSW	5, C2
Oxted	S	CO	5, C4
Oxwellmains	Sc	NB	31, B2
Paddington	W	GW	5, B2; 39, C5 and Inset, C3
Paddock Wood	S	SEC	5, D5
Padgate	LM	CLC	20, C2; 24, G2; 45, C4
Padiham	LM	L & Y	24, D1
Padstow	W	LSW	1, C2
Paignton	W & DVR	GW	2, D3
Paisley Canal	Sc	GSW	29, C4; 44, F3
Paisley Gilmour St	Sc	G & P	29, C4; 44, F3
Paisley St James	Sc	CR	29, C4; 44, G3
Paisley West	Sc	GSW	29, C4; 44, G3
Paisley Underwood	Sc	Cal	44, G3
Palace Gates	A	GE	40, A5
Palmers Green & Southgate	E	GN	5, A3
Pangbourne	W	GW	4, A2
Pannal	E	NE	21, C3
Pant (Glam)	Ind	BM	43, C1
Panteg Works	W	GW	8, B3 and 43, A2
Pantyffynnon	W	GW	7, A4; 43, G1
Par	W	GW	1, D3
Parbold	LM	LY	20, B3; 24, F3; 45, E1
Park (Manchester)	LM	LY	45, A3
Parkandillack	W	GW	1, D2
Parkend	DFR	SVW	8, A1; 9, E2
Park Royal	LUL	Dist	39, C3
Park Royal		GW	39, C3
Parkstone	S	LSW	3, F5
Park Street & Frogmore	LM	LNW	11, G1
Parracombe		LB	7, E4
Parsons Green	LUL	Dist	39, D4
Parson Street	W	GW	3, Inset
Partick	Sc	Cal	44, E4
Partington	LM	CLC	24, G1 and 45, B3
Parton (Cumb)	LM	LNW	26, E4
Patchway	W	GW	8, C1; 9, G1
Pateley Bridge		NE	21, B2
Patricroft	LM	LNW	20, B2; 24, F1; 45, B3
Patterton	Sc	Cal	29, C4; 44, E2
Peak Forest	LM	Mid	15, A5
Pear Tree	LM	Mid	16, D5; 41, G2
Peckham Rye	S	LBSC	40, D4
Peebles	Sc	NB & Cal	30, D2
Peel (IoM)	IoMR		23, B2
Pegswood	E	NE	27, A5
Pelaw	TWM		28, C5
Pemberton	LM	LY	20, B3; 24, F2; 45, D2
Pembrey & Burry Port	W	GW	7, B2
Pembroke	W	GW	7, D2
Pembroke Dock	W	GW	7, D2
Penallta Colliery	W	RR	43, B3
Penally	W	GW	7, D3
Penarth Dock	W	TV	43, B5
Penarth Town	W	TV	8, D4; 43, B5
Pencader	W	GW	13, F4
Penicuik	Sc	NB	30, C2
Pendleton	LM	LY	45, B3
Pendre	Tal		13, B5
Pengam	W	Rhy	8, B4; 43, B2
Penge East	S	SEC	40, F4
Penge West	S	LBSC	40, F4
Penheley	W	Cam	13, B5
Penistone	E	GC & LY Jt	21, F3; 42, E3
Penkridge	LM	LNW	15, E3
Penmaenmawr	LM	LNW	19, D3
Penmere	W	GW	1, F1
Pen Mill	W	GW	3, D2; 8, G2
Penyfford	LM	GC	20, E4
Penrhiwceiber	W	TV	43, C2
Penrhyn	Fest		19, F2
Penrhyndeudraeth	LM	Cam	19, F2
Penrith	LM	LNW	27, E1
Penryn	W	GW	1, F1
Pensarn	LM	Cam	19, G2
Penshurst	S	SEC	5, D4
Pensnett	LM	GW	15, G3
Pentewan	Ind		1, 2E
Pentre-bach	W	TV	8, A5; 43, C2
Pen-y-bont	W	LNW	14, D3
Penybont	Ind	GW	13, G4
Penychain (for Pwllheli Holiday Camp)	LM		19, F1
Penzance	W	GW	1, Inset F4
Percy Main	TWM	NE	28, B5
Perivale	LUL	GW	39, C2
Perranwell	W	GW	1, E1
Perry Barr	LM	LNW	13, B3; 15, G4
Pershore	W	GW	9, C4
Perth (General)	Sc	Cal	33, F5
Perth (Princes St)	Sc	Cal	33, F5
Peterborough (East)	E	GE	11, A2; 17, F2
Peterborough (North)	E	GN	11, A2; 17, F2
Peterhead	Sc	GNS	37, D5
Petersfield	S	LSW	4, D2
Petts Wood	S		40, G1
Pevensey & Westham	S	LBSC	5, F5
Pevensey Bay	S	LBSC	5, F5
Pewsey	W	GW	4, B5
Pickering	NYMR	NE	22, A5
Picton	E	NE	28, F5
Piddington		Mid	10, B2
Pigs Bay	A		6, A4
Pilmoor	E	NE	21, B4
Pilning	W	GW	8, C2; 9, G1
Pilot Halt	RHD		6, E3
Pilsley	LM	GC	41, D3
Pinhoe	W	LSW	2, B3
Pinner	LUL	Met & GC Jt	39, A1
Pinxton		GN	16, C4; 41, E3
Pitlochry	Sc	HR	33, C4
Pitsea	A	LTS	6, A5
Pittenweem	Sc	NB	34, G3
Plaistow	LUL	LTS	40, C2

Station	Region	Pre Group	Map Ref.
Plean	Sc	Cal	30, A5
Pleasington	LM	LY	20, A2; 24, E2
Pluckley	S	SEC	6, D4
Plumley	LM	CLC	15, A2; 20, D2; 45, B5
Plumpton (Sussex)	S	LBSC	5, F3
Plumstead	S	SEC	40, D1
Plymouth	W	GW & LSW	1, D5 and Inset
Plymouth Friary	W	LSW	1, D5 and Inset
Plymstock	W	LSW (GW)	1, D5 and Inset
Poplar	DLR		40, C3
Pokesdown	S	LSW	4, F5
Polegate	S	LBSC	5, F5
Polesworth	LM	LNW	16, F5
Polkemmet Colliery	Sc	NB	30, C4
Pollokshaws East	Sc	Cal	44, E3 and Inset F1
Pollokshaws West	Sc	GBK	44, E3
Pollokshields East	Sc	Cal	34 Inset
Pollokshields West	Sc	Cal	44, E3 and Inset F1
Polmont	Sc	NB	30, B4
Polsloe Bridge	W	LSW	2, B3
Ponder's End	A	GE	5, A3; 11, G3
Ponsandane	W	GW	1, Inset
Pontarddulais	W	GW & LNW Jt	7, A3
Pontefract (Baghill)	E	SK	21, E4; 42, C1
Pontefract (Monkhill)	E	LY	21, E4; 42, C1
Pontlottyn	W	Rhy	8, A4; 43, C2
Pontlottyn & Rhymney		BM	43, C2
Pontrilas	WR	GW	14, G1
Pontsticill	Ind	B & M	43, C1
Pont-y-Pant	LM	LNW	19, E3
Pontypool	W	GW	8, B3; 43, A2
Pontypool Road	W	GW	8, B3; 43, A2
Pontypridd	W	TV & BRY	8, B5; 43, C3
Pool Dam	LM	NS	15, C3; 20, F1
Poole	S	LSW (SD)	3, F5
Poplar	DLR	NL	40, C3
Poppleton	E	NE	21, C4
Port Carlisle	Sc	NB	26, C2
Portchester	S	LSW	4, E2
Port Clarence	E	NE	28, E4
Port Dundas	Sc	Cal & NB	44, E4
Port Elphinstone	Sc	GNS	37, F3
Port Erin (IoM)	IoMR		23, C1
Portessie	Sc	GNS & HR	37, C1
Port Glasgow	Sc	Cal	29, B3
Porth	W	TV	8, B5; 43, C3
Porthcawl	W	GW	7, C5; 43, E4
Portlethen	Sc	Cal	34, A1
Porthmadog	LM & Fest	Cam	19, F2
Portishead	W	GW & WCP	3, A2; 8, C2
Port Patrick	Sc	P & W	25, C1
Portreath		GW	1, Inset E5
Portslade	S	LBSC	5, F3
Portsmouth Arms	W	LSW	7, G3
Portsmouth Harbour	S	LSW & LBSC Jt	4, E2
Portsmouth & Southsea	S	LSW & LBSC Jt	4, E2
Port Sunlight	LM	BJ	20, C4; 45, F4
Port Talbot Docks	W	GW	7, B4 and 43, F3
Port Talbot Parkway	W	GW	7, B4; 43, F3
Potterhill	Sc	GSW	44, G3
Potters Bar	E	GN	11, G2
Poulton-le-Fylde (Lancs)	LM	PWY	24, D4
Poynton	LM	LNW	15, A3; 20, C1; 45, A4
Prees	LM	LNW	15, D1; 20, F3
Prescot	LM	LNW	20, C3; 24, G3; 45, E3
Prestatyn	LM	LNW	19, C5
Prestbury	LM	LNW	15, A3; 20, D1; 45, A5
Presteign		GW	14, D2
Preston	LM	LNW & LY	24, E3
Prestonpans	Sc	NB	30, B1
Preston Park	S	LBSC	5, F3
Prestwich	LM	LY	20, B1; 24, F1; 45, B2
Prestwick	Sc	G & SW	29, E3
Priestfield	LM	GW	15, Insert E3
Primrose Hill	LM	LNW	39, B5
Prince of Wales Colliery	E	L&Y	42, C1
Princes Dock	Sc	PDJ	44, E3
Princes Risborough	W	GW & GC Jt	10, F2
Princetown		GW	2, C5
Prittlewell	A	GE	6, A4
Prudhoe	E	NE	27, B4
Pulborough	S	LBSC	5, E2
Purfleet	A	LTS	5, B5
Purley	S	LBSC	5, C3
Purley Oaks	S	LBSC	5, C3
Putney	S	LSW	39, E4
Putney Bridge	LUL	Dist	39, D4
Pwllheli	LM	Cam	19, F1
Pye Bridge	LM	Mid	16, C4; 41, E3
Pyle	W	GW	43, E4
Quainton Road	W	Met & GC Jt	10, E2
Quaker's Yard (HL)	W	GW	8, B5; 43, C2
Quaker's Yard (LL)	W	GW & TV Jt	8, B5; 43, C2
Queenborough	S	SEC	6, B4
Queensbury	E	GN	21, D2; 42, B5
Queensbury	LUL		39, A3
Queen's Head	LM	GW	13, B3
Queen's Park (Glasgow)	Sc	Cal	44, E3
Queen's Park, West Kilburn	LM & LUL	LNW	39, B5
Queen's Rd (Peckham)	S	LBSC	40, D4
Queensferry	LM	LNW	20, D4
Queenstown Road	S	LSW	39, D5 and Inset E4
Quidhampton	S	GW	4, C5
Quintrel Downs	W	GW	1, D1
Quorn & Woodhouse	MLST	GC	16, E4
Radcliffe (Black Lane)	LM	LY	20, B1; 24, F1; 45, B2
Radcliffe-on-Trent	LM	GN	16, D3
Radford	LM	Mid	16, D4; 41, G4
Radlett	LM	Mid	11, G1
Radley	W	GW	10, F4
Radstock		SD	3, B3; 8, E1
Radway Green & Barthomley	LM	NS	15, C2; 20, E1
Radyr	W	TV	8, C4; 43, C4
Rainford Jcn	LM	LY	20, B3; 24, F3; 45, E2
Rainham (Essex)	A	LTS	5, A4
Rainham (Kent)	S	SEC	6, B5
Rainhill	LM	LNW	20, C3; 24, G3; 45, E3
Raisby	E	NE	28, D5
Ramsbottom	ELR	LY	24, E1 and 45, B1
Ramsey	E	GE & GN	11, A2/B2
Ramsey (IoM)	IoMR & ME		23, A3
Ramsgate	S	SEC	6, B1
Rannoch	Sc	NB	32, D1; 33, D1
Ratcliffe Power Stn	LM		16, D4
Ratho	Sc	NB	30, B3
Rauceby	E	GN	16, C1; 17, C1
Ravenglass	LM & RE	Fur	26, G3
Ravensbourne	S	SEC	40, F3
Ravenscourt Park	LUL	LSW & Dist	39, D4
Ravenscraig	Sc	Cal	44, A2
Ravensthorpe	E	LNW	21, E2; 42, C3
Ravenstruther	Sc	Cal	30, D4
Rawcliffe	E	LY	21, E5
Rawdon Colliery	LM	Mid	16, E5
Rawtenstall	ELR	LY	20, A1; 24, E1
Rayleigh	A	GE	6, A5
Raynes Park	S	LSW	39, F4
Reading	W	GW	4, A2
Reading Central (Goods)	W	GW	4, A2
Reading Southern	S	SEC	4, A2
Reading West	W	GW	4, A2
Rectory Rd	A	GE	40, B4
Redbridge	LUL		40, A2
Redbridge	S	LSW	4, E4
Redcar (Central)	E	NE	28, E3
Redcar (East)	E	NE	28, E3
Redcar Ore & Mineral Terminals	E	NE	28, Inset
Reddish North	LM	GC & MidJnt	45, A3
Reddish South	LM	LNW	45, A3
Redditch	LM	Mid	9, B4
Redhill (Surrey)	S	SEC	5, C3
Redland	W	CE	3, Inset
Redmire	E	NE	21, A1; 27 G4
Redruth	W	GW	1, Inset E5
Redwharf Bay & Benllech	LM	LNW	19, C2
Reedham (Norfolk)	A	GE	18, F2
Reedham (Surrey)	S	SEC	5, C3
Reedsmouth	Sc	NB	27, A3
Regent Centre	TWM		27, B5
Reigate	S	SEC	5, C3
Renfrew (Fulbar Street)	Sc	G & SW	44, F4
Renfrew (South)	Sc	G & SW	44, F4
Renfrew (Wharf)	Sc	G & SW	44, F4
Renishaw Park Colliery	E	Mid	41, B3
Renton	Sc	D & B	29, B3
Resolven	W	GW	7, A5; 43, E2
Reston	Sc	NB	31, C3
Retford	E	GN	16, A3
Rhayader	W	Cam	14, D4
Rheidol Falls	LM	VR	14, C5
Rhiwbina	W	CDF	8, C4; 43, B4
Rhiwfron	W	VR	14, C5
Rhosguch	LM	LNW	19, C1
Rhosneigr	LM	LNW	19, D1
Rhydyronen		Tal	13, B5
Rhyl	LM	LNW	19, C5
Rhymney	W	Rhy	8, A5; 43, C2
Rhymney Bridge	W	LNW & Rhy	8, A5; 43, C1
Ribblehead	LM	Mid	24, A1
Riccarton Jcn	Sc	NB	31, G1
Riccarton & Craigie	Sc	GSW	29, E4
Rice Lane	LM	L&Y	20, C4; 45, F3
Richmond (Surrey)	S	LSW	5, B2; 39, E3
Richmond (Yorks)	E	NE	27, F5
Rickmansworth	LUL	Met & GC Jt	5, A2; 10, F1
Riddings Jcn	LM	NB	26, B1
Riddlesdown	S		5, C3
Ridgmont	LM	LNW	10, C1
Ridham Dock	S	SEC	6, B4
Riding Mill	E	NE	27, C4
Ringwood		LSW	4, E5
Risca	W	GW	8, B4; 43, A3
Rishton	LM	LY	24, D1
Rishworth	LM	L & Y	21, E1
Robertsbridge	S	SEC & KES	6, E5
Robeston	W	GW	7, Inset
Roby	LM	LNW	20, C4; 24, G3; 45, E4
Rocester		NS	15, D5
Rochdale	LM	LY	20, A1; 21, E1; 45, A1
Roche	W	GW	1, D2
Rochester	S	SEC	6, B5
Rochford	A	GE	6, A4
Rock Ferry	LM	BJ	20, C4; 45, F4
Rockingham	LM	LNW	16, F2
Roding Valley	LUL		5, A4
Rogart	Sc	HR	36, A5
Rolleston Jcn	LM	Mid	16, C2
Rolvenden	KES		6, E5
Romaldkirk	E	NE	27, E4
Roman Bridge	LM	LNW	19, E3
Romford	A	GE & LTS	5, A4
Romiley	LM	GC & Mid Jt	21, G1
Romney Sands	RHD		6, E3
Romsey	S	LSW	4, D4
Roose	LM	Fur	24, B5
Ropley	MHR	LSW	4, C2
Rosedale	E	NE	28, F3
Rose Grove	LM	LY	24, D1
Rose Heyworth	W	LNW	8, A4
Rose Hill (Marple)	LM	GC & NS Jt	21, G1
Roseisle	Sc	HR	36, C2
Roskear	W	GW	1, Insert E5
Rossington Main Colliery	E	GN	21, F5
Ross-on-Wye	W	GW	9, D1
Rosyth	Sc	NB	30, B3
Rosyth Dockyard	Sc		30, B3
Rothbury	E	NB	31, G4
Rotherham (Central)	E	GC	21, G4; 42, F1
Rotherham (Masboro)	E	Mid	42, F1
Rotherham (Westgate)	E	Mid	21, G4; 42, F1
Rotherhithe	LUL		40, C4
Rothes	Sc	GNS	36, D1
Rothesay Dock	Sc	NB	44, F4
Rothley	MLST	GC	16, E4
Roughcastle	Sc	NB	30, B5
Roughton Road	A	N&S Jt	18, D3
Round Oak	LM	GW	15, G3
Rowland's Castle	S	LSW	4, E2
Rowley	E	NE	27, C4
Rowley Regis	LM	GW	13, C2; 15, G4
Rowsley		Mid	16, B5
Royal Oak	LUL	GW	39, C5 and Inset, C1
Roy Bridge	Sc	NB	32, B2
Roydon	A	GE	11, F3
Royston (Herts)	E	GN	11, D3
Royston (S. Yorks)	E	Mid	42, D2
Royton	LM	LY	21, F1; 45, A2
Royton Jcn	LM	LY	21, F1
Roxburgh	Sc	NB	31, E2
Ruabon	LM	GW	20, F4
Ruddington	LM	GC	16, D4
Rufford	LM	LY	20, A3; 24, E3; 45, E1
Rufford Colliery	E	GC	16, B3 and 41, D5
Rugby (Central)		GC	10, A4
Rugby (Midland)	LM	LNW	10, A4
Rugeley Town	LM	LNW	15, E4
Rugeley (Trent Valley)	LM	LNW	15, E4
Ruislip	LUL	Dist	5, A2
Ruislip Gardens	LUL		5, A2; 39, B1
Ruislip Manor	LUL		5, A2
Runcorn	LM	LNW	15, A1; 20, C3; 45, D4
Runcorn East	LM	LNW Jt	15, A1; 20, C3 and 45, D4
Runcorn Folly Lane	LM	LNW	45, E4
Ruskington	E	GN	17, C1
Ruswarp	E	NE	28, F2
Rutherglen	Sc	Cal	44, D3
Ryburgh	A	GE	18, D5
Ryde (Esplanade)	S	LBSC & LSW Jt	4, F3
Ryde (Pier Head)	S	LBSC & LSW Jt	4, F3
Ryde (St John's Road)	S	IWLBSC & LSW Jt	4, F3
Ryder Brau	LM		45, A3
Rye	S	SEC	6, E4
Rye Harbour	S	SEC	6, E4
Rye House	A	GE	11, F3
Rylstone	Ind	Mid	21, C1
St Albans Abbey	LM	LNW	11, F1

Station	Region	Pre Group	Map Ref.
St Albans City	LM	Mid	11, F1
St Andrews	Sc	NB	34, F4
St Andrew's Road	W		8, C2
St Annes-on-Sea	LM	PWY	24, E4
St Austell	W	GW	1, D2
St Bees	LM	Fur	26, F4
St Blazey	W	GW	1, D3
St Boswells	Sc	NB	31, E1
St Botolph's	A	GE	12, E4
St Budeaux	W	LSW	1, D5 and Inset
St Budeaux Ferry Road	W	GW	1, D5 and Inset
St Budeaux Victoria Road	W	GW	1, D5 and Inset
St Columb Rd	W	GW	1, D2
St Combs	Sc	GNS	37, C5
St Davids (Exeter)	W	GW & LSW	2, B3
St Denys	S	LSW	4, D4
St Erth	W	GW	1, Inset F4
St Germans	W	GW	1, D5
St Helens Jcn	LM	LNW	20, C3; 24, G3; 45, D3
St Helens Central		GC	20, C3; 24, G3; 45, D3
St Helens Central	LM	LNW	20, C3; 24, G3; 45, D3
St Helens Ravenhead	LM	LNW	45, E3
St Helier	S		39, G4
St Ives (Cornwall)	W	GW	1, Inset E4
St Ives (Hunts)		GN & GE Jt	11, B2
St James	TWM		28, Inset
St James Park	LUL	Dist	40, D5
St James Park (Exeter)	W	LSW	2, B3
St James St (Walthamstow)	A	GE	40, A3
St John's (IoM)	IoMR		23, B2
St John's (London)	S	SEC	40, E3
St Keyne	W	LL	1, D4
St Leonards (Warrior Square)	S	SEC	6, F5
St Leonards (West)	S	SEC	6, F5
St Margaret's (Herts)	A	GE	11, F3
St Margaret's (Middx)	S	LSW	39, E2
St Mary Cray	S	SEC	5, B4; 40, G1
St Michael's	LM	CLC	45, F4
St Neots	E	GN	11, C2
St Pancras	LM	Mid	5, A3; 40, C5
St Rollox	Sc	Cal	44, D4
St Thomas (Exeter)	W	GW	2, B3
Sale	LM	MSJA	20, C1; 24, G1; 45, B3
Salford	LM	LY	45, A3
Salford Crescent	LM	L&Y	45, B3
Salfords	S	LBSC	5, D3
Salhouse	A	GE	18, E2
Salisbury	S	LSW	4, C5
Saltaire	E	Mid	42, A5
Saltash	W	GW	1, D5
Saltburn	E	NE	28, E3
Saltcoats	Sc	G & SW	29, D3
Saltend	E	H&B	22 Inset
Saltley	LM	Mid	15, G5
Saltmarshe	E	NE	22, E5
Salwick	LM	PWY	24, D3
Sandall & Agbrigg	E	GN	21, E3; 42, C2
Sandbach	LM	LNW	15, B2; 20, E2
Sanderstead	S	CO	5, C3
Sandgate	S	SE	6, D2
Sandhills	LM	LY	45, F3
Sandhurst	S	SEC	4, B1
Sandling for Hythe	S	SEC	6, D3
Sandown	S	IW	4, F3
Sandplace	W	LL	1, D4
Sandsend	E	NE	28, F2
Sandside	LM	FR	24, A3
Sandwell & Dudley	LM	LNW	13, B2
Sandwich		SEC	6, C2
Sandwich Road	S	EK	6, C2
Sandy	E	GN & LNW	11, D2
Sankey	LM	CLC	20, C3; 24, G2; 45, D4
Saundersfoot	W	GW	7, D3
Saunderton	W	GW & GC Jt	10, F2
Savernake for Marlborough	W	GW	4, A5
Sawbridgeworth	A	GE	11, F3
Saxilby	E	GN	16, A1
Saxmundham	A	GE	12, C2
Scarborough	E	NE	22, A3; 28, G1
Scotscalder	Sc	HR	38, D3
Scotgap		NB	27, A4
Scotstounhill	Sc	NB	44, F4
Scotswood	E	NE	27, B5; 28 Inset
Scunthorpe & Frodingham	E	GC	22, F4
Seaburn		NE	28, C5
Seacombe		WR	45, F3
Seafield Colliery	Sc	NB	30, A2
Seaford	S	LBSC	5, G4
Seaforth & Litherland	LM	LY	45, F3
Seaforth C.T.	LM		45, F3
Seahouses	E	NSL	31, E5
Seaham	E	NE	28, C5
Seamer	E	NE	22, A3
Sea Mills	W	CE	3, A2; 8, C2
Seascale	LM	Fur	26, F3
Seaton Carew	E	NE	28, E4
Seaton (Devon)	Ind	LSW	2, B1
Seaton Jcn (Devon)	W	LSW	2, B1
Seaton-on-Tees	E	NE	28, E4
Seer Green	W	GW & GC Jt	5, A1; 10, F1
Selby	E	NE	21, D5
Selhurst	S	LBSC	40, G5
Selhurst Depot	S		40, G4
Sellafield	LM	Fur	26, F3
Selling	S	SEC	6, C3
Selly Oak	LM	Mid	9, A4; 15, G4
Selkirk	Sc	NB	30, E1
Selsdon	S	CO/WSC	5, C3
Selsey	SL		4, F1
Senghenydd	W	Rhy	8, B4; 43, C3
Settle	LM	Mid	24, B1
Seven Kings	A	GE	5, A4
Sevenoaks	S	SEC	5, C4
Sevenoaks Bat & Ball	S	SEC	5, C4
Seven Sisters (London)	A	GE	40, A4
Severn Beach	W		8, C2; 9, G1
Sevington	S		6, D3
Severn Tunnel Jcn	W	GW	8, B2; 9, F1
Shackerstone	Ind	AN	16, F5
Shadwell	LUL/DLR		40, C4
Shakespeare Staff Halt	S	SE & C	6, D2
Shalford	S	SEC	5, D1
Shanklin	S	IW	4, G3
Shap	LM	LNW	27, F1
Sharlaston Colliery	E	L&Y	42, C1
Sharpness	W	SVW	8, B1; 9, F2
Shaw	LM	LY	21, F1
Shawford	S	LSW	4, D3
Shawlands	Sc	Cal	44, E3
Sheepbridge	E	Mid	16, A5; 41, B2
Sheerness-on-Sea	S	SEC	6, B4
Sherwalton Moss	Sc	GSW	29, E3
Sherwood Colliery	E	Mid	16, B4 and 41, D4
Sheffield (Midland)	E	Mid	16, A5; 21, G3; 41, A2; 42, G2
Sheffield (Victoria)	E	GC	16, A5; 21, G3; 41, A2; 42, G2
Sheffield Park	BBL	LBSC	5, E4
Shelford	A	GE	11, D3
Shenfield & Hutton	A	GE	5, A5; 11, G4
Shenstone	LM	LNW	15, F5
Shepherds Bush	LUL	H & C	39, C4
Shepherd's Well	S & EK	SEC	6, D2
Shepley	E	LY	21, F2; 42, D4
Shepperton	S	LSW	5, B2
Shepreth	A	GN	11, D3
Shepton Mallet (Charlton Road)		SD &	3, C2; 8, E1
Sherborne	W	LSW	3, D2; 8, G1
Sherburn	E	NE	21, D4
Sheringham	A & NNR	MGN	18, D3
Sherwood Col	LM	Mid	16, B4; 41, D4
Shettleston	Sc	NB	29, C5; 44, C3
Sherwalton Moss	Sc	GSW	29, E3
Shifnal	LM	GW	15, F2
Shildon	E	NE	27, E5
Shiplake	W	GW	10, G2
Shipley	E	Mid	21, D2; 42, A5
Shippea Hill	A	GE	11, B4
Shipston-on-Stour	W	GW	9, C5
Shipton	W	GW	10, D5
Shirebrook	E	Mid & GN	16, B4; 41, C4
Shirebrook Colliery	E	Mid	41, C4
Shirehampton	W	CE	8, C2; 9, G1
Shiremoor	TWM		28, B5
Shireoaks	E	GC	16, A4; 41, A4
Shirley	LM	GW	9, A5
Shoeburyness	A	LTS	6, A4
Sholing	S	LSW	4, E3
Shoreditch		NL	40, B4
Shoreditch	LUL	EL	40, B4
Shoreham (Kent)	S	SEC	5, C4
Shoreham-by-Sea (Sussex)	S	LBSC	5, F3
Shortlands	S	SEC	40, F2
Shotton High Level	LM	GC	20, D4
Shotton Low Level	LM	LNW	20, D4
Shotts	Sc	Cal & NB	30, C4
Shrewsbury	LM	S & H & S & M	15, E1
Sidcup	S	SEC	5, B4; 40, E1
Sidmouth		LSW	2, B2
Sighthill	Sc	NB	44, E4
Sileby	LM	Mid	16, E3
Silecroft	LM	Fur	24, A5
Silkstone	E	L & Y	21, F3; 42, E3
Silkstone Common	E	GC	21, F3 and 42, E3
Silloth	LM	NB	26, C3
Silverdale Colliery	LM	NS	15, C3
Silverdale (Lancs)	LM	Fur	24, B3
Silverhill Colliery	LM	Mid	41, D3
Silver Street	A	GE	5, A3
Silvertown & London City Airport	A	GE	40, C2
Silverwood Col	E	GC/H & B	21, G4; 42, F1
Sinclairtown	Sc	NB	30, A2
Sinfin Central	LM	Mid	16, D5
Sinfin North	LM	Mid	16, D5
Singer	Sc	NB	29, C4; 44, F5
Sittingbourne	S & S & KL	SEC	6, C4
Skegness	E	GN	17, B4
Skelmersdale	LM	L & Y	20, B3
Skinningrove	E	NE	28, E3
Skipton	LM	Mid	21, C1
Slade Green	S	SEC	5, B4
Slaggyford	Ind	NE	27, C2
Slateford	Sc	Cal	30, Inset
Sleaford	E	GN	16, C1; 17, C1
Slaithwaite	E	LNW	21, E2 and 42, D5
Slamannan	Sc	NB	30, B5
Sleights	E	NE	28, F2
Sloane Square	LUL	Dist	39, D5
Slough	W	GW	5, B1; 10, G1
Small Heath	LM	GW	13, C4; 15, G5
Smeaton	Sc	NB	30, B2
Smeeth	S	SEC	6, D3
Smethwick Rolfe Street	LM	LNW	13, B2; 15, G4
Smethwick West	LM	GW	13, B2; 15, G4
Smith's Park	TWM		28, B5
Smitham	S	SEC	5, C3
Smithywood	E	GC	21, G3 and 42, F2
Smithy Bridge	LM	L&Y	21, E1
Snaith	E	LY	21, E5
Snailbeach		SBH	14, B1
Snailwell	A	GE	11, C4
Snape		GE	12, C2
Snaresbrook	LUL	GE	40, A2
Snodland	S	SEC	6, C5
Snowdon Summit	SMR		19, E2
Snowdown	S		6, C2
Snow Hill		GW	13, C3; 15, G4
Soho & Winson Green	LM	GW	13, C3; 15, G4
Sole Street	S	SEC	5, B5
Solihull	LM	GW	9, A5
Somerleyton	A	GE	12, A1; 18, F1
Somersham		GN & GE Jt	11, B3
South Acton	LM	NSW	39, C3
Southall	W	GW	5, B2; 39, C1
Southam & Long Itchington	LM	LNW	10, B5
Southam Road	LM	GW	10, B5
Southampton Parkway	S	LSW	4, D3
Southampton	S	LSW	4, E4
Southampton Terminus	S	LSW	4, E4
South Bank	E	NE	28, E4
South Bermondsey	S	LBSC	40, D4
Southbourne	S	LBSC	4, E1
Southbury	A	GE	5, A3; 11, G3
South Croydon	S	LBSC	5, C3
South Ealing	LUL	Dist	39, D2
Southease	S	LBSC	5, F4
South Elmsall	E	WRG	21, F4; 42, D1
Southend-on-Sea, Central	A	LTS	6, A4
Southend-on-Sea East	A		6, A4
Southend-on-Sea Victoria	A	GE	6, A4
Southfields	S	LSW	39, E4
South Gosforth	TWM	NE	27, B5
South Greenford	W		39, C2
South Gye	Sc	NB	30, B3
South Hampstead	LM	LNW	39, B5
South Harrow	LUL	Dist	39, B1
South Kensington	LUL	Dist	39, D5
South Kenton	LM		39, A2
South Kirkby Colliery	E	GC/GN	42, D1
South Lynn	A	MGN	17, E4
South Merton	S		39, G4
South Milford	E	NE	21, D4
Southminster	A	GE	12, G5
Southport (Chapel St)	LM	LY	20, A4; 24, E4; 45, F1
South Quay	DLR		40, C3; 45, F1
South Ruislip	W & LUL	GW & GC Jt	39, B1
South Shields	TWM	NE	28, B5
South Tottenham	A	THJ	40, A4
South Snowdon		NWNG	19, E2
South Wigston	LM	LNW	16, F3
Southwell		Mid	16, C3
Southwick (Sussex)	S	LBSC	5, F3
Southwick (T&W)	E	NE	28, C5
Southwold		SWD	12, B1
Sowerby Bridge	E	LY	21, E1; 42, C5
Spalding Town	E	GN & Mid	17, E2
Spean Bridge	Sc	NB	32, B2
Spey Bay	Sc	GNS	36, C1
Spiersbridge	Sc	GSW	44, E2
Spilsby	E	GN	17, B3
Spital	LM	BJ	20, C4; 45, F4
Spondon	LM	Mid	16, D5; 41, G2
Spooner Row	A	GE	12, A4; 18, F4
Springbank	E	NE	44, A4
Springburn	Sc	NB	44, D4
Springfield	Sc	NB	34, F5
Spring Road	LM	GW	15, G5
Spring Vale	LM	LNW	13, A1
Sproxton	E		16, D2
Squires Gate	LM	LY & LNW	24, D4
Stacksteads	LM	LY	24, E1
Stafford	LM	LNW	15, E3; 20, G1
Stafford Common		GN	15, D3; 20, G1
Stainby	E		16, D2
Staines	S	LSW	5, B2
Staines West	S	GW	5, B1
Stainforth & Hatfield	E	GC	21, F5
Stainland	E	L & Y	21, E2; 42, C5
Stairfoot	LM	Mid/GC	42, E2
Stallingborough	E	GC	22, F2
Stalybridge	LM	GC & LNW Jt & L & Y	21, F1 and Inset A2
Stamford Brook	LUL	Dist	39, D4
Stamford Hill	A	GE	40, A4

Station	Region	Pre Group	Map Ref.
Stamford Town	E	Mid & GN	16, F1; 17, F1
Stanford-le-Hope	A	LTS	5, A5
Stanhope	E	NE	27, D4
Stanlow & Thornton	LM		20, D4; 45, E5
Stanmore	LUL	LNW	5, A2
Stansted	A	GE	11, E4
Staplehurst	S	SEC	6, D5
Stapleton Road	W	GW	3, Inset
Starbeck	E	NE	21, C3
Starcross	W	GW	2, C3
Staverton Bridge	DVR	GW	2, D4
Staveley	LM	LNW	27, G1
Staveley Central	E	GC & Mid	16, A4; 41, B3
Stechford	LM	LNW	15, G5
Stepney Green	LUL	WB	40, C3
Stevenage	E	GN	11, E2
Stevenston	Sc	G & SW	29, D3
Stewartby	LM	LNW	11, D1; 10, C1
Stewarton	Sc	GBK	29, D4
Stirling	Sc	Cal & NB	30, A5
Stockport (Edgley)	LM	LNW	20, C1; 45, A4
Stockport (Tiviot Dale)	LM	CLC	20, C1; 45, A4
Stocksfield	E	NE	27, C4
Stocksmoor	E	LY	21, F2; 42, D4
Stockton-on-Tees	E	NE	28, E5
Stogumber	WSR	GW	8, F5
Stoke Canon	W	GW	2, B3
Stoke Ferry		GE	11, A5; 17, F5
Stoke Mandeville	W	Met & GC Jt	10, E2
Stoke Newington	A	GE	40, B4
Stoke-on-Trent	LM	NS	15, C3; 20, F1
Stone	LM	NS	15, D3; 20, F1
Stonebridge Park	LM	LNW	39, B3
Stone Crossing	S		5, B5
Stonegate		SEC	5, E5
Stonehaven	Sc	Cal	34, A1
Stonehouse (Glos)	W	GW & Mid	9, E3
Stonehouse (Lanarks)	Sc	Cal	30, D5
Stonehouse Pool	W	LSW	1, D5 and Inset
Stoneleigh	S		5, C3
Stourbridge Jcn	LM	GW	9, A3; 15, G3
Stourbridge Town	LM	GW	15, G3
Stowmarket	A	GE	12, C4
Stranraer Harbour	Sc	P & W	25, C2
Stranraer Town	Sc	P & W	25, C2
Strata Florida	W	GW	14, D5
Stratford	A/DLR/LUL	GE	40, B3
Stratford Market	A	GE	40, B2
Stratford-upon-Avon	LM	GW	9, B5
Strathaven Central	Sc	Cal	29, D5
Strathcarron	Sc	HR	35, E2
Strath Isle	Sc	GNS	37, D1
Strathord	Sc	Cal	33, E5
Strathpeffer	Sc	HR	35, D5
Strawberry Hill	S	LSW	39, E2
Streatham	S	LBSC	40, F5
Streatham Common	S	LBSC	40, F5
Streatham Hill	S	LBSC	40, E5
Stretford	LM	MSJA	45, B3
Stretton	LM	Mid	16, B5; 41, D2
Strines	LM	GC & Mid Jt	15, A4
Stromeferry	Sc	HR	35, E1
Strood	S	SEC	6, B5
Stroud	W	GW	9, E3
Stroud Midland	W	Mid	9, E3
Sturry	S	SEC	6, C2
Styal	LM	LNW	45, A4
Sudbury & Harrow Rd		GC	39, B2
Sudbury Hill	LUL	GC	39, B2
Sudbury Hill (Harrow)	W	GC	39, B2
Sudbury (Suffolk)	A	GE	12, D5
Sudbury Town	LUL		39, B2
Summersent	ELR	LY	24, E1 and 45, B1
Sunbury	S	LSW	5, B2
Sunderland	E	NE	28, C5
Sundridge Park	S	SEC	40, F2
Sunningdale	S	LSW	5, B1
Sunnymeads	S		5, B1
Surbiton	S	LSW	5, B2; 39, G2
Surrey Docks	LUL	EL	40, D4
Sutton-in-Ashfield		GC	16, B4; 41, D4
Sutton Coldfield	LM	LNW	15, F5
Sutton Colliery	LM	Mid	41, D3
Sutton Common	S		39, G5
Sutton Jcn	LM	Mid	41, D4
Sutton Park	LM	Mid	15, F5
Sutton (Surrey)	S	LBSC	5, C3
Swaffham	A	GE	18, F5
Swale	S		6, B4
Swanage	Ind	LSW	3, G5
Swanley	S	SEC	5, B4
Swanscombe	S	SEC	5, B5
Swansea Burrows Sdg	W	GW	43, F3
Swansea Docks	W	GW	43, G3
Swansea East Dock	W	GW, RSB & Mid	7, B4; 43, G3
Swansea Eastern Depot	W	GW	43, G3
Swansea	W	GW	7, B4; 43, G3
Swansea Rutland Street		Mum	7, B4; 43, G3
Swansea St Thomas		Mid	7, B4; 43, G3
Swansea Victoria		LNW	7, B4; 43, G3
Swan Village	LM	GW	13, B2
Swanwick	S	LSW	4, E3
Sway	S	LSW	4, E5
Swaythling	S	LSW	4, D4
Sweet Dews	E	H&B	22, Inset
Swinderby	E	Mid	16, B2
Swindon	W	GW	9, G5
Swineshead	E	GN	17, D2
Swinton (Lancs)	LM	LY	20, B2; 24, F1; 45, B2
Sydenham	S	LBSC	40, F4
Sydenham Hill	S	SEC	40, F4
Sylfaen	W & L		14, B2
Symington	Sc	Cal	30, E4
Syon Lane	S		39, D2
Syston	LM	Mid	16, E3
Tackley	W		10, D4
Tadworth & Walton-on-Hill	S	SEC	5, C3
Taffs Well	W	TV	8, C4; 43, C4
Tain	Sc	HR	36, B4
Tallington	E	GN	17, F1
Talsarnau	LM	Cam	19, F2
Talybont	LM		13, A5; 19, G2
Tal-y-Cafn & Eglwysbach	LM	LNW	19, D4
Talyllyn Jcn		BM	14, G3
Tamworth	LM	LNW & Mid	15, F5
Tan-y-Bwlch	Fest		19, F3
Tanygrisiau	Fest		19, F3
Taplow	W	GW	5, B1; 10, G2
Tattenham Corner	S	SEC	5, C3
Taunton	W	GW	8, F4
Taynuilt	Sc	Cal	32, E3
Tebay	LM	LNW	27, F1
Teddington	S	LSW	39, F2
Tees Dock	E	NE	28, Inset
Teesside Airport	E	NE	28, E5
Tees Yard	E	NE	28, E4 and Inset
Teignmouth	W	GW	2, C3
Telford Central	LM	GW	15, E2
Templecombe	S	LSW	3, D3; 8, G1
Temple Meads (Bristol)	W	GW & Mid Jt	3, A2 and Inset; 8, C2
Tenby	W	GW	7, D3
Tenterden		KES	6, E4
Tetbury	W	GW	9, F3
Teynham	S	SEC	6, C4
Thame	W	GW	10, E3
Thames Ditton	S	LSW	39, G2
Thameshaven	A	LTS	6, A5
Thatcham	W	GW	4, A3
Thatto Heath	LM	LNW	20, C3; 24, G3; 45, E3
Thaxted		GE	11, E4
Theale	W	GW	4, A2
The Dell (Falmouth)	W	GW	1, F1
The Lakes	LM	GW	9, A5
The Mound	Sc	HR	36, A4
Theobalds Grove	A	GE	11, G3
Thetford	A	GE	12, B5; 18, G5
Theydon Bois	LUL	GE	11, G3
Thirsk	E	NE	21, A4
Thoresby Colliery	E	GC	16, 33 and 41, C5
Thornaby	E	NE	28, E4
Thorne North	E	NE	21, E5
Thorne South	E	GC	21, F5
Thornbury	W	Mid	8, B1; 9, F2
Thorney Mill	W	GW	5, B2
Thornford	W	GW	3, E2
Thornliebank	Sc	Cal	44, E2
Thornton Abbey	E	GC	22, E3
Thornton (Goods)	Sc	NB	30, A2 and 34, G5
Thorntonhall	Sc	Cal	29, D5; 44, E2
Thornton Heath	S	LBSC	40, G5
Thornton-in-Craven	LM	Mid	21, C1 Inset
Thornton Jcn	Sc	NB	30, A2; 34, G5
Thorpe Bay	A	LTS	6, A4
Thorpe Culvert	E	GN	17, C3
Thorpe-le-Soken	A	GE	12, E5
Thorpe Marsh Power Station	E	GC	21, F5
Thrapston		LNW & Mid	10, A1
Three Bridges	S	LBSC	5, D3
Three Oaks	S		6, F5
Three Cocks Jcn	W	Mid & Cam	14, F2
Three Spires	LM	LNW	10, A5
Thurcroft Colliery	E	S Yks Jt	21, G4
Thurgarton	E	Mid	16, C3
Thurgoland	E	GC	42, E3
Thurscoe	E	NE & Mid	21, F4; 42, E1
Thurso	Sc	HR	38, C3
Thurston	A	GE	12, C5
Tidenham	W	GW	8, B2; 9, F1
Tidworth		MSW	4, B5
Tilbury (Riverside)	A	LTS	5, B5
Tilbury (Town)	A	LTS	5, B5
Tile Hill	LM	LNW	10, A5
Tilehurst	W	GW	4, A2
Tillynaught	Sc	GNS	37, C2
Timperley	LM	MSJA	20, C1; 24, G1; 45, B3
Tintern	W	GW	8, B2; 9, F1
Tipton (Owen Street)	LM	LNW	13, B1; 15, F4
Tipton St John's		LSW	2, B2
Tir Phil	W	Rhy	8, A4; 43, B2
Tisbury	S	LSW	3, D4
Titley	W	GW	14, E1
Tiverton	W	GW	2, A3; 8, G5
Tiverton Jcn		GW	2, A2
Tiverton Parkway	W	GW	2, A2 and 8, G5
Tivetshall	A	GE	12, A3; 18, G3
Todmorden	LM	LY	20, A1; 21, E1
Toddington	G & WR	GW	9, D4
Tollesbury		GE	12, F5
Tolworth	S		39, G3
Tomatin	Sc	HR	36, E4
Tonbridge	S	SEC	5, D5
Tondu	W	GW	7, C5; 43, D4
Tonfanau	LM	Cam	13, B5
Ton Pentre	W	TV	8, B5 and 43, D2
Tonypandy & Trealaw	W	TV	8, B5; 43, D3
Tooting	S	LBSC & LSW Jt	39, F5
Topley Pike	LM	Mid	15, A4
Topsham	W	LSW	2, B3
Torness	Sc	NB	31, B2
Torquay	W	GW	2, D3
Torpantau		BM	8, A5; 43, C1
Torrance	Sc	NB	44, D5
Torre	W	GW	2, D3
Torrington	W	LSW	7, G3
Totnes	W	GW	2, D4
Totnes Riverside	DVR	GW	2, D4
Tottenham Hale	A	GE	40, A4
Totteridge & Whetstone	LUL	GN	5, A3; 11, G2
Totton	S	LSW	4, E4
Towcester		SMJ	10, C3
Tower Colliery	W	GW	43, A1
Tower Gateway	DLR		40, C4
Town Green	LM	LY	20, B4; 24, F3; 45, F2
Trafford Park	LM	CLC	45, B3
Trawsfynydd	LM	GW	19, F3
Treamble		GW	1, D1
Trefforest	W	TV	8, B5; 43, C3
Trefforest Estate	W		43, C3; 8, B5
Trehafod	W	TV	8, B5; 43, C3
Treherbert	W	TV	43, D2
Trentham	LM	NS	15, C3; 20, F1
Trentham Park	LM	NS	15, D3; 20, F1
Treorchy	W	TV	8, B5; 43, D2
Tresavean		GW	1 Insert, E5
Trimley	A	GE	12, E3
Tring	LM	LNW	10, E1
Tring Cutting	LM	LNW	10, E1
Troed-y-rhiw	W	TV	8, B5; 43, C2
Troon	Sc	G & SW	29, E3
Trostre Works	W	GW	7, B3
Trowbridge	W	GW	3, B4
Trowell	LM	Mid	16, C4; 41, F3
Truro	W	GW	1, E1
Tufnell Park	LM	GE	40, B5
Tulloch	Sc	NB	32, B1
Tulse Hill	S	LBSC	40, E5
Tunbridge Wells (Central)	S	SEC	5, D5
Tunbridge Wells (West)	S	LBSC	5, D5
Tunstead	LM	Mid	15, A5
Turkey Street	A	GE	11, G3
Turnham Green	LUL	LSW	39, D3
Turnchapel		LSW	1, D5 and Inset
Tuxford	E	GN	16, B2
Tweedmouth	E	NE	31, D3
Twickenham	S	LSW	39, E2
Twyford (Berks)	W	GW	4, A1
Ty Croes	LM	LNW	19, D1
Ty Glas	W	CDF	43, B4
Tygwyn Halt	LM		19, F2
Tyldesley	LM	LNW	20, B2; 24, F2; 45, C2
Tyndrum Lower	Sc	Cal	32, E1
Tyndrum Upper	Sc	NB	32, E1
Tyne Dock	TWM	NE	28, B5
Tynemouth	TWM		28, B5
Tyseley	LM	GW	15, G5
Tytherington	W	Mid	8, C1 and 9, G2
Tywyn	LM & Tal	Cam	13, B5
Uckfield	S	LBSC	5, E4
Uddingston	Sc	Cal	44, C3
Ulceby	E	GC	22, E3
Ulleskelf	E	NE	21, D4
Ulverston	LM	Fur	24, A4
Umberleigh	W	LSW	7, F3
University	LM	Mid	13, C3
Uphall	Sc	NB	30, B3
Upholland	LM	LY	20, B3; 24, F3; 45, D2
Upminster	A	LTS	5, A5
Upminster Bridge	LUL		5, A5
Upney	LUL		5, A4; 40, B1
Upper Bontnewydd	W	GW	8, B3; 43, A3
Upperby	LM	LNW	26, Inset
Upper Halliford	S		5, B2
Upper Holloway	LM	THJ (LTS)	40, B5
Upper Warlingham	S	CO	5, C3
Uppingham		LNW	16, F2
Upton (Ches)	LM	GC	20, C4; 45, F4
Upton Park	LUL	LTS & LNW	40, B2

Station	Region	Pre Group	Map Ref.
Upwell		WUT	17, F4
Upwey	S	GW	3, F3
Urmston	LM	CLC	20, C1; 45, B3
Uskmouth	W	GW	8, C3 and 43, A4
Uttoxeter	LM	NS	15, D5
Uxbridge	LUL	GW & Dist	5, A2; 10, G1
Valley	LM	LNW	19, B2
Vauxhall (London)	S	LSW	40, D5
View Park	Sc	Cal	44, B3
Velindre Works	W	GW	43, G2
Ventnor	S	IW	4, G3
Verney Jcn	LM	LNW	10, D3
Victoria Basin		GW	15, F3 Inset
Victoria Dock			40, C2
Victoria (London)	S	LBSC SEC & Dist	5, B3; 39, D5
Victoria Rd, St Budeaux	W	GW	1, A1, D5
View Park	Sc	Cal	44, B3
Vobster		GW	3, B3; 8, E1
Virginia Water	S	LSW	5, B1
Waddon	S	LBSC	5, C3
Waddon Marsh	S	LBSC	40, G5
Wadebridge	W	LSW	1, C2
Wadhurst	S	SEC	5, E5
Wainfleet	E	GN	17, C4
Wakefield (Kirkgate)	E	LY & GN Jt	21, E3; 42, C2
Wakefield (Westgate)	E	GN & GC Jt	21, E3; 42, C2
Walkden (High Level)	LM	LY	20, B2; 24, F1; 45, B2
Walkergate	TWM		28, B5
Wallasey (Grove Road)	LM	Wir	20, C4; 24, G4; 45, G3
Wallasey Village	LM	Wir	20, C4; 24, G4; 45, G3
Wallingford	W	GW	10, F3
Wallington	S	LBSC	5, C3
Wallsend	TWM	NE	28, B5
Walmer	S	SEC	6, C1
Walsall	LM	LNW & Mid	13, Inset A2; 15, F4
Walsingham	WWL	GE	18, D5
Waltham Cross & Abbey	A	GE	11, G3
Weltham-on-the-Wold		GN	16, D2
Walthamstow Central	A	GE	40, A3
Walthamstow Queens Rd	A	TFG	40, A3
Walton Jcn	LM	LY	45, F3
Walton-on-Naze	A	GE	12, E3
Walton-on-Thames	S	LSW	5, C2
Wanborough	S	LSW	5, C1
Wandsworth	S	SEC	40, E5
Wandsworth Common	S	LBSC	39, E5
Wandsworth Road	S	LBSC	39, Inset
Wandsworth Town	S	LSW	39, E5
Wansbeck Road	TWM		27, B5
Wansford	NVR	LNW	11, A1; 17, F1
Wanlockhead	Sc	Cal	30, F4
Wanstead	LUL		40, A2
Wanstead Park	A	TFG	40, B2
Wantage		WT	10, F5
Wantage Rd	W	GW	10, F5
Wapping	LUL		40, C4
Warblington	S	LBSC	4, E2
Warcop	LM	Mid	27, E2
Ware	A	GE	11, F3
Wareham	S	LSW	3, F4
Wargrave	W	GW	4, A1; 10, G2
Warminster	W	GW	3, C4
Warnham	S	LBSC	5, D2
Warren	S	SEC	6, D2
Warrington Bank Quay	LM	LNW	15, A1; 20, C2; 24, G2; 45, D4
Warrington Central	LM	CLC	15, A1; 20, C2; 24, G2; 45, D4
Warsop Main Colliery	E	GC	41, C4
Warwick	LM	GW	10, B5
Warwick Road Old Trafford	LM	MSJA	45, B3
Washford	WSR	GW	8, E5
Washington	E	NE	28, C5
Watchet	WSR	GW	8, E5
Waterbeach	A	GE	11, C4
Waterhouses	E	NE	27, D5
Waterhouses (Staffs)		L & M	15, C5
Wateringbury	S	SEC	6, C5
Waterloo (Aberdeen)	Sc	GNS	37, G4
Waterloo (Lancs)	LM	LY	20, B4; 24, F4; 45, F3
Waterloo (London)	S	LSW	5, B3; 40, D5
Waterloo East	S	SEC	40, D5
Water Orton	LM	Mid	15, F5
Waterside	Sc	G & SW	29, F4
Waterston	W	GN	7, Inset
Waterton (Fords)	W	BR	7, C5 and 43, D4
Watford High St	LM	LNW	5, A2; 11, G1
Watford Jcn	LM	LNW	5, A2; 11, G1
Watford North	LM	LNW	5, A2; 11, G1
Watford West	LM	LNW	5, A2; 11, G1
Watlington	W	GW	10, F3
Wath		HB	42, F1
Wath North	E	Mid	42, E1
Wath-on-Dearne	E	GC	42, F1
Watton-at-Stone	E	GN	11, F2
Waun-gron Park	W		43, B4
Waun Llywd	W	GW	43, B1
Waverley (Edinburgh)	Sc	NB	30, B2 and Inset
Wearhead	E	NE	27, D3
Wedgewood	LM		15, D3; 20, F1
Wednesbury	LM	GW & LNW	13, A2
Weeley	A	GE	12, E3
Weeton	E	NE	21, C3
Wellbeck Colliery	E	GC	16, B3 and 41, C5
Welham Green	E	GN	11, F2
Welling	S	SEC	5, B4; 40, E1
Wellingborough	LM	Mid	10, B1
Wellington Telford West	LM	SWN	15, E2
Wells-next-the-Sea (Norfolk)	WWL	GE	18, C5
Wells (Som)	W	GW	3, C2; 8, E2
Welshpool	LM & W & L	Cam	14, B2
Welton	E	GC	17, B1
Welwyn Garden City	E	GN	11, F2
Welwyn North	E	GN	11, F2
Wem	LM	LNW	15, D1; 20, G3
Wembley Central	LM & LUL	LNW	39, B2
Wembley Stadium	W	GC	39, B3
Wembley North	LM & LUL	LNW	39, B2
Wembley Park	LUL	GC	39, B3
Wembley Stadium	LM	GC	39, B3
Wemyss Bay	Sc	Cal	29, C2
Wendover	W	Met & CG Jt	10, E2
Wenford Bridge	W	LSW	1, C3
Wennington (Lancs)	LM	Mid	24, B2
West Allerton	LM		20, C4; 45, E4
Werneth	LM	L & Y	45, A2
Westbourne Park	W & LUL	GW & H & C	39, C5 and Inset C1
West Bay		GW	3, F1
West Bridge	LM	GC	16, F3
West Brompton	LUL	Dist & WLE	39, D5
West Bromwich	LM	GW	13, B2; 15, G4
Westbury (Salop)	LM	SWP	14, A1
Westbury (Wilts)	W	GW	3, B4
West Burton Power Station	E	GC	16, A2
West Byfleet	S	LSW	5, C1
West Calder	Sc	Cal	30, C4
Westcliff	A	LTS	6, A4
Westcombe Park	S	SEC	40, D2
West Croydon	S	LBSC	40, G5
West Depot (Bristol)	W	GW	3, Inset
West Drayton	W	GW	5, B2; 10, G1
West Dulwich	S	SEC	40, E4
West Ealing	W	GW	39, C2
Westenhanger	S	SEC	6, D3
Westerfield	A	GE	12, D3
Wester Hailes	Sc	Cal	30, C3
Westerham	S	SEC	5, C4
Westerleigh	W	Mid	8, C1 and 9, G2
Westerton	Sc	NB	29, C4; 44, E5
West Ferry	DLR		40, C3
Westfield	Sc	NB	30, A2 and 34, G5
West Finchley	LUL		5, A3
Westgate-on-Sea	S	SEC	6, B2
West Ham	A & LUL	LTS & Dist	40, C2
West Horndon		GE	5, A5
West Hampstead	LM/LUL	LNW & Met	39, B5
West Hampstead Thameslink	LM	Mid	39, B5
West Harrow	LUL	Met	39, A1
Westhoughton	LM	LY	45, C2
West India Quay	DLR		40, C3
West Jesmond	TWM		28, Inset
West Kensington	LUL	Dist	39, D4
West Kilbride	Sc	GSW	29, D2
West Kirby	LM	BJ & Wir	20, C5; 24, G5 and 45, G4
West Malling	S	SEC	5, C5
Westminster	LUL	Dist	40, C5
West Monkseaton	TWM	NE	28, B5
West Norwood	S	LBSC	40, F5
Westoe Col	E		28, B5
Weston Milton	W	GW	3, B1; 8, D3
Weston-super-Mare	W	GW & WCP	3, B1; 8, D3
West Ruislip	W & LUL		5, A2
West Runton	A	MGN	18, D3
West St Leonards	S	SEC	6, F5
West Sutton	S		5, C3
Westward Ho!		BWHA	7, F2
West Wickham	S	SEC	40, G3
West Worthing	S	LBSC	5, E5
Wetheral	E	NE	27, C1
Wetherby	E	NE	21, C4
Weybourne	NNR	MGN	18, D4
Weybridge	S	LSW	5, C2
Weymouth Town & Quay	W	GW	3, G3
Whaley Bridge	LM	LNW	15, A4
Whatley Quarry	W	GW	3, B3
Whatstandwell	LM	Mid	16, C5; 41, E2
Whimple	W	LSW	2, B2
Whimsey	W	SVW	8, A1; 9, E2
Whitacre	LM	Mid	15, F5
Whitby	E	NE	28, F2
Whitchurch (Glam)	W	Car	8, C4; 43, B4
Whitchurch (Hants)	S	LSW & GW	4, B3
Whitchurch (Salop)	LM	LNW	15, C1; 20, F3
Whitechapel	LUL	EL & WB	40, C4
White City	LUL		39, C4
Whitecraigs	Sc	Cal	44, E2
Whitefield	LM	LY	45, B2
White Hart Lane	A	GE	40, A4
Whitehaven (Bransty)	LM	LNW & Fur Jt	26, E4
Whitehaven (Preston Street)	LM	Fur	26, E4
White Notley	A	GE	11, F5
Whiteinch (Riverside)	Sc	Cal	44, F4
Whitland	W	GW	7, A1; 13, G2
Whitley Bay	TWM	NE	28, B5
Whitley Bridge	E	LY	21, E5
Whitlocks End	LM	GW	9, A5
Whitlingham	A	GE	18, F3
Whitstable & Tankerton	S	SEC	6, B3
Whittington	A	GE	11, A2; 17, F2
Whittlesford	A	GE	11, D3
Whitton	S		39, E1
Whitton (Lincs)	E	GC	22, E4
Whitwell	E	Mid	41, B4
Whitworth	LM	L & Y	45, A1
Whyteleafe	S	SEC	5, C3
Whyteleafe South	S		5, C3
Wick	Sc	HR	38, D2
Wickford	A	GE	6, A5; 11, G5
Wickham Market	A	GE	12, C2
Widdrington	E	NE	27, A5; 31, G5
Widnes	LM	LNW	15, A1; 20, C3; 45, D4
Widnes, Central	LM	GC & Mid Jt	15, A1; 20, C3; 45, D4
Widnes, North	LM	CLC	15, A1, 20, C3; 24, G3 45, D4
Widney Manor	LM	GW	9, A5
Wigan Central		GC	20, B3; 24, F2; 45, D2
Wigan North Western	LM	LNW	20, B3; 24, F2; 45, D2
Wigan, Wallgate	LM	LY	20, B3; 24, F2; 45, D2
Wigston Magna	LM	Mid	16, F3
Wigton	LM	M & C	26, C2
Wigtown	Sc	P & W	25, C4
Willesden Green	LUL	Met	39, B4
Willesden Jcn	LM & LUL	LNW	39, C4
Williamwood	Sc	Cal	44, E2
Williton	WSR	GW	8, E5
Willoughby (Lincs)	E	GN	17, B3
Wilmcote	LM	GW	9, B5
Wilmslow	LM	LNW	15, A3; 20, C1; 45, A5
Wilnecote	LM	Mid	15, F5
Wilton Works	E	NE	28, Inset
Wimbledon	S & LUL	LSW & LBSC & LSW Jt	5, B3; 39, F4
Wimbledon Chase	S		39, F4
Wimbledon Park	LUL	LSW	39, E4
Wimborne		LSW	3, F5
Winchcombe	G & WR	GW	9, D4
Winchelsea	S	SEC	6, E4
Winchester	S	LSW & GW	4, D3
Winchfield	S	LSW	4, B1
Winchmore Hill	A		5, A3
Windermere	LM	LNW	26, G1
Windermere Lakeside	L & HR	Fur	24, A4
Windsor & Eton Central	S	GW	5, B1
Windsor & Eton (Riverside)	S	LSW	5, B1
Winfrith	S	LSW	3, F4
Wingate	E	NE	28, D5
Wingfield	LM	Mid	16, C5
Wingham	S	EK	6, C2
Winnersh	S	SEC	4, A1
Winnersh Triangle	S	SEC	4, A1
Winsford	LM	LNW	15, B2; 20, D2
Winsford & Over		CLC	15, B2; 20, D2
Wirksworth	LM	Mid	16, C5; 41, E1
Wisbech East	A	GE, WUT & MGN	17, F3
Wisbech St Mary		MGN	17, F3
Wishaw (Central)	Sc	Cal	30, C5; 44, A2
Wishaw South	Sc	Cal	44, A2
Witham (Som)	W	GW	3, C3
Witham (Essex)	A	GE	12, F5
Withernsea	E	NE	22, E2
Withymoor Basin	LM	GW	13, C1
Witley	S	LSW	5, D1
Wittersham Road	KES		6, E5
Witton	LM	LNW	13, B4
Wivelsfield	S	LBSC	5, E3
Wivenhoe	A	GE	12, E4
Woburn Sands	LM	LNW	10, C1
Woking	S	LSW	5, C1
Wokingham	S	SEC	4, A1
Woldingham	S	CO	5, C3
Wolverhampton High Level	LM	LNW	15, F3
Wolverhampton Low Level	LM	GW	15, F3
Wolverton	LM	LNW	10, C2
Wombwell	E	Mid	21, F3; 42, E2
Woodbridge	A	GE	12, D3
Wood End	LM	GW	9, A5